Searching for Dunderhead

An American Story

h. Alton Jones

54 Candles Publishing
Scottsdale, Arizona

Copyright © 2016 by h. Alton Jones

Requests for permission to make copies of any part of the work should be submitted online at info@54Candles.org or mailed to the following address:

54 Candles Publishing Company
8369 N. Via Linda
Scottsdale, AZ 85258

www.54Candles.org

ISBN 978-0-9845545-3-9

Library of Congress Control Number: 2016902694

To all of those I have ever wounded. May this book shed light on the collective foolishness and folly of the human race and provide at least a glimmer of hope that we can overcome our foibles. With a humble smile, I reach out my hand.

There is so much good in the worst of us,
And so much bad in the best of us,
That it ill behooves any of us
To find fault with the rest of us.

Anonymous

About this book ...

When I was a child, my father had pet names for his boys. When we did something that fell short of his high expectations, he would refer to us by these pet names. They were nuanced so each one carried a slightly different meaning. At first glance, "meathead", "gordhead" and "dunderhead" might seem little more than derogatory terms, but in our household, they weren't. If you were a meathead, you lacked the capacity for prescient thought, i.e., you might be doing your best, but you just didn't have the mental horsepower needed for the task at hand. On the other hand, "dunderhead" suggested you had the capacity to think clearly and cogently, but you simply weren't using that capacity to its fullest extent. In our household, neither was truly a derogatory name. They were actually terms of endearment if not affection. They merely said, "Hey, you can do better than that."

There were times I felt compelled to check my birth certificate to verify that I was in fact named "Howard Alton Jones" rather than "Dunderhead Jones". When I was Dunderhead, I knew my father was simply extolling me to reach higher and to accomplish more. Strange as it may sound, when I was Dunderhead, I knew he truly cared and wanted me to take longer strides toward my full potential.

In 2011, my mother died. Twelve months later, my father died. I was deeply saddened by their passing. Like everyone, I dealt with the losses as best I could. Their memories live on not only in my heart and mind, but in my sheer existence. I *am* my parents, both genetically and as a result of the years of exposure and learning how to be Howard Jones.

I cognitively understood that once they were gone, they would never again be available to answer questions and provide those little snippets of wisdom and knowledge that parents impart. I didn't grasp the completeness of that loss until it was too late.

Never again could I turn to my mother and ask her about something or someone from a time long before I was born. Never again would my father be around to tell me about the emotions of a young man about to enter the fray that became World War Two. Any information about life during the Great Depression now had to come from books rather than from the lips of my parents.

For someone whose thirst for knowledge and understanding was insatiable, the absence of these two great resources left a bigger void than I'd ever dreamed. I miss them for the love and caring guidance they gave me over the years. But I miss them even more for their oracle like qualities. The knowledge and wisdom they carried with them is now gone forever with only some remnants remaining in the form of a few pictures and a rare letter or school paper left behind.

Now I'm at the vanguard. I'm the oldest surviving member of my family. It may be arrogant to assume that there may be something to learn from my life. Even if it's only the answers to questions about what it was like to be a college student in the sixties or what was it like to grow up in a city that was once a vibrant American megalopolis, I hope the reader finds something of value. I hold the answers to many questions about living through the past eight decades. When I'm gone, another resource will be permanently checked out of the library of humanity.

My goal in producing this book is not to suggest my life experience is more worthy than anyone else's. It is to chronicle the times in which I lived. Perhaps when I'm gone, someone will have a question that I have answered herein. If so, if only just once, I have attained my goal.

The book was written from my memory, aided from time-to-time, by access to old photographs or documents. In that my memory has been squeezed for its recollection of events that covered eight decades, two centuries and two millennia, the accounts presented in this book may not be one-hundred percent accurate. I have endeavored to tell everything with as much veracity as humanly possible. However, in the hopefully rare case where truth deviates from my telling, I hereby declare my version the true and correct version. After all, it is my book. If someone's recollection differs, I will anxiously await his or her book.

I have chosen not to tell my story as a chronological trek through time. Instead, I have selected what I consider life's more significant topics and dealt with them on a chapter-by-chapter basis. In that way, I accomplish two things. I can deal with sociological, cultural and philosophical issues from the context of my living them. I also make it easier for the reader to forego any chapter that doesn't pique his curiosity.

It would be nice if my views on topics like marriage, religion, education or family was somehow more significant than the views of others, but such is not the case. I present them solely because I lived through them. Presumably, they reflect to a greater or lesser extent the times in which I lived. The house in which I lived in 1954 was not significantly different than the houses millions of other Americans enjoyed at that time. However, my life in that house did reflect the social structure of a large American city. It did reveal cultural views on everything from education to racism. Today's society was built upon a foundation constructed from the building blocks we created in years past. For that reason, my house in 1955, my classroom in 1963 and my boat in 2006 are significant in their own small ways.

As you read through these pages, you will exalt in the things we had in common and recoil from our differences. It's a story of a common post-World War II boy who grew up and gradually woke up to the world around him. I hope you enjoy the adventure.

h. Alton Jones – March 2016

So who is Howard Jones today? He's sort of an "older guy". The calendar works on all of us. If Einstein was so damn smart, why couldn't he have dealt with this better? Nonetheless, Jonesy has white hair (what's left of it), a white beard, a gait that hides far too many hard slides into third base and a normal façade with a Scottsdale demeanor that masks his real persona. He lives in a quaint, yet substantial cabin with Liz in an up-scale neighborhood in one of America's most affluent communities.

He's happily married to Liz McCarty. He can't speak for Ms. McCarty, but after more than thirty years, he's content – probably overly so. She does a great job of appearing content too. Frankly, if life's success is based on that metric, you can put this manuscript down now and go to bed. Jonesy's life has been a success. He's smiling and happy. Is there more?

So meet Dunderhead.

Chapter One - Trauma Center

I'm sure no life has ever existed where fate didn't administer a regular dose of trauma. I don't really remember it, but I suspect my passage through the birth canal was tough. I'm still recovering from that one. It was also one of the few that didn't involve other people (other than my mother). People can sometimes be rather inconvenient. Consider some examples.

Scars of Honor - I've never met the person that has miraculously gone through life without a fair share of trauma. Some of the "beautiful people" of Scottsdale, Beverly Hills and other Botox Meccas, spend time and money to cover up scares and other imperfections. I can't tell you how far I am on the opposite end of the spectrum. I have many scars and I earned every one of them. Don't you dare try and tell me I should try to hide them. Do you know how much effort I went through to get them? They're my badges of honor and accomplishment. They're my battle ribbons. I wear them with pride.

My first big, memorable scar came from a knife in the middle of Detroit. I was four, maybe five. My mother had a pocket knife. For some inexplicable reason, it intrigued me. Maybe she told me not to touch it, so of course... when she wasn't nearby, I opened her purse and stealthily removed the jackknife.

We lived in an old flat in the early fifties. I vividly recall many things about the place as if I'd lived there last week. We had a milk-chute where the milkman dutifully brought quart bottles from his horse-drawn wagon and replaced the empty bottles. Later in the day, another horse drawn cart came rumbling down the street. The Italian merchant would sing out the day's best deals. His voice still echoes in my memory, "Strawberries, tree quartza fora dolla." The iceman also delivered block ice from his horse drawn wagon. Electric refrigerators weren't found in every home in 1951. The house was heated by coal. For that, we needed a coal-chute. Hinged at the bottom, you pull it open and dump wheel barrow loads of anthracite coal into it.

The coal bin in the basement was a good sized room, at least it was to a four year old boy. It was also a great place to hide and play with a heisted jackknife. I snuck down the stairs and went into the coal bin. It was there my excitement overwhelmed my sense of guilt. I tried to pull the blade from the knife. For a little guy, it took some strength. I had it partially opened when a suspicious mother announced her presence. She figured something from the "no good" side of boyhood was up and had followed me down the stairs.

"Howard!" she said from behind me. I jumped. So did the knife. All's well that ends well. This wasn't one of those times. When I dropped the knife, it snapped shut like a rat trap. I'm afraid the rat was me. It caught me at the base of the thumb and opened it up half way to the knuckle. I learned a lot that day. I learned (1) mothers are everywhere, (2) jackknives are very, very sharp, (3) large pools of blood mixed in coal dust aren't pretty and (4) little boys should do what they're told by their mothers. Alright, the first three are true. I'm not sure I ever really grasped the fourth one.

Well, I recovered. I still carry a significant scar on that thumb, but I was just beginning. I was very fortunate to have been born with far more natural athletic ability that the average boy. I played baseball nearly constantly from spring through fall. In the winter, I was usually found on the ice with a hockey stick and puck. My talents led me onto the high school football field. I did a lot of swimming and diving. My skills in that arena earned me intercollegiate letters as a diver at one of the nation's more reputable swimming schools. I also played a year of college hockey, but found that as much as I loved the game, I'd be better off sticking with my strongest sport which was unquestionably baseball.

The Brotherhood of the Breens - It's funny how some of our early childhood experiences ultimately provide us with some of life's greatest lessons, useful long into our adult lives. One of my most memorable lessons involved human nature, loyalty, danger, stress under pressure and leadership. Clearly, these are all matters with boundless impact on one's future in the business world and life in general.

Before I talk about the Breen brothers, I need to tell you a little about the structure and dynamics of an eleven year old's world when growing up in a city like Detroit, Michigan. The neighborhood consisted of "blocks" with roughly forty houses, twenty on each side of the street facing each other. The block was your world. You knew the kids on your block. You played with them, socialized with them, knew their brothers and sisters. It was your nation-state. There were other blocks nearby, each its own nation-state with its own social hierarchy and power structure. Much like the countries in medieval Europe, there was occasional contact between blocks, some trade and commerce, but for the most part, you stayed in your world. After all, you had to cross streets to get into other blocks and Mom knew that's when you could be hit by a car. If you were on another block, you couldn't hear the nightly call from Mom. "Dinner's ready. Come home." Life was good on your block; it was also relatively safe.

However, there were certain cultural institutions essential to the lives of young boys that didn't exist on your block. You needed to engage in world travel to reach them. Other than school, the most important institution to the boys on my block was "Al's Drug Store". Al's was the Macys, the Herrod's of the neighborhood. It stocked all of the things that were essential in the life of an eleven year old. Pea shooters, candy, caps, baseball cards with bubble gum – everything of value in life was sold at Al's. He also had a soda-fountain and served the planet's finest milkshake for twenty-five cents. Al's was the center of the universe as we knew it.

Here's the problem, Al's Drug Store was at the corner of Washburn and Puritan, two blocks east and one block south of our border at Griggs and Florence. No matter how you cut it, that meant we had to travel through one other nation-state's territory to get there. We could go due south for a block. Oh how boring. Nothing ever happened there. We could actually see that block from our homes, hence there was nothing exotic about it. It was almost like not leaving home. There was no allure to traveling Griggs south of Florence.

We could travel two blocks along the side-street of Florence and drop one block south on Washburn. We actually did that fairly often, but that block was like south Griggs. It was sterile, not much to see, rarely anything eventful. And it didn't seem as much like world travel because the Washburn route, like the Griggs route, only involved one turn. How can a kid consider it a big trip with only one turn?

The solution ... the Ilene route. Travel one block east on Florence – turn right – one block south the length of the Ilene nation-state – turn left – one block further east to Washburn and we were in baseball card heaven. And who knew, you might find a Mickey Mantle card in your next nickel pack of baseball cards. Ilene was the path of choice, except that's where the Breen brothers lived.

Billy and Bobby Breen were twins. They were about a year older than me. They were roughhousing bullies who lived for a scrap. Even in appearance, they reminded me of Butch of Little Rascals fame (a man that fifty years later, I would get to know in San Diego). The Breen brothers hung around with a couple of other kids from their world and when some of the Griggs boys would wander past their house, they acted as the neighborhood "unwelcoming committee". They would greet the Griggsians, block their way and put fist-to-face as a way of saying "Hello". It was not uncommon to see one of our boys running home, scuffed up and bloodied after attempting passage through the turbulent land of Ilene. Frankly, it got old.

One day, what later in life proved to be some innate leadership skills began to surface in the mind of the young Jones boy. He called a counsel of the Griggs boys together to discuss the problem. He met with Jimmy Foley, Harvey Solomon, John Paul and others from the block. "Look, the Breen brothers always attack when you guys go over there one or two at a time."

A plan came together. We would all go over together. I believe there were seven of us. "Even if they do try to block our way, they'll be no match for the seven of us. We can leave their bruised bodies in the gutter and they'll never be crazy enough to mess with us ever again!" Problem solved. Some of the boys expressed some fear and concern, but I talked them through it and we would present a unified front that would bring nothing to the Breen boys other than lumps, bumps and tears. Tomorrow, the sun would dawn on a new world order.

When the appointed hour arrived, all seven of us stood together and reviewed our plan. We began our trek turning left on Florence bravely marching to the corner of Ilene. We crossed the street and turned south. As our force marched confidently down the block, we saw movement near the Breen house. We were twenty feet from the house when they appeared. The bullies blocked the sidewalk.

"What do you think you're doing here?" bellowed one of the twins. "I thought we told you not to come back."

"We're going to Al's" I said with an over-confident smirk. I puffed out a bit like a banty rooster.

"Try it Jones. You'll be meeting Mr. Fist if you do."

I was almost smug when I said, "Give it a try. We'll pound you guys like a tambourine at a gypsy convention."

One of the Breens snarled and said, "Oh really? Who's going to do that?"

"We are and you're not going to like it" bragged the brash boy from Griggs. With that I slowly turned my head and said, "Aren't we boys?" Time to rally the troops.

As I looked to my rear, about four houses down the street, I saw twelve elbows and six asses running as fast as they could bound for the security of the Griggs border. My forces had mutinied.

They'd gone AWOL. They were running so fast, their shadows seemed to be racing to catch up with them.

I stood alone! Well, not totally alone; there were the Breen brothers. They were identical twins and I was seeing double. And that was before the first punch was thrown. I fought back, but was no match for a double dose of the Breens. I finally managed to break free and ran as fast as I could to the closest sanctuary – Al's Drug Store. I holed up in Al's for a couple hours while the Breens waited patiently outside. They must have finally heard the call, "Billy – Bobby. Dinner's on the table," because they disappeared. I took the Washburn route home. It was boring, but that was OK. It gave me time to reflect on the lessons I'd learned that day. When you're the lead buffalo, you need to look behind you from time to time. It's wise to make certain the herd is still there.

Things that go lump in the night - Through all those years of athletic activity, I picked up more scuffs, bruises, bumps and lumps than I could even begin to remember, but a couple stand out. I spent part of my freshman year in high school playing on the junior varsity football team and part of the year on the varsity squad. During a practice session, I was designated as the punt return guy as the varsity players practiced their punting game. I stood at one end of the practice field guarded by ten puny, inexperienced freshman blockers as the ball would come spiraling high in the air. I was to catch the ball and run up the field with it – if I survived the catch. The kicking team wanted nothing more than to dismember a freshman. There were no referees watching the kicking team to prevent them from leaving early and half of them were in full gallop before the ball was even snapped. Just before the ball reached me, more than two tons of blood thirsty football players running at full throttle greeted me. My helmet had a plastic face-guard. I was hit so hard, the guard snapped off and entered my upper lip. My nose was so badly broken, I could pretty well put it most anywhere on my face. When the coaches saw the magnitude of that train wreck, they came running onto the field to tend to the dead and dying. I was bleeding profusely, but they wanted to make sure all the parts stayed in one place just in case my head had actually been removed from my body. They held me down and kept saying, "Just stay down. You'll be alright."

I wanted to say, "Like hell I will", but I couldn't speak. They were drowning me. Not until I started overflowing did they figure it out and let me sit up. Now all of this may seem a little gory, especially if you've never played a violent sport, but believe me, it wasn't all that big of a deal. At least it wasn't until the following day.

I remember being taken to the hospital that evening and the doctor running down a list of the injuries not the least of which was the nose was not only broken, it was broken in

Diving for a ball in a high school game

three places. A broken nose isn't something you put in a cast to heal. The doctor said to just be careful. Don't move it around. And "Don't blow your nose" he said. This was going to be fun. I could feel a cold coming on.

Now the bad part. My father thought guys like John Wayne weren't tough enough. He was from the world where a hockey player could take fifty stiches and come back ten minutes later and finish the game. If you weren't losing at least a pint of blood every minute, you weren't hurt. By the next morning, my nose had swollen up so big I could barely see around it. It hurt. It throbbed. And I had a head cold. "You're going to school" he said. "You're not that hurt."

I went to school and for a week held a cloth handkerchief over my face. I didn't blow my nose. I just sat there hanging my head knowing I must be tougher than John Wayne or dumber. For the rest of my life, I had nostrils of two very different sizes. But the truth be known, the biggest injury I suffered was the embarrassment of sitting in class for a week like a neighborhood dog that had been mauled by a bigger dog. And all the girls were watching.

Over time, the list of physical trauma events grew without bound. Catastrophic demolition of my knee was a lot of fun. The other knee had to be completely replaced. A part of my big toe was actually shot off by a blazing slap shot in a hockey game. More nose breaks, but unfortunately none that ever put the nose back into its original condition. Broken arms, broken legs, torn rotator cuffs, rarely a dull moment. In reality, I don't regret any of the things the led up to the trauma. The joy of playing the game more than compensated for the little bit of suffering that came from the injuries.

Life's biggest traumas result from head injuries. Not the lumps and bumps kind; from the injuries of the mind and the spirit. Heartbreaks. Irretrievable losses. Truly, our greatest traumas are associated with our greatest regrets. It leads me to the story of Norman Appel.

Remember that growing up in a midst of a blue collar neighborhood in Detroit meant I lived on a "block" where the kids knew each other, played together, went to the same school, celebrated birthdays together and learned about life together. There were feuds and fights, but for the most part, we got along. We had to. But there were exceptions.

Norman Appel lived across the street from me. His family was from someplace in the Middle East. They were Jewish. Norman wasn't very athletic. He had some difficulty fitting in with the other boys socially. His complexion was quite dark. His hair was dark and extremely curly. In a world that was categorized as black and white, Norman could easily have been identified as black.

In the mid-1950s in Detroit, racial integration was on the march, but huge barriers still existed. There were no blacks in our lily-white neighborhood. A ten year old boy in a segregated neighborhood had little to base his world views on other than the actions of those around him. Those around me weren't long on life experience and weren't especially worldly in their views. Racism was ubiquitous. It was implicit. It was taken for granted. The mind of a ten year old isn't typically an expansive playground for liberal thought.

When Norman tried to participate in a street ball game, his lack of natural ability invariably led to a costly error or strike-out. His teammates weren't patient. Little boys can be downright mean, especially when infected with the herd mentality of collective meanness. After a skill failure, invariably one of the meaner boys would verbally abuse Norman. From time-to-time, it would lead to fisticuffs and Norman would head home crying. After a while, Norman no longer wanted to play in the games. If the boys were a player short, even Norman was a sought after asset. When he declined the demand that he play, the boys would become increasingly abusive and would taunt Norman. One boy would start in – "Norman's a nigger. Norman's a nigger" went the chant. I joined in the rhythmic chant.

At that time, I had never felt the cold, cutting blade of racism. I had no understanding of the sting of words like nigger. As I chanted, I wasn't trying to indict an entire race. I didn't hate or even dislike blacks in general. I was merely joining with the crowd in trying to hurt someone who had rejected us. I wasn't trying to be racist. I had no concept of how mean I was being. Norman did. He was hurt and he didn't deserve to be. When I went home, it was forgotten. It didn't amount to a hill of beans to me. But it did to Norman.

I ultimately moved away from Detroit and into the lily white, affluent suburbs. As I matured and grew, I underwent a gradual awakening. I came to believe that not only were all men created equal, I grew to believe all living things deserved my respect and reverence. But occasionally from the deep recesses of my memory, I could hear the chant. "Norman's a nigger. Norman's a nigger." It haunted me. I felt a great sense of shame that I had participated in such a reprehensible act of cruelty to an undeserving person. I felt a great sense of shame in using a term that denigrated an entire group of people without regard to fairness and justice. It bothered me more and more as time went on.

I don't remember when I first felt the need to actually reach out and atone for my actions, but I had a burning need to find Norman and to apologize. Even if he couldn't find it within himself to forgive me, I needed to give him that apology so I could forgive myself.

For the next forty-five years, I looked for Norman. In the days before the internet, such a search was a challenge. Even after the arrival of the cyber-world, it wasn't easy. I kept up my search until I found him. He had moved to New York. I would finally escape the shackles that had bound me for fifty years. The elation I felt when I realized I'd found him were short lived. I discovered Norman had been struck by a car while crossing a Manhattan street. He had died a couple of months before I could give him my heartfelt apology. So like the wound from the jackknife, I have another scar that will never heal. It may not be a visible scar, but it's there. It's still tender to the touch. I hope I suffered more for my transgressions than did Norman. In an odd way, Norman did more for me than he could ever possibly imagine. He helped me recognize that all mankind deserves respect. It's just too bad I couldn't share that with him personally.

Guess again - Race relations led to another major trauma in my early years. My mother's mother was Tennessee born and bred. She was a racist, but until I was twelve, I had no concept of how deeply racism was ingrained in her. I spent most of my summers living at my grandmother's house on Green Lake. R.J. and Douglas were there too. My cousin Douglas was my age; R.J. was a year older. We were inseparable friends spending our days swimming, turtle hunting and playing baseball. The small town of Union Lake was about a five mile drive from our house. We lived at the far end of Warner Drive, about a half mile from the highway that took us to what my grandmother called "the little city". Warner Drive was a dead end road and was private. It was maintained by the property owners. A sign at the highway said,

"Private Drive". The implication was that not everyone was welcome. I guess you had to guess if you were one of the welcomed people. I remember the day someone guessed wrong.

My grandmother was driving her blue 1947 Buick. She was one of the worst drivers in the history of the internal combustion engine. She would usually get in the left lane, i.e., the "passing lane" and drive thirty-five miles per hour in a fifty-five mile per hour zone. I remember so well how people would pass her in the right lane and always wave to her, usually with the middle finger. Nonetheless, on

Tella Jane Radcliffe

this summer day she was blazing along doing at least fifteen miles per hour, maybe sixteen, down Warner drive. There were nice lake houses along the left and apple orchards on the right. In the distance, I could see a white, 1957 Ford station wagon coming toward us. As it came closer, I saw four adult men, two in the front seat and two in the back. My grandmother's vision was abysmally poor and she didn't see them until they were about fifteen yards away. She instantly realized all four men were black. Without hesitation, she jerked the wheel to the left and drove directly in front of the Ford. The driver turned his wheel hard to the left to keep from hitting my grandmother's car. They narrowly missed an apple tree as they came to a stop in the orchard.

My grandmother threw open her door and bolted from the car which still blocked the road. As the driver of the station wagon got out of the car, he towered over my grandmother. He looked down at her in shocked amazement as she railed on. "What are you niggers doing here? Didn't you see the sign that said private drive? You niggers get out of here." Her assault was unrelenting. The large black man looked at her with a stunned expression, "Mam, we're just here to cut Mrs. Carpenter's lawn."

It didn't stop little Madam Compassion, "You niggers get out of here!" she shouted.

All four men were stunned silent now, but no one was more stunned than was I. I was truly traumatized. I couldn't fathom how a little woman could so viciously attack four men she had never met. The experience made a lasting impression on me. To this day, blind hate makes no sense to me whatsoever. It may also be of interest to note that R.J. and Douglas, the two cousins with whom I shared the back seat of the car, grew up to be ultra-religious evangelicals and ardent racists.

Adolescence – Touchy, touchy, touchy. As a boy child approaches manhood, sensitivities are heightened. After all, it's tough to know how to act when you've never been that person before. It seems all eyes are upon you. Popularity in school can affect your sense of self-worth. I was a freshman in high school. I was new to the area and although I would have denied it at the time, I wanted to be accepted and respected by my new classmates. As a result of test scores, I had been placed in a "special" class for "gifted" students. Miss Dorian was a hard driving task mistress and expected high performance in her freshman English class. She had made it clear on the first day that "class participation" would be a factor in the grade her student's ultimately earned. That wasn't my favorite activity, but a month or so into the semester, she asked a question of the class. I knew the answer. It was a chance to "participate". I was the only one to raise a hand. Miss Dorian looked my way and called on me.

Jerry Burns and I played on the football team. He was a big boy, a tackle on the team. He sat behind me in class. He was slouched down in his seat. The room went dead quiet as I prepared to answer the question. All eyes were trained on the new student. As I collected my thoughts and prepared to speak, Jerry farted. I don't mean a little "fudgy fart"; I mean a window rattling, two second blast of an ill-wind that bounced off the walls like a drum roll. A fourteen year old boy has not spent a lot of time anticipating such an event. I was at a loss for words and could only turn around and look at him. He had a slight grin on his face as he spoke with Shakespearean clarity, "Nice going Howie."

I remember the laughter in the classroom and I remember my intense desire to vaporize and disappear from the world. Miss Dorian wanted class participation. She got it from Jerry Burns. I wonder if it helped his grade.

Girls – The root of all evil. Gail was a nice enough girl. She was attractive in a plain sort of way. She was friendly, smiled easily and was enthralled with boys that played sports. We were in the ninth grade at Northville High School. I had just moved to Northville from Detroit and was on the football team. Gail thought that was wonderful. We got along well and we both liked each other. I was sufficiently obtuse that I didn't realize she liked me in a way that wasn't shared by me. As it turns out, she had quite a romantic crush on me. I hadn't developed that level of affection.

After every football game was the Friday night dance. The Jones boys aren't dancers. Outfit them with boxing gloves or a hockey stick and dancing became second nature, but to simply stand out in front of a crowd and attempt to contort your body rhythmically to the sound of *Danny and the Juniors* or *Elvis Presley* just seemed to be an affront to the laws of nature. Gail certainly knew I wasn't a dancer and that I had no designs on becoming one. I attended the Friday night dances, but only to strut in front of the girls so they could inflate my ego by saying "Great game, Howie."

The "Senior Prom" has been a cultural institution for generations. It is intended primarily to lubricant the wheels of courtship for seniors, hence the name "senior" prom. The "Junior Prom" or "J-Hop" was the minor league version of the senior prom and again as the name suggests, is intended for the high school juniors. We were freshman. To me the concept of attending either one of these events was so ridiculous and outrageous that any talk of doing so would clearly fall into the realm of the theater of the absurd. I didn't dance. I was a freshman. I didn't drive. And I didn't have a crush on Gail Nirider.

Under those conditions, when I smiled and with a hyperbolic sense of sarcasm, said "We should go to the junior prom", no rational person would think I was being serious. I'm afraid I falsely made an assumption that Gail was a rational person. My oops. Gail went home and apparently told her mother she'd been asked to the junior prom by Howie Jones. This was big in the Nirider household. Together, Gail and her mother designed a dress, bought the material and spent many days and nights making the gown she would wear to the ball. Meanwhile, I played football.

My next-door neighbor, Susie Eastland, was a junior and was in fact going to the prom. She also played the saxophone and sat next to Gail in band practice. About a week before the prom, I ran into Susie. "Hey, I hear you're taking Gail Nirider to the prom" she said.

I thought she was joking and responded with a cavalier, "Yea right." She put somewhat of a quizzical look on her face and hesitated slightly, "No, seriously. I think that's great. She's been making a dress for it."

Now I'm starting to worry. I think she's serious. Egad. We cut the innuendo out of the conversation and bore right to the core. The remark I had made many weeks back had been taken seriously and Gail and all of her friends were under the impression I was going to the prom. As a fourteen year old boy, I had yet to hone my decision making skills and as I thought about the problem, I concluded that if I simply said nothing and didn't show up on prom night, everyone would figure things out and live happily ever after. I said nothing to Gail, my parents or any of my friends. My silence precluded me from receiving any advice from someone wiser in the ways of the world except Susie and I could ignore her; she was blond. I had no idea how important such an event could be to a high school age girl, not to mention her mother who fronted the money and labor to build the dress.

I stood her up.

It was one of the few times that the royal carriage turned into a pumpkin before the stroke of midnight; it was a jack-o-lantern before it even got to the ball. Gail was crushed. Her mother was pissed. When I told my friends about it, they'd look at me like someone who was just going into an appointment with a Mafia bill collector. Their faces were pained, but the pain was mine. I had committed a social faux-pas worse than any in the history of Northville High School and – if the rumor mill were given credence – worse than any in the history of the human race, a race from which my membership had been revoked in the eyes of all of Gail's friends.

For the next three years, not one of a group of about eight or ten girls who were Gail's friends would speak a word to me. In some respects, the retribution was noteworthy, but I pretty much welcomed the silence. They tended to fall into the cheerleader set. One of the "pep" customs in high school was on the morning before a football game, the cheerleaders would make cute little signs and tape them to the lockers of the football team. I suspect it was just a ploy for the girls to get into the boy's locker room, but it was what it was. I'd go to my locker to get ready to suit-up before the game and there'd be the quaint little sign saying something like, "Go Howie, Yes! Fight for NHS." But I knew that without the supervision of Miss Dorian, the cheerleader coach, my locker sign would have said something more along the lines of "Die you scumbag dog. I hope the kicker boots both your balls."

It was in the latter half of my senior year that a thaw seemed to be underway. A few of Gail's friends were now speaking to me, admittedly to tell me what a shithead I was for standing her up three years before, but progress is progress. Things had almost returned to normal by the time we graduated. Gail herself was even speaking to me. I started to realize that despite having to maneuver through the rubble of a social and emotional minefield, she still had a crush on me.

Some of the guys decided it would be fun to get dates and spend a day at Edgewater Park, an old fashioned amusement park not far from Northville. I thought I might not only have a nice time taking Gail, I could also score some much needed political points with the girls if I asked her to go. She couldn't say yes fast enough. After three and a half years, we were finally going to have our first date. I was hoping she wouldn't wear her prom dress.

The day went well. We hit most of the rides, ate cotton candy and generally had a grand time. We rode the roller coaster a number of times. I had fun even though a good roller-coaster barely got my heart rate up. Then fate set out to even the score for prom-night past.

As we approached the Ferris wheel, Gail exclaimed, "Oh look! I just love Ferris wheels. Let's go on it."

I guess it's possible she knew; a woman scorned . . . but it didn't matter. Although I could almost nap on a roller coaster, I must have been born with some internal mechanism whereby my body doesn't suffer Ferris wheels well. In fact, in every instance during my childhood where I found myself on one of those wheels of death, I also found myself deathly ill, violently sick. But now I was stuck. I was eighteen and a macho young stud whose primary mission in life was to impress the girls in general and Gail in particular that I was the epitome of a "He Man". In the wake of the events of the past three-and-a-half years, how could I now possibly face a date with my lip quivering, fighting back my tears and tell her I was actually a super-wimp and not worthy of adulation? Oh my! What a conundrum.

By the time of my eighteenth summer, my talent for rationalization had become fairly refined. I put it to work. Surely, my fears were based upon circumstances that were only operational as a little child and now that I was a full grown bundle of masculinity, I had outgrown them. I also knew that I was tough, a real gamer that could overcome any and all obstacles. I cast my fears overboard and headed toward the ticket counter. Two please.

Carney operators rarely have graduate degrees in physics or philosophy. Most don't have roots in middle class American society. They're not usually the most polished members of our world. As I walked past the operator of the Ferris wheel I was about to board, he was the image of what I imagined to be the body-double for Boris Karloff in a 1930s vintage horror movie. He was tall, emaciated, a little hunched over and had a sadistic smile cut into his face. I had a feeling of unease and I had yet to take my seat.

Gail and I were locked into place and soon began our joyful ride to traumaville. The Ferris wheel gained speed as we rose up the backside. As we approached the zenith, I was vividly reminded of why I had never liked Ferris wheels. At the top, there is a brief moment of weightlessness where you seem to be floating a hundred or so feet above the ground. I had been designed to not enjoy that feeling. Every part of my being was weightless, especially my stomach. My body was offering counsel to my head. Every sense in me said, "Get off of this thing. Now is much better than later."

As we descended, I could see Igor the operator looking my way. "You really need to stop and let me off" I hollered as I approached him. He smiled diabolically and pulled back on the long metal lever that controlled the ride. We sped up. I briefly saw into the future and it wasn't pretty. As we approached the zenith for the second time, my mind was no longer in control of my body. In fact my mind had morphed into a trembling pulp of fear and panic. At that moment of weightlessness, my stomach took control of all that was meaningful. I threw up violently. I also threw down, over, back and forward. Gail looked on in abject horror as she was covered from head to toe with that which my body had so graciously ejected. I was also successful in thoroughly decorating the couple sitting in the chair in front of us and I saved plenty for the couple sitting behind.

The only good thing that came out of this bit of misfortune was that I also made a substantial deposit on Igor himself. He quickly decided to honor my request to let me off the ride, albeit one revolution too late. As they unlocked the gate on our seat, Gail bolted for the restroom presumably to shower. I don't know if it was traumatic for her, but it damn sure was for me. It would only be another thirty years before I'd see her again.

Sometimes, "cool" just isn't. The following fall, I became a freshman at Western Michigan University in Kalamazoo. Like almost all freshmen, I lived in a dormitory. Like almost all freshmen, I had an insatiable hunger for the opposite sex. And like some freshman, I took up smoking cigarettes so I could be cool, just like the Marlboro man (who later died of lung cancer), the Tareyton man who'd rather "fight than switch" and the guy that would walk a mile for a Camel. I asked Linda Beckler out on a date.

I met Linda in one of my classes at WMU. Had I been more attentive to my studies, I might even remember which one. She was a pleasant girl, fairly pleasing to the eye and offered promise in the arena in which most college boys hoped to perform sooner or later. You had to be twenty-one in Michigan to buy alcohol so we weren't going to any bars or clubs. The social center of the campus was the "student union", a huge almost cafeteria looking place where students met, socialized, ate the infamous "Bronco Burger" (a hamburger with a ton of peanut butter slathered on it), smoked cigarettes and told lies.

I walked to Linda's dorm. From there we walked to the student union. The temperature hovered near zero so we welcomed the warmth of the union. It was a Friday night and the union was nearly packed with students staying out of the snowy frigid weather. We managed to find a table, shed our bulky coats and sat down to make ourselves comfortable. Linda was about to witness an act of such ultra-coolness she would swoon dangerously out of control. I had practiced and practiced. No more rehearsal; this was the time the bumbling freshman would demonstrate to Linda Beckler in particular and the hundreds of young women in the union that night that he was the alpha-male, the one most worthy of being first selected in any future breeding activities.

A pack of Tareytons sat at the ready in my shirt pocket. At the perfect moment, I brought my right hand up and pulled the pack from my pocket. I tapped the pack lightly upon the table so a cigarette protruded slightly. I slowly raised the pack toward my lips and drew the cigarette from the pack. I returned the pack to my pocket. Linda had to be thinking, "Wow, if he can do all of this with just one hand, imagine what he could do with two."

With the cigarette dangling from my lips like a limp sex toy, I pulled an old fashioned book of matches from my pocket. My left hand remained immobile. I held the book of matches between the tip and the base of my index finger. My thumb was then available to casually flip open the book of matches. The one-handed performance was moving forward flawlessly and I suspect a couple dozen young women watching from nearby tables were already contemplating leaving their boyfriends as they looked on with unbridled lust and envy.

Still holding the now opened matchbook in one hand, I used my thumb to pull one and only one match forward and folded it such that its head rested directly above the strike-pad. "Please hold your applause until the show is complete", I thought to myself. With my thumb, I pressed the head of the match onto the strike-pad. With a quick flip of the match and even quicker removal of the thumb, the match ignited. I furtively glanced toward Linda to see if she was already beginning to disrobe as I slowly and coolly brought the match to the end of the cigarette dangling from the corner of my mouth. In an act worthy of Clark Gable's finest performance, I lit the cigarette. My God! This was a performance that would be etched into the memories of all the now helpless and lustful women watching.

I could see people standing out of the corner of my eyes, undoubtedly preparing for the standing ovation or to simply walk over and introduce themselves to me. I was totally cool, so damn cool. All that remained was for me extinguish the match. I hoped the level of sex hormones in the air wasn't so great that the room would explode. I slowly moved the flaming match from the tip of the cigarette toward the other corner of my mouth so I could blow it out with a barely perceptible move of my lips.

It all went so well until an ever so slight misjudgment caused me to lay the flaming ball of molten sulfur directly onto my lip. The pain was instant and it was intense. The flaming match fell into my pants. I don't mean onto; I mean into. It landed between my shirt and belt. The freshly lit cigarette fell into my crotch area. I let forth with a yelp that drew the attention of everyone in the student union as I jumped violently out of my seat tipping over the table and everything on it. As our drinks blanketed Linda with their sugary, syrupy contents, I jumped up and down frantically grabbing my crotch to extinguish a match and a cigarette.

The blister was instantaneous. And it was huge. I was afraid I'd have another scar for life, but it ultimately healed. The emotional trauma was long lasting. I truly don't remember if I escorted Linda back to her dorm, but I do remember that was the last time I ever saw her. I haven't smoked in over forty years, but if you do and you're looking for another reason to quit, you might consider giving this circus stunt a try. Hey, you never know. You might be the alpha-male.

I think it's fair to say I've experienced my share of trauma over my lifetime. I probably haven't made much of a dent in the list. Everyone has his own list. And when you really get to thinking about it, we've all had some doozies. The uniqueness of our individual experiences is what we have in common. All of us are to a greater or lesser extent the products of our traumas.

Chapter Two - Marriage – More is Better

I'm "happily married". What the hell does that mean? To me, it's obvious. But to someone reading this missive, it leaves a great deal to interpretation. If ten thousand people were surveyed as to what it means to be happily married, chances are, you'd end up with ten thousand opinions.

I've got a girl that's spunky, indomitable, intelligent, and fun. Forgive me for trivializing one of life's monumental issues, but I'm not sure what more I could possibly ask for, other than maybe having a phenomenal chef. Oh my! Now that you ask – she was hall-of-fame in the kitchen before she attended countless cooking schools all over the world. Ok – so I won the lottery. You can't win if you don't play.

What gives me the right to define marital "happiness"? What gives you the right? Believe the media or the preacher? It's got to be defined somewhere. Maybe the Bible. Maybe the statutes. If you don't believe in either one, maybe somewhere else.

I learned about marriage in the traditional way – watching my parents and watching TV. When I was born, TV existed, but not in the home. My mother learned about marriage from her parents, the same way everyone has learned about it since Piltdown Man. This isn't an anthropological treatise, so let's jump to the twentieth century and just say. . . man was the physically dominant animal. Despite Hollywood's best attempts to paint a different picture, size matters.

Frank Jones married his high school sweetheart Jean Elizabeth Radcliffe in 1945. Frank was a young Army lieutenant. Elizabeth was a young, naïve girl delighted to have

Frank Jones in 1944

someone's attention and happier still to leave the home of a cold and demanding mother. Frank was the apple of his mother's eye and as a result, he was quite spoiled and indulged. He was the center of his own universe. He was a football player in high school, a young officer in the Army, a respectable student and he was in love or lust or possibly both. Elizabeth may have been in love or lust herself. In her later years following the bitter break-up with Frank, she swore Frank wasn't the love object of her youth. Rather he was her ticket out of the dysfunctional Radcliffe home. Regardless, both settled into their defined roles as husband and wife.

Initially, they moved in with Frank's parents, Howard and Helen Jones. They stayed there while Frank attended the University of Detroit and received his degree as a civil engineer. For the first four years of my life, I had two couples as role models for the way a marriage was "supposed" to operate. I watched as my grandfather, Howard, worked and brought home the bacon. Helen's role was to have the kids and raise them. She was to be subservient, have the meals prepared, do the laundry and keep

Elizabeth Radcliffe 1943

the house clean. In exchange for being the bread winner, Howard was afforded "privileges" commensurate with his role in American society in 1950. He would stop by "the Eagles" club after work and have a beer or six and chase the "girls". On Friday nights, it wasn't uncommon for him to arrive home, drunk and covered in blood following the fight that ended the evening. He was never one to back away from a scrap, but he didn't win them all.

He gave my grandmother an allowance from which she was to buy the food and all the household supplies. This assumed he hadn't been rolled outside the beer parlor after having too many and lost the week's pay. Groceries were a high priority, nearly as high as beer (Pabst Blue Ribbon) and cigarettes (Chesterfields or Pall Malls or Lucky Strikes). Saturday nights usually involved a card game at the house. The whole adult family participated, aunts, uncles and cousins. Pinochle was usually the preferred game. In our family, it was almost a rite-of-passage, the entry into adulthood, to be allowed to participate in the game. For my grandfather, Sunday was usually reserved for fishing or hunting. He was considerate that way. He got out of my grandmother's hair while she cleaned up the house and dishes following Saturday night's card playing train wreck. Monday morning, Howard went to work on the railroad, the New York Central, and the cycle began again.

That is the model upon which my father built his perception of a marriage. Once he was out of college and gainfully employed in the construction field, he became the bread winner. He set the rules, made the decisions and became the ever more brightly burning star at the center of his universe. My mother was given a rather paltry allowance out of which she had to buy groceries and maintain the household. My father had a car; my mother did not. A woman didn't need a car in those days. Where was she going to go? Her job was at the home. My grandmother, Helen, never had a driver's license in her life.

Frank tried to be a beneficent monarch in the early years of his marriage. He actually had most of his dinners at home around the family table. We had moved into a "flat" in Highland Park, a small section in northern Detroit. He worked. He came home. His life and hence our lives were all built on the family model we had watched in the generations before us. Frank didn't belong to the Eagles lodge and didn't copy his father's lifestyle of carousing in the evening. He worked. He came home.

After a year and a half, Frank borrowed the down payment for a new house on Detroit's west side. He was now a superintendent for a general contractor (Walter L. Couse & Co.) and his income was beginning to rise. He bought a new 1957 Buick; he believed he had to look successful. But for the most part, the model was intact. Frank gave Elizabeth a nearly pathetic allowance to run the household. She continued to try and live the model, subservience, stay at home, clean the house, have the meals prepared, take care of the kids (now three boys) and serve at the pleasure of the bread winner.

I say this not to indict my parents or grandparents for having the marriages they did. That was the way it was for most marriages of the era. I knew this because by 1955 or 1956, we had joined the crowd and now had a television. It broadcast in black-and-white on a screen that may have been seventeen inches on the diagonal – nineteen at the most. And with that tool, we validated our perceptions of how a marriage should work.

The Nelsons, Ozzie, Harriet, David and Ricky, were America's family. They defined the institution of marriage for countless Americans who watched their weekly show. Ozzie went to work every morning and came home every evening to a dedicated housewife, Harriet, who was generally preparing the meal, no doubt paid for out of the allowance given to her by Ozzie. She didn't work outside the house. Who would have taken care of the boys? She took off her apron after serving the meal and the entire family sat down

Ozzie, Harriet, David and Ricky Nelson

together to have dinner and discuss their middle-American lives. Harriet wore a nice dress. Her hair was done. Her make-up was always in place. Ozzie actually wore his sport coat and tie at the table. Obviously, that was the way it was supposed to be. I'm not sure if Ozzie ever came home from the Eagles lodge three sheets to the wind. If he did, they kept it out of the show. I don't know if he was banging his secretary, but we were led to believe he would never consider such a thing. Perhaps the Nelson family had roots not stained by the coal dust of the mines of central England as were my family's. It could have been that we were just a touch more "blue collar", but the family model was pretty much the same as the one we came to know.

The Nelsons weren't the only ones validating our family structure. Other shows gave the same support to our way of life. Everyone with a television knew "Father Knows Best". Jim Anderson wore his coat and tie to the dinner table and broke bread with the entire family every night. The Cleavers had a little more discord, no doubt because of that damned troublemaker Eddie Haskell. I'll bet his father was at the Eagles lodge with my grandfather on Friday nights. Nonetheless, Ward Cleaver wore shirt and tie to the dinner table and June's makeup was always flawless. She did at one point have a part-time job, but was fired, probably because her natural role was to tend the home of Ward and the boys. Even Ralph Cramden, the bluest of blue collared heads of family in the fifties, had a wife who stayed home to tend the apartment. She had an allowance generously awarded her by the bread winner. She prepared dinner and dressed appropriately. No slacks, makeup in place. She did the dishes. That's the woman's job.

One more little observation on the Frank and Elizabeth show before moving on. By the time we purchased a television and I began watching Ozzie and Harriet, Leave It to Beaver and other primers of cultural indoctrination, Frank wasn't home as much in the evenings. The demands of being the General Superintendent of a sizable construction company began putting greater and greater demands on his time. With an increasing regularity, he had to work late. He had to review bids, go over drawings, deal with labor matters and otherwise deal with all the challenges of being a construction "big shot". Some of the jobs were out of town. I remember one in Kokomo, Indiana and another in Tennessee. The demands were so great that he needed help in dealing with them. Who better equipped to assist than a large breasted secretary? More on this set of adventures later, but suffice it to say, this soap opera also weighed heavily in the design of my idea of a domestic partnership.

As a product of that time period, it should come as no surprise that in 1966 when my first marriage was just around the corner, my model wasn't going to be significantly different than the entirety of what I had observed up until that time. Compound that reality with the fact that at the ripe old age of nineteen, maturity wasn't my long suit. And without a doubt, a hormone cluttered mind didn't help strengthen my analytical skills.

By now, you've got a pretty good idea of what my expectations were for the future when on November 19, 1966, I married Lucy Llewellyn Byard. I dropped out of my

Howard and Lucy – November 19, 1966

sophomore year at Western Michigan University. Lucy left her freshman year at Olivet College. I was in love. The question was "With what was I in love?" Lucy had a rack that made Dolly Parton look like a candidate for a training bra. As far as having things in common, we both lived in Northville, Michigan, both immature teenagers and both driven by a near lethal concentration of hormones. The stage was set for a great adventure. Some of it was good, but much of it could have been better. Off we rode into the sunset seeking the bliss that existed only in our youthful imaginations.

Before I leave this model-building part of my life's adventures, I'll point out a couple of the final building blocks that were cemented in place on that fateful fall day. They completed the marriage model I was about to implement.

In Michigan that year, November 19th happened to be the opening day of the deer hunting season. In scheduling the wedding, I had overlooked that fact. My father was faced with a great dilemma: attend the wedding of his oldest son or go hunting for yet another of an endless succession of deer that had passed through our freezer over the years. Clearly, the question was which event was most important? He had only one oldest son. That oldest son would never again get married (at least for the first time); it's a once-in-a-lifetime event. Deer season is an annual event wherein you get to struggle in the dark through thickets of thorns and stickers, fall through frozen ice into freezing water and kill things in the snowy woods. I'm sure to most of you, the choice would be apparent. My father did not attend my wedding.

I should also mention that if I had known then what I know now, I would have given him the benefit of the doubt and realized that he had a higher calling. He had a way to stay warm even during the coldest hunting situations. It's amazing how warm a great bwana can feel when snuggled up with his large breasted secretary. I do not know beyond a shadow of a doubt that hooters came into play in his decision making process, but I can almost guarantee it. Either way, my father was absent from the wedding. I suspect that it gave me a subconscious realization that the institution of marriage wasn't all that important.

One other little thing shed light on the significance of marriage on that fall day in 66. Avid football fans may remember that on November 19, 1966, a college football game that to this day is generally acknowledged as "the game of the century" was played. The two major football polls differed because the top two teams were so closely matched. Associated Press had Notre Dame ranked number one in the nation and Michigan State ranked second. United Press International ranked Michigan State number one and Notre Dame number two. They would play each other on the final day of the season to settle the dispute. Both teams were so strong that The Sporting News later rated them the 11th and 13th greatest individual teams of the twentieth century. Many future professional football stars played that day.

The All-American quarterback from Michigan State, Steve Juday, was from Northville and was a good friend of mine. The teams ended up playing to a 10-10 tie, hardly a good omen for the newlyweds.

So what does all this have to say about my marital future? Half the guests weren't going to come to the wedding because they didn't want to miss the game. We ended up working the phones that morning to call everyone involved and delay the wedding three hours. Yes, the marriage was off to a good start. It wasn't as important as deer hunting, college football or oversized breasts, but it was as important as the cider tasting event going on down the road at Parmenter's Cider Mill and "The Professionals" starring Burt Lancaster, Lee Marvin and Jack Palance which was playing at the Northville Theater – at least for the dozen or so people who attended the wedding. From that day forward, Howard and Lucy would be "playing house" together.

Living with Lucy - I'd love to tell you about our blissful life together. However, despite the fact that we did have a lot of good times together, let's cut to the chase. The marriage ended in bitter failure after about eleven years. I won't pretend we cruised on autopilot with a setting of "happy" for all those years and suddenly dropped off into grumpiness. The marriage was pretty well doomed from the start. Unfortunately, both Lucy and I were the last to recognize it.

There was one complication. Eight months, thirty days and a few hours after the wedding, Lucy gave birth to Amy, our first and only daughter. Had we not delayed the wedding three hours due to the Michigan State/Notre Dame game, we might have hit nine months right on the button. It might make you wonder what we did during the delay time. The fact is Amy was three weeks overdue, but who's counting.

So there we were, a young, immature, married couple with a child. I had always been successful at whatever I put my mind to (baseball, turtle hunting, throwing snowballs and those other useful trades learned as a boy). There was certainly no question in my mind that I would be a highly sought after asset to whatever company was lucky enough to win the race for my talents. It hadn't dawned on me that after one year of poor performance at one of the nation's great party schools and no significant experience aside from working as a construction laborer during the summers, the bag containing all of my marketable skills was completely empty. I didn't let that reality interfere with my willingness to grace the Detroit work world with my presence. I got an entry level job at a floor covering company. With an income barely adequate to buy groceries and pay the rent on our two-room, attic apartment, I set out to build our future with my marriage model as my guide.

I would be the patriarch, the breadwinner and "head" of our household. As President Bush the Younger said during his term, I was the "decider". Lucy would be the docile, subservient, apron wearing housewife. I would be Ozzie. She would be Harriet.

It didn't take long for some design flaws to come to the surface. First of all, Lucy came from a fairly well-to-do family. She was accustomed to having servants, not being one. I've got to give her credit; she at least gave it the old college try. She tried to prepare meals just like Harriet would have, but she really didn't know how to cook. Maybe that's an overstatement, but without a doubt, cooking wasn't her strength and it damn sure wasn't her passion. I was self-centered and demanding. I had the culinary tastes of a street beggar and expected Lucy to cater to my every dining (and other) desire. I'm sure it's not going to come as a big surprise to find out that this course wasn't a sustainable one. As time went on, it led to some friction. How's that for understatement?

As the years went by, so did a number of jobs (more on that later), apartments and adventures. We had good times. We had bad times. But all in all, we struggled to make it work to the best of our limited abilities. We had the "important things", a TV, a bed, a 1966 Volkswagen. Is there more to life than that?

After a couple years had passed, I returned to the broadcast world. I had worked part-time while in college at radio stations and had done some announcing. Apparently, I had a good radio voice and some talent for using it. I ended up on-the-air as a radio "personality" in Ann Arbor, Michigan. I hosted a fairly popular jazz program in the evenings and worked as a news reporter and broadcaster when I wasn't entertaining my small cadre of jazz followers at night. This meant that I was becoming a "celebrity". I was my biggest fan, but there were others. As my fame grew in my own mind, I started hanging out in the jazz clubs of Ann Arbor after my show was over. Some of the ladies thought I was appealing and were more than willing and anxious to spend their time with me. It would have been selfish of me to deny my fans. And surely it was acceptable behavior on my part. After all, my father and his father before him had been beacons guiding me into the ports of infidelity.

I'm not going to give you a blow by blow description of each day of my tumultuous eleven year relationship with Lucy, but clearly we weren't on the smoothest road to bliss. Lucy was temperamental, moody, immature, self-centered, somewhat air-headed at times and lived to be spoiled. At the time we ultimately split up, I was convinced she was the complete embodiment of the world's biggest bitch. And she was. She did things that were as rotten as rotten could be. At times, she was a devious, diabolical, scheming, dishonest sewer rat. However, as I look back with introspective honesty, she was married to an immature, self-absorbed, narcissistic asshole. Why should she have been any different? There was enough dirty laundry to go around. Some of it was mine; some of it was hers.

As I pen this, we would have been married for nearly fifty years if we had stayed together. But for all the aforementioned reasons, we're not together. Although at the time of our breakup, she undoubtedly blamed me and I certainly blamed her. The truth is we were both at fault. If one of us had to accept more blame than the other, I guess I'd have to step forward. It's neither here nor there. It was destined to fail. In part due to our youth and immaturity. In part due to our selfishness. But above all other reasons, it failed because we went into the marriage with unreal expectations based upon a flawed model. I've since learned that any woman that could make that model function wouldn't be a woman with whom I could spend any time. It took a while, but one of my greatest realizations in life is that with any successful relationship, it must be based upon mutual respect. Had I know that nearly fifty years ago, maybe Lucy and I would still be together. More than likely, Lucy and I wouldn't have been married. Either way, after fifty years, I've forgiven Lucy. More importantly, I've forgiven myself. A lot of good things did come from the marriage. And I'm sure we're both much wiser for the experience. Happy anniversary Lucy. It's just too bad Michigan State didn't win the game.

On the Dark Side of the Moon with Eleonor - After the bitter divorce from Lucy, my "model" for marriage changed dramatically. Unfortunately, it wasn't necessarily for the better. Lucy taught me the value of getting the best and the most ruthless attorney when engaged in legal proceedings. I'm sure her lawyer kicked little children and ate the neighbor's dogs and cats without even skinning them. The only animal he skinned was me. When I drove off into the sunset, everything I owned was in the new compact car I had just purchased. I still had room to pick up a hitchhiker if I had wanted to. I had to buy the new car because Lucy's attorney gave her a trick to keep both of the family cars. For my transportation, Lucy left me a pair of shoes. Lucy kept things that she needed to survive, like my hockey gear and all of the heirlooms acquired from my family.

Another thing I lost in the war was my belief in love and marriage. Relationships had value. I mean who doesn't like a party? And the recent legal conflagration hadn't dampened the wants and needs with which nature had endowed the human animal. It's just that I had concluded a legally binding marital relationship was no different than a hot burner on a stove. It was something that was to be avoided at all costs. It was something with little or no meaning and offered nothing but the potential for pain and discomfort.

I met her at the Chevron refinery where I worked. Leonor de la Torre (Eleonor) was a friendly, exotic, department secretary. Eleonor always had a smile on her face. She was quick to laugh. She had stories of her past that were interesting and intriguing. She was married, but her husband was a professional musician. She worked days; he worked nights. Their relationship was distant. It was as if they never saw each other and lived in parallel worlds that rarely overlapped. She was pleased when I showed interest in hearing her stories of growing up, the daughter of a Yaqui Indian from the area of Ciudad Obregón, Sonora, México. We hit it off well. We had lunch a couple of times. Then we begin having lunch most days. Then dinner. We hit it off quite well. Then she moved her husband out and moved me in.

Actually, I must confess. There was one evening she moved me in before her husband had moved out. As luck would have it, the crowd was unusually light at the club showcasing Bruce's band and he came home a couple hours earlier than his customary 2:30 a.m. arrival time. I managed to get to the back door and made a hasty exit as I heard the sound of the hammer on his 38 caliber revolver clicking into the firing position. It was a chilly night as I beat a retreat down the street clad only in Eleonor's husband's bathrobe. That was so long ago, I don't remember how I managed to retrieve my car keys and clothes and get home that night. The memory of the deafening sound of the gun's hammer locking into place seems to have nudged some of the other details of that night off of that particular shelf in my memory bank.

Even to me, it sounds cold to say that my feelings for Eleonor were rooted in something other than a burning love. We got along well. We enjoyed each other's presence. It was a good life when we were together, but coming on the heels of implosion of my relationship with Lucy, I really don't think I was capable of a deep emotional relationship at that time. Eleonor was a wonderful, sincere and charming person. I wasn't. As time went on, she began to hint at the idea of marriage. Unfortunately, it was as if she were talking to someone in a foreign language, a language I didn't speak or understand. My "model" of the institution had been blown off the face of the earth. Looking back at that model, it was probably a good thing. It needed to be destroyed. But at that time, I hadn't even begun to clean up the rubble that remained, let alone begun to reconstruct the concept in my mind.

When the Twin Towers of the World Trade Center collapsed in 2001, not only were they left in a pile of rubble, the collapse caused a lot of damage to the things around them. So it was with my divorce from Lucy. There was a lot of collateral damage. My concept of marriage was an integral part of my concept of "self". I was now a thirty year old, single man living in the exotic land of Northern California. I was a very employable chemical engineer making a good living. I was in a relationship. But my dock lines had been broken and my ship was adrift in a confused sea. I could go in any direction I wanted to, but when I looked at my various horizons, I really didn't know where they were or what was beyond them. The Firesign Theater had a great line in one of their performances many years ago. "How can you be in two places at once when you're not anywhere at all?" That pretty well summed up my life at that moment in time.

I had parted ways with Chevron Research and gone to work for Radian Corporation as part of a traveling research team studying "fugitive emissions". The job took me to various locations up and down the west coast for a couple months at a time. When not on assignment, I lived with Eleonor in Pinole, California near San Francisco. After about a year, I took a job with Union Oil near home so I could have a bit more of a "normal" life. One thing led to another and I worked my way into a position where I solved a couple of complex technical problems for Union Oil. The work resulted in some rather lucrative patents in the world of crystallization. I have the pride of knowing my work ended up having great commercial value to my employer, but Union Oil retained those rights. And they should have; they were paying me to do that work. They invested in me. They should reap the rewards.

One thing I did get from the work was a little bit of notoriety in the world of science. The next thing you know, I had received an offer to study for my Ph.D. through a grant from the National Science Foundation under the wing of world's foremost expert in the field, Dr. Alan Randolph of the University of Arizona. The attention felt good and the prospect of becoming Dr. Howard Jones had a certain charm. I agreed to begin my doctoral studies in Tucson, Arizona in the summer of 1979. I was starting to regain a little bit of focus in my life. I still had a long way to go.

Eleonor and I were still together, getting along well, enjoying life. I'm sure I loved her – sort of in the way I would love a new driver in my golf bag or a new car. I cared about her and always will. She was a wonderful person. But she was living with damaged goods. I had still done little to begin rebuilding my marriage model. That didn't stop her. She wanted to get married. She had a good job at Chevron. She knew I would be leaving for Arizona and that she would be staying behind. But she still wanted to get married. She seemed to truly believe that the marriage would somehow survive the long separation and that "Dr. Jones" would ultimately return to the Bay Area and everyone would live happily ever after.

Eleonor was the product of a traditional Mexican family. To explain that in greater detail would require another set of books. Let's just say her "model" of the institution of marriage was a bit different than mine had been or would ultimately become. She believed that it was a wife's role to serve. In retrospect, it's funny because her perception isn't all that far from my father's and my grandfather's dreams. A woman to serve your every need. I could do no wrong. If I was hungry, I was fed. Every household chore was her responsibility. If my seat wasn't comfortable, she would bring the cushion. If I had an itch, it was her job to scratch it. On the surface, this may sound like man's version of heaven and to the chauvinist, maybe it is. But to me, it was the beginning of discovering who I really was. And I was not an Egyptian Pharaoh. Frankly, the incessant attention and servitude drove me crazy. I had long known that I was not the type of person that was willing or capable of bowing to power, but now I knew I couldn't have a deep and lasting relationship with anyone else that was capable of being subjugated. It's ironic that the beginning of my long walk to maturity began not with someone showing me what I was; rather it began with someone inadvertently showing me what I wasn't.

Nonetheless, by March of 1979, with a June departure for Tucson looming, Eleonor continued to lobby hard for marriage. My thinking, foolish as it may have been, was . . . marriage means nothing, I have no intention of ever believing in the institution again, I don't even know what it's supposed to be. I only knew from recent experience, it doesn't work in the way in which I was led to believe over the past thirty years. It meant something to her, but nothing to me. What could it hurt?

I told her that I would go ahead and marry her, but only on the condition the wedding take place on April Fool's Day. I entered into my second marriage on the first day of April 1979. A couple weeks later, I left for Tucson, Arizona. Eleonor stayed behind.

The Death of a Born Again Spirit – R.I.P. Life as a doctoral candidate amounted to a monumental change. No longer was I bringing in the big oil company paycheck. No longer did I have a secretarial pool that would perform my clerical duties and more mundane tasks. It was more like I had entered a monastery. I was now a slave to my major professor. I had my laboratory in which I faithfully performed my research on the kinetics of the crystallization of potassium chloride in a classified reactor. I was being paid enough to survive, but just barely. I had no extra income for any form of entertainment, but that really didn't matter because it was expected that I would have no time available for any form of entertainment. All of my waking hours were to be dedicated to study and research. It was such a monastic lifestyle, that the only entertainment I afforded myself was on Sundays when I would go to the Tanque Verde Swap Meet and wander about looking at the people and at the merchandise which even if I had wanted, I couldn't have afforded to buy. A Ph.D. student truly must grasp the concept of deferred gratification. There sure as hell wasn't much instantaneous pleasure unless discovering you had a great fit of your data with a non-linear multiple regression analysis was the source of euphoria. (I'm almost embarrassed to admit that even to this day, I do find it nearly euphoric).

I had a lot of time for introspection during my time at the University of Arizona. I was still somewhat bitter and disillusioned in the wake of my divorce. Technically, I was married to Eleonor even though we were nearly a thousand miles apart. But the reality was I was a cloistered grad student with most of the trappings of my previous existences gone and becoming increasingly forgotten. I immersed myself in my studies. I was far more concerned with the present than I was with a future. I knew parts of myself very well, but other areas of my being had not been revealed to anyone including myself.

On a chilly day in November, a chance meeting would turn my life upside down. I walked out of my little apartment and headed toward my motorcycle. (I had opted for the fuel efficiency of a motorcycle; what grad student could afford to put gas in a car?) It dawned on me I had left a needed book on my table. I returned to get it. As I hurried back, a woman with a small child emerged from one of the other apartments. I glanced her way; she mine. She struck me as one of the most beautiful woman I had ever seen. She had long black hair, an exotic appearance almost Asian, but not. Her complexion was dark. Clearly, she was non-European. She could have been from anywhere. The U of A drew students from all over the world. I moved on to retrieve my book.

As I rushed back toward the parking lot, the woman unlocked her car which happened to be parked next to my motorcycle. Perhaps I had been spending far too much time in my laboratory, too much time in the books. Perhaps not. As I approached, she turned and smiled. It was as if a flash of light suddenly illuminated my universe. I was blinded by a beauty that seemed to go beyond the physical world. Far smarter and more eloquent people than I have dedicated their lives to explaining and writing about such things. I can't begin to explain what happened there.

Actually, that's not true; I can "begin" to explain it, but I'm certain I can't complete the task. We exchanged a casual "Hi" and we both went on our ways. However, with a smile more lethal than the rock that slew Goliath, I had been smitten.

I saw her again a couple days later and we said hello. Her image was burned into my mind. I thought about her when I was supposed to be thinking about my studies. At night I would wonder who she was. In my lab, I would adjust the laser crystal counter I used in my research and be thinking about this woman I didn't know. I wondered if she was on campus studying while I labored over my data.

After about a week, I ran into her again in the university housing complex in which we both lived. This time, I took the time to engage. I found out she was a nursing student at the university. She was Native American. She was born and raised on the Navajo reservation in Northeastern Arizona. Her family and her ancestors had lived in Ganado, Arizona for roughly seven hundred

Roberta LaRose in native dress

or so years. She was single, divorced and intent on earning her nursing degree and returning to help her people. She was torn between two worlds, that of the Navajo and that of the Anglo. She was intelligent and fun to be around. Our relationship quickly intensified.

I soon learned that she had had a bout with breast cancer nearly five years prior, but had tenaciously overcome it. It had no bearing on our budding romance. It only served to prove what a great sense of will she had.

Over the course of the next six months, we became inseparable. Although a permanent relationship was problematic, it started to become a very real possibility and then a probability. We faced numerous challenges of more than trivial magnitude. I was still legally married. She was bicultural and if I was to spend a serious amount of time with her, it quickly became apparent I too would have to be bicultural. I'd have to learn the Navajo language, the culture, their ways and the lifestyles. But somehow, the barriers seemed small when compared to the fulfillment we both felt when we were together. A heart frozen in bitterness had finally begun to thaw.

I ordered a do-it-yourself divorce kit and filed all the papers necessary to legally dissolve my marriage to Eleonor. She put up a nominal fight, but soon realized our relationship was not destined to last. The divorce was quick and relatively painless, a far cry from the Armageddon like battle with Lucy. I began to learn Navajo, spent time on the reservation and let my Ph.D. studies slip away from me. On a sunny Saturday afternoon in June of 1980, Roberta LaRose and Howard Jones were married in Tucson, Arizona.

Less than forty-eight hours later, Roberta went for her annual physical checkup. The honeymoon was brought to an abrupt end when the doctor told her the cancer had returned with a vengeance. Without treatment, she might survive one to two years. With aggressive treatment, she could conceivably live three to four years. It was under those circumstances that I entered into my third marriage. It was under those circumstances I would endeavor to bring forth from the emotional ruins of my past a new model of marriage. It was to be a bigger construction project than I had ever dreamed possible.

Over the next three years, my perception of marriage was tossed and turned in every direction imaginable and in many ways unimaginable. Even after nearly thirty-five years, the events that

followed remain tender to the touch and difficult to discuss. I'll
try and summarize them by stating the obvious.

When someone is given an irrevocable sentence of death, it is an
indescribably heavy emotional and physical burden to carry.
Now complicate the situation by placing the onus of raising three
young children on that person's shoulders. Consider what it's
like living with a constant fear that when you're gone, no one
will care for the little ones. If the load is still manageable, take it
a step further by putting that person in a situation where one foot
is in the Anglo world and the other one is firmly embedded in
the Navajo world where life views, beliefs, medicine, culture and
history share little in common with mainstream America. Throw
in the issue of the effects of the anti-cancer medications under
which much of life goes on. Now give that person no quarter, no
respite, no escape from these monumental burdens. They stalk
the person day after day, twenty-four hours a day. Every time the
victim looks into a mirror, she sees her ghost bearing down on
her. It was such an incredible situation, it was described in a
nearly full front page story on a Sunday edition of Tucson's
primary newspaper. Even the National Enquirer contacted us
wanting interviews for a feature story. We turned them down.

As you might guess, the marriage wasn't something you'd be
inclined to call "average". The range of emotions seemed to have
no bounds. There were many tender, loving moments. We had
lots of tumultuous times where the anger of being "selected" to
die couldn't be contained any longer. Anglo medicine and
hospitals accounted for a lot of our time. So did traditional
Navajo healing ceremonies with medicine men chanting, sand
paintings and native blessings. Life on the reservation was hard.
In the winter months, merely getting enough wood to stay warm,
water to drink and food to eat accounted for much of our time.
Sheep needed to be tended. There were always jobs to be done
just to stay alive.

Sadly, no matter the circumstances at any given moment in time,
everything was converging on a point in the future called death.
Elisabeth Kubler Ross wrote a classic book entitled "On Death

and Dying". In it, she talked of the various stages one goes through as life's end approaches. She talked about the stress and trauma that go hand in hand with the journey. She talked of the great difficulties of dealing with such things. But she didn't begin to address the sequence for someone with so many complications.

It was a wild ride. It was an education. It was trauma. It was sweetness, bitterness, tenderness, a warm caress, wrath, a torrent of tears, pain, suffering, conflict, joy and enlightenment. It was a dark hell. It was the light of wisdom. It was an ever so fleeting eternity.

As her condition progressively worsened and the cancer metastasized further and further, the conflict between her two cultures intensified. Forty generations of her ancestors rested in the hills of Ganado. Obviously, Anglo medicine wasn't going to save her. More and more, her need was to have the comfort of tradition as she advanced toward the darkness. We had to be in Ganado for that. But we also had to eat and without an income, that can be difficult. I needed to keep my job at the "dynamite factory" in Benson, Arizona to pay the bills and buy the groceries. We would spend two or three weeks in one place and two or three more in the other. That made the burden even heavier. The stresses increased exponentially.

We both professed to love one another deeply, but our emotional load carrying capacities weren't without limit. After hours of stressful and emotional talks, we agreed the only reasonable approach would be for her to go back to the reservation permanently and for me to stay in Benson permanently. My presence brought her worlds into conflict. She wanted them both, but could have neither. She came into the Navajo world when she was born. She wanted to leave the world under the light of a Navajo moon. Even though by then, I could speak Navajo decently and I had become very familiar with the culture, I wasn't Navajo. It was best that I not clutter the end. I had to honor her wishes and let her die. "Girlie" (her family's nickname for her) went to Ganado for the last time. Although I spoke with her a number of times after that, I never again saw her. She is buried along with her ancestors on the hilltop near the place of her birth.

Even before she physically died, I began mourning her passing. I drew myself inward, dedicated myself to my work and frankly, spent a lot of time feeling sorry for myself. What had happened to my concept of marriage? I really didn't know. I knew Ozzie and Harriet had flat out lied to me. It wasn't all that easy. The events of the past few years had educated me and I now knew that no one person in a relationship was any more important than the other. My father's idea that the man is to be the beneficent ruler of the relationship was debunked. It was a two party deal, each the ruler of his or her own domain, but willing to share life with an equal who would synergistically enhance the relationship and bring pleasure and success to both parties.

However, I had also learned marriage could lead to immeasurable pain and suffering. No one wants to lose a loved one. Loving someone could be dangerous and risky. To give love, you make yourself vulnerable. As I faced the future, I wasn't sure I would ever have the ability to share on that level again.

As I did battle with my emotions to overcome the hurt and grief, I got a phone call one day that again would change the course of my life. A paper mill in northern Arizona had somehow heard about my work at Apache Powder Company in Benson. The caller wanted me to go to work for him. I thanked him for his kind words, but assured him I was happy with my present job. He told me he was willing to more than double my current salary. I hung up the phone and wrote my resignation letter. Ironically, the job would put me two hundred miles closer to Ganado. Had the offer come a couple months earlier, we may have been enticed into trying to live the dual life between the two worlds. But by now, choices had been made. I moved to the White Mountains of Arizona.

From out of the Darkness – Spunky and Her Gang -
Fortunately, the new job took most of my time. It was an all-

consuming job riding herd over nearly 500 men in the engineering and maintenance world of a big paper manufacturer. In my off hours (which were few and far between), I largely kept to myself. I would treat myself to dinner half the evenings and indulge myself with gourmet TV dinners on the others. I had one and only one real friend and we spent all my non-working hours together. "FatBoy" was half English bulldog and half St. Bernard. He was a great friend in an otherwise empty and lonely world.

Before returning to grad school, I used to play a lot of golf. When I moved to Pinetop, Arizona, I hadn't picked up a club in five years. Between working at the paper mill and helping FatBoy do the crossword puzzles in the New York Times, I was doing little to break my self-imposed exile from the real world. I needed to do something to claw my way back to normalcy. I thought, why not get the clubs out and play a little golf.

I saw an announcement in the local newspaper about a tournament for some charity. It was being held at the most exclusive country club in the area. It would be fun. I found my way to the office of Marv Rollo, the man who was putting the event together. "I'd like to sign up for the tournament", I told him.

"Great!" said the man. "Who's on your team? Each team has to have three men and one woman."

I explained I was new to the mountain and not only wasn't on a team, "I don't even know anyone here. Can't you just put me on a team?"

I paused before displaying my slightly perverse sense of humor. "Just pair me up with a beautiful woman, around thirty years old, about a six or seven golf handicap, wealthy and architecturally well designed and constructed."

Marv didn't hesitate. "Liz!" he said as he wrote my name on the sign-up sheet. I was to be on a team with two other guys and some young woman named Liz.

Unbeknownst to me, Liz McCarty had recently started a real estate company and although she was in a relationship, she wanted to play in the tournament in the hope of meeting some bachelor with a lofty income who might be interested in buying a house. Her boyfriend was a sleazy insurance salesman and would be playing in another foursome hoping to meet a victim for his business pleasure.

The night before the tournament, there was a Calcutta auction to raise money for the charity. This is a marginally legal event where teams are auctioned, sometimes for substantial amounts of money. A portion of the auction proceeds are paid to the owners of the tournament's winning teams. These auctions can be quite lucrative. As a result, they tend to draw every cheater and golf hustler within two hundred miles. Frankly, an honest golfer doesn't stand much of a chance. Fortunately, I was there just for the fun of playing golf.

When I arrived at Mario's Restaurant and Club, I was introduced to some of the locals who would be playing. I met a young woman named Trish Fagan. Even though she was barely thirty years old, she was a widow. And this woman had her laser sights on high alert scanning the room looking for eligible bachelors. When Marv introduced me to her, she quickly processed the data – single, engineer, single, high income, single, not bad looking, athletic, single – oh yes, and not married. She immediately staked out her territory. She surrounded me with hormonal traffic cones, but they were only visible to other women. She sat next to me at a table and we enjoyed a pleasant conversation. I'm afraid I wasn't wise to the ways of widows and was totally oblivious to the fact that she had laid claim to me as if I was the Lotto Jackpot. Trish had a herding instinct every bit as strong as Major, our collie on the farm of my childhood. Major kept the cows together as we brought them in for milking early every morning. Trish was just as skillful, but did it without barking.

It wasn't long before Liz, along with her boyfriend Mike, arrived. Marv escorted her to my table to introduce us as playing partners. We exchanged cordial greetings. Trish smiled, but extended her claws and said, "Hi. I'm Trish Fagan. I'm with Howard."

Liz assumed Trish was my wife. I assumed the auction would be starting soon. And it did.

Most teams were selling for five or six hundred dollars each. When our team was finally put up for auction, I thought, "What the hell. I'm making good money. Even though we undoubtedly have no chance of winning, I'll squander a couple hundred dollars just to own the team."

I had briefly met our third player, a local florist who was not the picture of a scratch golfer. In fact, he seemed to bring our team into question as possibly violating the three men/one woman team composition. Liz had played some golf when she was in high school and college, but really hadn't spent any time on the golf course in ten years. I hadn't touched a club for five years. Even if I had, no one in town had a clue who I was. I had no idea about our fourth player. He wasn't coming into town until the next morning. No sane, reasonable, prescient human being would invest in our team, especially knowing the field was packed with sandbagging experts and certified cheats.

Our team went on the auction block. I offered the opening bid of two hundred dollars. Sold! Or so I expected. Two-twenty-five was shouted with a high pitched voice somewhere in the room of two to three hundred golfers and guests. "What the hell?" I thought. Maybe this guy doesn't realize which team is up for auction.

"I have two-twenty-five" bellowed the auctioneer. "Do I have two-fifty?"

I considered letting the bimbo live with his mistake, but went ahead and got him off his hook. I raised my hand. "Two-seventy-five" shouted the voice from the darkness. I thought, "What a dumb shit. He's bidding on a losing team."

"Do I have three-hundred?" The auctioneer started to sense he had the makings of a bidding war. One last bid. "Three-hundred" said I in a voice that dripped with a tone that suggested I'd go no higher. Surely I didn't look stupid?

"Three-twenty-five!" "Three-fifty!!" "Three-seventy-five!!!" This is getting insane. This other guy's got to be drunk, stupid, mentally ill or extremely confused. I would later meet him and learn I was right on all counts. Nonetheless, I bid four-hundred dollars and Lee Larsen jumped the bid to four-fifty. This for a team without a ghost's chance in hell of finishing within hearing distance of the tournament leaders. Lee Larsen now owned our team. The goal had been to have fun playing golf. I'd have to do so without any financial interest in our team.

The next morning, I arrived at the golf course to loosen up. Trish was waiting. I went to the practice putting green. I thought I heard the sound of plastic traffic cones falling to the ground nearby. Trish dressed herself in a smile and hovered like a chicken-hawk wherever I went. When Liz and her boyfriend arrived, Trish was only too happy to tell Liz where I was and to suggest that she hoped our team did well.

It was then I discovered why little Lee Larsen was willing to bid the team up as high as necessary for ownership. Our fourth player was to be some linebacker for the University of Arizona football team that was supposedly an excellent golfer and a gorilla. It was said that he had to tuck his prehensile tail in his pants to hide it. He ate bananas without pealing them. He shaved his palms every morning. He hit his drives three-hundred-eighty yards. And he was absent. Our gorilla didn't show up. Lee Larsen was devastated.

The club and the tournament organizers had a problem now. The format of the tournament was a "scramble" where each player hit his or her shot. The team picked the best of the four shots and everyone hit again from that spot. With only three players, our team couldn't compete fairly (as if competing with a field full of cheats and crooks was fair to start with). They'd have to refund our money or they'd have to find us a fourth. Jack Bartko, the club pro, went into the club house and found a member and told him he desperately needed someone to play. Out came Jack with the member in tow. We looked at our new partner and concluded he had probably gone to school with Teddy Roosevelt and had been sitting in the club house because he was too tired to get up and go home, a place that's location he'd probably forgotten long before. We also thought it was possible he was already dead and that we were only witnessing post-mortem twitching. We later concluded he was still clinically alive; no dead person could possibly have had such a grumpy and contrarian personality.

Due to the delay we had in getting a fourth player, our group was put as the last to tee off. We all hit our balls on the first hole and we were underway. I shared a cart with the florist. Liz rode with the dead guy. I hit a fairly good drive and we quickly agreed it was that spot from which we would all hit our next shots. First the florist, followed by the dead guy, then Liz. She struck her ball well, but not perfectly. As she turned and faced us, she released a little bit of what I would call a "nervous chuckle".

Again my perverse sense of humor bubbled to the surface. With an absolutely straight face, I looked at her and said, "We're not out here to enjoy ourselves. We're here to win a golf tournament."

She looked directly into my eyes and I into hers. More than thirty years later, I can still see her face as her mind ran through all of the options. Was I serious? Was I joking? Was I simply socially challenged? I could see her turning the pages in her mind. After a second or so had passed, it appeared she suspected I must be joking, but she covered all the bases when she said, "How would you like me to slap the shit out of you?"

We had just met. We really didn't know each other at all. It's not clear to me how she thought that statement would help her sell a house to a stranger. Given the manner in which it was phrased, it wasn't clear to me if she was saying she was contemplating some form of corporal punishment or if she had already decided and she was merely questioning "How?" or with what technique she should proceed. Either way, it was clear to me this girl had spunk. I liked it. I really liked this early indicator of an indomitable spirit. It was to be a fun day.

Without any ownership in our team, we felt little pressure to perform well. We were committed to nothing beyond a day of enjoyment. The dead guy had left his sense of humor on the bench back in the club house. On more than one occasion, he informed Liz that the laughs and fun moments that she shared with that guy in the other cart (me) had no place on the golf course. The cart-girl came by with great regularity. We did our best to make sure her day was not spent in vain. We had a couple – on the front nine and a couple – on the back nine. Not only was I passing the time on the golf course, the beer caused me to develop a need to pass more than just the time. It was obvious no one was home and there were lots of big pine trees in his yard. So I excused myself to pee in the backyard of Tom Weiskopf, one of the most famous professional golfers of the time. For some reason, Liz found this to be humorous. A while later with another beer knocking on the exit door, I spotted another house where the owners weren't home and there was heavy tree cover in the yard. I quickly relieved myself in the backyard of Bob Goldwater, the brother of former Arizona Senator and Presidential candidate Barry Goldwater. To this day, Liz rolls her eyes and laughs about my bouts with the famous on the day we met.

As the tournament progressed, I seemed to be playing quite well. Liz was doing well herself. She'd made a couple of exceptionally long putts. The florist may have helped a little bit. The dead guy stayed dead. As we approached the 18th green, it was clear to me that our score would be good enough to be in contention. I had played enough golf over the years to know that if we didn't win the tournament, we most assuredly would finish in the money. And we didn't own our team. Someone else would take the money and run.

We birdied the last hole and walked off the green headed for the club house. I noticed Lee Larsen walking behind the green. He looked even smaller than he actually was. He was hunched over and had a dejected look on his face. When his pet gorilla failed to show up, he knew he had thrown four-hundred-fifty dollars down the drain. I thought there is no way he would consider it, but I asked him if he'd like to sell the team. He looked at me as if he'd just met the village idiot.

"Sure. I've got four-fifty in it" he blurted. He didn't seem to find it suspicious that we'd be willing to buy our team after we'd finished playing. Lee may not have been NASA scientist material.

Without hesitation, I reached into my pocket and started doling out money. As it happened, I had four-hundred-ten dollars. I quickly handed it to Larsen. I turned to Liz and said "Give me forty dollars quickly."

She gave me two twenties and we walked into the club house with full ownership of a team of unknowns consisting of a lacy type guy with flowers, a dead guy who made the Grinch seem like a goodwill ambassador, a rusty thirty-six year old engineer and a cute twenty-nine year old, curly headed sweater full of twenty-four carat spunk.

As the last group in, there was only one team whose score had yet to be posted. With a quick glance at the scoreboard, it was obvious our investment would pay off. Liz went off into the crowd to join her boyfriend for the awards dinner and celebration. I found a chair at another table. Well, not exactly. I found that Trish had saved the final chair at the dinner for me. I sat down surrounded by invisible cones.

The tournament organizers picked up the microphone and called for the attention of the two-hundred-fifty attendees. They announced the third place team; it wasn't us. Next the second place team was introduced. Oh oh, maybe our investment wasn't so good after all.

"And the winners of the tournament and $3,000 in prize money are . . . Howard Jones, Liz McCarty, phuff the florist and the dead guy!" Well, maybe that's not exactly the way he phrased it, but the payout was the same. And it was in my pocket. It was celebration time. Trish was delighted. Her future husband was richer. I was elated. I had just spent a wonderful day with Madam Spunk and got paid for the privilege. The dead guy was nowhere to be seen. To this day, I'm not certain if the dead guy ever knew he actually played in a tournament. The florist was probably in the ladies room.

I partied throughout the dinner and the charity auction that followed. As the end of the evening approached, I knew I didn't want this to be the last time I saw Liz. I was determined to see her again. I approached the table at which she was seated between her boyfriend on one side and her friend, Gail Turney, on the other. Someone was speaking at the front of the room. I didn't want to obstruct anyone's view so I knelt down across the table from Liz.

Howard and Liz on the day they met

"I really enjoyed myself today" said her suitor. "I'd love to see you again. Perhaps we can get together for dinner sometime next week."

Her eyes widened with the audacity of the man kneeling in front of her. She turned and looked emphatically at her boyfriend, then swung her head in my direction with theatrical emphasis. It was as if she was saying, "Look stupid. Can't you see I'm in a relationship?" I waited for the sequel to "How would you like me to slap the shit out of you?" but it never came. All she said was "I'm busy."

Having more than my share of a theatrical talent and not one to be out-performed, I upped the ante. I widened my eyes. I suddenly shifted my head to the right and looked directly into the face of her boyfriend (I would have looked into his eyes, but he averted his glance to the side). After a moment, I dramatically brought my face back in line with hers. I smiled and said, "Well, get rid of him!"

For the first and possibly the last time in four decades, Liz was speechless. Gail broke the silence. "I think you should" she said. With that, I smiled and left. Little did I know that when I jokingly described a partner as I signed up for the event that wishes do sometimes come true.

I didn't know Liz's home phone number, but I did know how to call her at the fledgling real estate company. "I'm not going to dinner with you. I'm busy" she said Monday afternoon when I called.

"We need to get together so I can deliver your share of the tournament winnings" I insisted. I used the same approach a couple days later when I called. I got the same response. Fortunately, caller-ID didn't yet exist. I got through a couple days later. Same question - same answer. The following week, I persisted with the same results.

But just like rock yielding to river, Liz finally agreed to have dinner. Maybe it was the forty dollars. Maybe it was my charm. Nah, forty dollars was a lot of money in 1983. We settled on The Paint Pony restaurant, Show Low's finest dinning establishment.

"I'll pick you up at six" I said. "Where do you live?"

"I don't like anyone coming to my house. I'll just meet you at the restaurant" insisted Madam Spunky. It didn't dawn on me she didn't want me at her house because she was in a "relationship" and he would be there.

"Well, OK" said I. "What's your home phone number in case I need to get in touch with you?"

"I don't have a home phone."

It sounded more than a bit fishy to me, but it's not like I had a choice. I'd meet her in the lounge area at six the following Friday. She seemed to be going to some great extremes to maintain an unusually high level of secrecy, but if I were to have the pleasure of her company, I had to live by her rules. But there was nothing that said I had to live silently by her rules. There were many ways to make a statement. In this instance, I purchased the props at the local dime-store.

I arrived at The Paint Pony early. I made it a point to get the table closest to the entry door. When I saw her approach, I donned the editorial prop I had purchased. She walked in and spotted me sitting at the table decked out with a black Lone Ranger mask. For the third time in our short relationship, I saw her with her eyes wide open. With a look of amazement, she said "What are you doing wearing that mask?"

I calmly explained "You seemed to be so set on secrecy and anonymity, I thought it would be appropriate to meet in the shadows under a vail of mystery and secrecy." I handed the other mask to her. She laughed and so began another wonderful evening together. After a toddy, we went into the dining room for dinner. As luck would have it, the man sitting directly behind her was an elderly man she knew quite well. His sense of humor was more than worthy of mine. He did his best to get her to turn around through most of her meal. I later told her I was having doubts about having any further relationship with her because I had seen so much of the back of her head that evening that I thought she had a beard.

The frost was off my heart. She was an absolute delight to be around. We saw each other more and more and with each meeting our feelings grew. The chemistry was exciting and invigorating. With each dose, I craved more. I was alive again. Life was good (except for the high paying job; it sucked!) and I couldn't get enough of Liz. She quickly took my advice from the first evening at the golf tournament. The boyfriend was given his walking papers shortly after our first dinner. We were seeing each other with great regularity.

We agreed to meet one evening at Charlie Clark's Steak House, a popular dining and "happy hour" spot in Pinetop. We planned on having a glass of wine and then I would go home while she would head off to Greer for a weekend business conference. One glass gave way to two then three. The conversation was delightful. Sips of wine were punctuated with bursts of laughter and the time passed far too quickly. When we finally left the table, I walked Liz to the parking lot. We enjoyed our first embrace. I watched as she opened the door, sat in her car and began to back out of her parking spot. Her vision has never been good, but looking through a lens colored with red wine, it was worse than usual. Behind her, two large cowboys sat on the tailgate of a pickup truck drinking bottles of beer.

My eyes widened as Liz backed ever closer to the cowpokes. They scrambled to avoid the impact. The sound of Liz's white Ford hitting the truck was loud and every one of the two dozen or so revelers in the parking turned to see the carnage. My protective instincts kicked in and I headed directly toward the scene of the crime thinking I may have a large problem – actually two of them – to deal with. As I approached, one of the cowboys bellowed at Liz, "Hey lady! You just hit my truck!"

I arrived at ground zero just in time to see Liz roll down her window and tell Tex, "I know that." Her voice had a tone of "You dumb ass. What fool didn't notice that wreck?" She then proceeded to pull off and point her wheels toward Greer. She left me standing there with a pair of livid cow punchers. They turned and faced me with a look of "Who the hell are you?" I gave them my best "I'm here to help you" look and hoped they didn't connect my face with Liz. I backed away and survived. Liz had to wait until Monday to find out if I was dead or alive. It was the first of many times in our four decade relationship when the dark clouds of trouble formed and Liz simply said, "I'm outta here."

Our times together were festivals of laughter. But there was still an air of defense that constantly hovered just out of sight. She had remedied a youthful mistake when she had married John, a nice enough guy, but one with which she shared little in common other than youth. She had gone through a troubled divorce from John and was still in the "once burned – twice shy" mode. As you can imagine, I was still more than gun-shy. I needed to revisit the hells of my connubial past about as much as I needed to perform my own root canal. As our love for each other grew, we frequently shared our concerns. "I'm not really looking for a long term relationship" I'd say.

"Either am I" she responded.

It was odd in a way. The stronger our feelings became, the more we felt compelled to erect our defensive barriers. I think it wasn't that we didn't trust each other; we didn't trust ourselves. Past decisions had resulted in hardship. Why should I believe my previously flawed decision making capabilities had suddenly attained a new found state of perfection? If I had been safe years ago, I never would have had to be sorry later. Nonetheless, after about six months, we moved in together. Life was good.

"I'm not really interested in getting married" I'd say. "Me neither" she'd respond. We were married September 15, 1984, almost one year to the day after we'd been introduced.

Clearly, I had some work to do. I had to put the pieces in place for a new marriage model. It was complicated by some other frighteningly grim realities (if you believe the experts). The psychologists and marriage "experts" have warned that when an oldest child marries an oldest child, you've got the makings of an explosion. Liz is the oldest of three girls separated by six years. I'm the oldest of three boys separated by seven years. We both have many of the stereotypical characteristics of oldest children. We're both independent. Both assertive. Some might say we're head-strong and stubborn, but I've refused to accept that assessment for my entire life. Yes, if you listen to the experts, our wedding was metaphorically no different than pulling the pin on a live grenade.

But from the rubble of previous models, I set about one more time to build a house of love and harmony. Who can say what tomorrow holds, but as of Christmas morning 2015, I can step back and say that with Liz's help, we've built a beautiful house. It's strong. It has withstood storms and hardships. It's a "rambler" with many additions. Constructed of the materials life has allotted us, it is colorful and unique, but strong.

This isn't the place to revisit every action we've taken to make it a great shelter from the storm, but I'll give you a couple of clues.

The foundation is constructed of mutual respect. We each realize that we are individuals in our own right. Our mission has never been to change our partner. We embrace each other for who we are rather than who we should be. That doesn't mean we always agree 100% on what to do, where to go or how to do things. It means we each respect the other and we respect each other's right to be an individual. We generally support each other's choices, even if we don't believe they're the best ones. We may talk about it, but we neither demand nor in many cases expect agreement.

The floor is built from learning how to share. I don't for a minute mean that all our cookies are split down the middle. Strange as it may seem, sharing in this instance may mean putting the entire burden on the other person. I may be more skilled in a given field, Liz in another. I may be better suited to certain tasks. I can get the pitcher off the top shelf. Liz needs a stool. We share by each doing what we can do best. We don't keep score. Liz is a master chef and enjoys cooking. We share her great strength. She prepares the meals. I happily eat them. If for any reason she doesn't feel like cooking, I am always ready and willing to make sure the task gets done. "Which restaurant would you like to go to tonight?" I'll ask. The things I'm good at and enjoy, I do. The things at which she excels and enjoys, she does. There is no keeping score.

The walls are built of laughter. Maybe we're just lucky. We both laugh easily and we both appreciate the other's sense of humor. Over the years, laughter has shielded us from the winds of injuries, cancer, family death and other disasters great and small. Laughter is the elixir that heals all wounds.

The roof is built of trust. After thirty-one years of togetherness, we know each other quite well. I have never violated her trust in any way. I believe she has never violated mine. The roof has never leaked. Trust is more than knowing the roof has never leaked. It's in knowing it never will.

The rooms of the house are decorated with the memories of the places we've been together, the things we've done and the people we've known. They don't always match, but they are decorated the way we wanted them to be. They are beautiful. We wouldn't trade them for anything. Our garden blooms with brilliant blossoms of all the colors of the rainbow. It is watered regularly with lots of love.

Yes, Liz is my girlfriend. The song of her laughter is wonderful. She's also a lot of fun to squeeze. I believe I know what it means to be happily married. There you have it. Marriage was the source of wisdom through repeated stress, pain and trauma in my life, but finally had a happy ending.

Chapter Three – The "W" Word (Work)

With the possible exception of my son-in-law, most people realize that survival requires some effort. "Signs of industry" as an Australian friend calls it. If you plan on eating, you'd better be prepared to grow it, hunt it or have something of value with which you can engage in trade for your burgers and beer. I'm of the belief that the need to work and produce something of value is bred into our genes. When little kids play, aren't they just laying the groundwork for a life of work later on? If you think about it, even sloths have to work to eat.

I shudder to think about the number of "jobs" I've had in my lifetime. I've earned money as a construction laborer, a carpenter, a disc-jockey, a chemical engineer, a writer, a scuba-diver, a computer programmer, a photographer, a baseball player, a music teacher, a newscaster, an office machines salesman, an auto assembly line worker, a real estate agent, a public speaker, a research scientist, a theater usher, a shoe salesman, a life insurance salesman, a golf caddy, a vacuum cleaner salesman, a dynamite maker, a swimming teacher, a gas station attendant, a mountain climber, a radio station engineer, a college instructor, a contractor, a janitor, a paper-boy and a gigolo. Ok, I made the last one up. But all the other ones and no doubt a few more are real. As I scan the list, it might have been easier to show the jobs I've never had. I've never waited tables, played professional basketball, been an astronaut or been a dance instructor.

I should probably make a small distinction between a "job" and a "job". The former being when I was earning money working for myself. I was the boss. I set my hours, defined the job and rounded up the customers. The second one being when I was collecting money while in someone else's employ. These were typically times when I allowed my employer to make all the wrong decisions, direct his business and keep most of the profits. In my early years, the first type of job, i.e., where I was the boss, was generally quite successful in most regards. The only thing usually lacking was a profit. I always loved the first type of "job". Not so much the second.

I guess I was born with the entrepreneurial spirit. I was always the first kid on the block to hawk Kool-Aid or lemonade. I remember setting up a little sports fair where kids paid admission to come into our yard and engage in a variety of sports activities, most of which they could have done outside the yard for free. It was all going pretty well until that one kid accidentally buried a golf club into the head of one of the other kids. Fortunately, that was back in the days when parents weren't as quick to file lawsuits. Nonetheless, the fair went under.

My first real venture into the world of business partnerships was a great learning experience and forced me into the realm of creative marketing at the ripe old age of nine. It was maybe a week after Thanksgiving and it was snowing. An inch or two had accumulated on the sidewalks leading to the doors of the forty houses on Griggs Street in Detroit. Jimmy Foley lived next-door. He may not have been the brightest kid on the block, but at least he was lazy. As we walked down the street, it occurred to me we could make a killing going door-to-door, shovels in hand and offer to shovel walks for twenty-five cents. If we hustled, we could handle five or six houses per hour. We'd make a fortune and split the proceeds. In 1956 my weekly allowance was twenty-five cents. I'd be making three times that much each hour. Jimmy and I agreed we'd run home, grab a snow shovel and meet at the end of the block where we would methodically go from one end of the block to the other knocking on doors and soliciting our shoveling jobs. Off we went.

Jimmy's shovel was easier to retrieve, probably because the lazy bastard hadn't put it away from the last time he used it. I had to climb down into the basement to retrieve mine. We didn't have a garage; only the rich people had garages. For whatever the reason, Jimmy was at the starting location three or four minutes before I got there. It seems that when he showed up with his shovel, Mrs. Greenspan saw him standing there and asked him if he would shovel her walk for fifty cents. He jumped right on it. He was almost done when I arrived.

"What are you doing?" I asked with a hint of consternation.

Jimmy told me the story and said "he" had just made fifty cents.

"What about our partnership?" I grumbled.

"Too bad on this one" my creepy friend said. "You're too late." Maybe I should have had an attorney draw up the paperwork, but all I could do now was fume and let him know where he could stuff his shovel. The business partnership broke up almost as soon as it had been formed. I was livid.

The little marketer in my mind kicked into overdrive. I turned and walked away. I walked all the way down to the other end of the block. I cleared the snow from the walkway of the first house. Mrs. Solomon came to the door. "What are you doing young man?" she said.

I gave her my best Mickey Rooney look of innocence and said, "I'm shoveling your walk, mam. It's been snowing."

"How much do I owe you son?"

I adjusted my halo and responded, "Oh nothing, mam. I'm just doing it to help you out."

She smiled as she spoke, "That's just not right. Here's fifty cents. You're such a nice boy."

I worked my way down the street as fast as I could. When Jimmy and I finally met, I had shoveled the walks of twelve of the twenty houses on that side of the street. I had four dollars and eighty-five cents. Jimmy had knocked on eight doors, gotten three jobs and had a dollar and a quarter (counting the half a buck he screwed me out of on the first house). The little son-of-bitch went home in defeat and the entire other side of the street was mine. Lesson learned and never forgotten.

Extra – Extra! My first "real job" was as a twelve year old in Detroit. I purchased a newspaper route. Seven days a week, rain or shine, I had to show up at the newspaper distribution office to buy roughly sixty copies of the Detroit News. I skillfully folded the papers and put them into the big canvas bag that I then mounted on the front of my bicycle. Off I would go peddling a mile and a half to Sorrento Street where my customers were awaiting the latest news. The "art" of being a paperboy called for excellent bike skills, a good cross-body throwing motion even with the big, bulky Sunday edition and some public relations and business sense. I had two out of three. I could ride faster than most while still throwing with good accuracy. Never mind the times when I missed the porch and threw the paper into the bushes. They knew where to look. Don't count the one time I threw the Wednesday edition with a little too much vigor and broke the window in the storm door. By and large, I was pretty good.

The business end of being a paperboy presented the greatest challenge. Once each week, usually on Thursday evenings, I had to collect from my customers. What a great learning experience that turned out to be. I went door-to-door ringing bells and knocking on doors. A subscription to the Detroit News in 1959 cost something on the order of fifty cents. Yet, it was amazing how many times I heard someone on the other side of the door say "Shhhh, it's the paperboy. Don't answer the door." Some paid and even threw in a nickel or a dime tip, but more often than not, I all but had to trap them into paying. Most waited until the holiday season and gave me a more substantial tip such as fifty cents. But it always seemed like the profits were so small, looking for lost change on the playground might have been more lucrative.

One day, my father asked to see the paperwork from the man from whom I bought the papers. I gave him my receipts. I couldn't explain them to him because they were confusing to a twelve year old. My father reviewed all the paperwork and concluded the distributor had been fleecing not only me, but a few of the other paperboys. He was charging us for more papers than we received. Rather than walk me through the process of verifying business income and expenses, my father went up to the paper distribution office and confronted the distributor. He taught me that if you threatened to relocate the guy's nose to the side of his face, he would quit cheating you. But I still couldn't have caught him if he started again. I guess there's more to business than bookkeeping.

In the summer between my high school freshman and sophomore years, my monetary needs had grown. I had just turned fifteen and I had places to go and things to do. I went to work as a golf caddie at Meadowbrook Country Club. It was big money by the standards of the fifteen year old in 1962. I was making better than a dollar per hour carrying a single bag for eighteen holes. When I learned more about the game of golf and how to be a better caddie, I occasionally carried a "double", two bags. For that I earned over two dollars per hour. Hell, retirement was within sight. It was a great job. I worked only when the weather was good. And Monday was "Caddie Day" at the club. Along with other club employees, we played golf for free. Although my father had taken me to the driving range from time-to-time beginning when I was around seven or eight years old, it was thanks to Caddie Day at Meadowbrook Country Club that I first began learning how to play the game of golf that would give me simultaneous feelings of pleasure and frustration for the next seven decades. It would be just like being married, but that was in a previous chapter.

When I graduated from high school and was college bound, I had the mixed blessing of having a father that owned a successful commercial construction company. I had access to a job that paid a veritable fortune, three-twenty-five per hour. Overtime was double-time. Holidays were triple-time. Work overtime on a holiday and I thought I'd never have to work again. My unofficial job title was to be "boss' son". My actual title was "laborer". It involved physical labor unlike any I had ever done. Most of the time that first year, I was a bricklayer's tender. I had to mix the mortar, carry it to the bricklayers and bring brick to the crotchety bastards. It was damn hard work. It involved unpleasant things like sweating, blisters and taking orders – all things that were acceptable when playing on a sports team, but totally unacceptable anywhere else.

My father believed that just because I was the boss' son, I shouldn't grow up with a silver spoon in my mouth. We weren't in agreement. I thought a suitable compromise would be for him to suspend that philosophy until his second son was able to work in the business. The latent scientist in me felt that it would be a great test of his theory. One son – silver spoon. The other son – no silver spoon. Compare the sons. Write it up and close the book.

Not only was I not getting good buy-in on my proposal, my father was determined that I would "work" my way up from the bottom. The only problem was there were no steps in place for me to climb up. In the ensuing years during which I would work summers in the construction world, I was forced to work hard physically. I learned that hard physical work sucks. It absolutely sucks.

I remember working one summer on a major expansion of Botsford Hospital in Farmington Hills, Michigan. We were to pour a colossal amount of concrete on a third floor deck. For those of you without the warm memories of working construction for a slave driver or who have never worked on a prison chain gang, I'll give you a taste of what it's like to pour a couple hundred yards of concrete in less than a day. First of all, it must be pumped to the third floor. In theory, you could put it in wheelbarrows and have a hundred or so laborers run it up the elevator, but that would take more time than it would to build the Great Pyramids with only The Dixie Chicks and a Waring Blender. A massive truck, pump and crane force massive amounts of heavy, wet concrete through a hose that's six or eight inches in diameter. But someone has to be at the other end of the huge hose. Enter Walter Coopwood.

"Coop" was a construction laborer like me. Scratch that. He was a construction laborer, but he damn sure wasn't like me. The hose through which countless tons of concrete were to be delivered had to be dragged around to whatever areas needed the "mud" at any given time. It was far too heavy for one person to manage the hose. There was a big rope attached to the end of the hose. The first man dragged the hose with that rope. The second man used another big rope that was maybe six feet behind the first. Between the two of them, they could usually manage the job.

Here was the problem. Walter stood seven feet plus an inch tall. Walter weighed three hundred pounds and it was a lean three hundred. Walter was in position one. I was in the number two spot. For the next twelve hours, whenever the foreman would shout "Get some mud over here", Walter would drag the hose, all the concrete that was in it and me, who was attached to the next location. On a number of occasions, Walter literally pulled me off my feet into and through the wet concrete. Walter did the work of three men that day, the one in first position, the one in second position and the work of a third guy that would have been hired to drag my sorry ass all over the deck at Botsford Hospital.

You may find it interesting to learn that a few years later, Walter left construction work to become a fire and brimstone inner-city preacher in Detroit. He had probably concluded that if he had witnessed the miracle of me surviving that day, he could probably conjure up a few more smaller miracles to keep his followers in the good graces of their eternal foreman in the sky.

I'm sure I could regale you with hours of stories from my life in the construction world, but let me just summarize the whole thing. I learned there are a lot of people without the good fortune of having a formal education that are sentenced to lives of hard, manual labor. Many of them are fine, decent and honorable human beings. In the decades that followed, I earned a substantial amount of fame and fortune mostly with my mind. I was paid more than the Walter Coopwoods and Willie Hardaways (another experienced and highly respected lifelong laborer) of the world. I'm glad I've got the material things and the security that my earnings buy, but I truly question whether or not I'm any more deserving or even as deserving of the "good life" than were some of the honorable men I met working in the trenches. Walter and Willie are both long dead, but they live on in me. They taught me the importance of hard work. They were decent and honorable men. I try to do them justice in my actions every day I live.

Oh yes . . . there's one other thing I learned. Hard manual labor is honorable and worthwhile, but it really sucks big time. I didn't mind watching it, but I didn't want any part of doing it. I wasn't up to it.

College students need money too. I was a scholarship athlete at Western Michigan University in Kalamazoo. As a diver on the swimming team, the assistance wasn't great. It probably covered books. My parents covered tuition and dormitory costs. That left beer and cigarette expenses as my responsibility. WMUK was the local radio station. It was and still is the NPR affiliate in Kazoo. They were looking for someone to spin records and do some basic announcing on the radio. I applied and got the job no doubt because I had a strong radio voice. I worked eight to sixteen hours per week for minimum wage, about two dollars per hour. I made money for beer, cigarettes and girls.

Get that will ya? I think it's my destiny calling. After a couple years of college, I dropped out. I've never been one to lack confidence in my ability to do something. There were many times I couldn't walk the talk, but it never kept me from trying. A lot of times I succeeded. I think it's safe to say that those successes never would have come to pass unless I was willing (and maybe dumb enough) to try.

It was probably a good thing I left college when I did; I wasn't mature enough to learn. I got married instead. But with marriage came the obligatory "breadwinner" role. I soon found that most companies weren't interested in how good I could be; they were more interested in how good I was. I actually was forced into taking work that was below what I thought was "my station" in life. There was always construction, but I'd already given that a rating of "sucks". I looked elsewhere.

The Parade of Jobs - First job after marriage – order taker and delivery scheduler for a floor covering company. Contractors would phone in their material orders. I would take them. Just before going home, we'd review the orders and schedule the delivery trucks on what seemed to be the best routes. This was long before the advent of computerized routing systems. We did it all manually. I performed well. It wasn't the most challenging job in the world and I saw no immediate path to fame and fortune. After a couple months, it was time to move on.

Second Job – Office Machines Salesman. Now I was moving into the big time. I actually had to wear a suit and tie. How much more important could I be? I was given a well-defined territory on Detroit's east side. I wasn't shy, had a fairly good command of the English language, could think on my feet and got off to a fast start. After a couple months, I made a cold call on a fairly large company along Gratiot Avenue. I hit it off well with the purchasing agent and the next thing you know, I had a substantial order. The following day I learned that my territory wasn't really "my" territory. Other salesmen in the company claimed they retained the rights to certain customers in "my" territory. I was told it was a big deal, I still had all the little, useless companies that couldn't scrape together enough money to pay their water bills, let alone buy state-of-the-art office equipment. That led to the next job.

Job Three – Life Insurance Salesman. The father of one of my high school girlfriends had an insurance agency for Great West Life of Canada. He had long known I had the requisite skills to learn the business and sell the product. He had hinted in the past that I should consider the profession. After meeting with Bob Bogart, I started the training regimen in a program that paid me commission advances for the first year. I was pretty much getting paid for doing nothing other than sitting on my ass and reading books. Now we're talking. We're getting closer to my true calling.

The problems didn't start until I had completed the training and earned my license with the State of Michigan. Now I had to actually work at the job. I don't mean real work like being a construction laborer. I did, however, have to start making phone calls to strangers and try and get them to grant me an appointment so I could browbeat them into buying my product. Nine out of ten calls resulted in rejection, some rather bluntly. I didn't like this at all. I was beginning to contemplate job number four, but I hung in there.

When you go into insurance sales, one of the first things you'll be asked to do is make a list of all of your friends and family members. Include your neighbors, former cellmates from the penitentiary, former classmates, illegitimate children, golf partners, ex-wives, future ex-wives and anyone else on the planet over which you might hold some sway or influence. You're strongly encouraged to contact them because, after all, they probably need life insurance. It's your moral calling to make sure they have it. I had one good friend from high school who had recently married. He was one of those guys liked by everyone. He was so well liked in part because he was a great accommodator. He hated to say no to anyone. To this day, I feel guilty for selling him so much life insurance that the only way he could ever pay for it was to die.

My father-in-law was on my list. He had more dough the Pillsbury and owned a company in Florida He did me a favor by purchasing a large life insurance policy on one of his key employees. In doing so, he inadvertently became the midwife to my next hair brained idea.

Job Four – Tropical Fish and Golf Balls. I'm reluctant to call it "thinking", but here's what I came up with. Lucy, our newborn daughter, Amy and I would move to Florida, sell a big insurance policy to each of the employees of my father-in-law and we'd be rich and live happily ever after. I could scuba dive and make money on the side selling tropical fish. I suspect I was subconsciously thinking, screw life insurance; I can scuba dive and have fun in the sun. Brilliant! Simply brilliant!

The fish business didn't pan out very well. I got an offer to work for a local dive shop that was owned by an officer on the

Hollywood, Florida Police Department. This pillar of morality and ethical behavior hired a couple of hungry divers and instructed them to meet a little after midnight at a back entrance to one of the local golf courses. We had to paint all stainless steel or other reflective surfaces black to reduce the chances of being spotted. Jim Burkett and his German Shepherd, Romel, patrolled the course perimeter while we dove in moonless darkness feeling our ways around the muddy bottoms of ponds and filling our lobster bags with the golf balls we found. I worked for a crooked cop stealing balls from ponds which other legitimate divers had spent thousands of dollars per year for the rights to dive for balls. The cop then sold the balls in his dive shop.

Job Five – How about a bag to go with your new shoes? My scuba diving career came to an abrupt end when I had to jettison my diving gear to save my life on a dive in *The Devil's Triangle* off the coast of Fort Lauderdale. No tank – no job. I had to find something to feed the family. I ended up with a job at Baker Shoes. I must have been important; I still wore a suit to work.

Although there was a little excitement every once in a while (helping a young mini-skirt clad woman into tight, knee high leather boots always offered the promise of excitement), this was definitely not my line of work. The pay was extremely poor, but the hours were miserable. I lasted nearly a month.

Job Six – I was Cleaning Up. Once again, Lucy's father stepped in to help the helpless. Perry Byard didn't like his son-in-law, but he did his best to hide it. With twenty-twenty hindsight, I've got to give him credit. If I would have been in his shoes, I would have put me to work digging a grave and I would have buried me in it.

By now, I'm thinking about returning to Michigan. Florida didn't seem to appreciate my skill set as much as I thought it should. But for now, Mr. Byard would give us a chance to feed ourselves by giving us a job as janitors at his factory. The money was better than shoe sales, but the similarity between this and real work was just too striking for me. We (Lucy and I) worked from about eleven at night until about four in the morning. I had to wax about five thousand square feet of floor every night. This was very difficult to do while I was asleep on my feet. The return to Michigan couldn't come soon enough – for me or for Mr. Byard.

Seventh Job – More Sweat. When we got back to Michigan, we needed money and needed it fast. I didn't really have time to cherry pick a job worthy of my immense talents. I jumped back into the position of "boss's son" and jumped back into the world of manual labor. I didn't like it when I left it. I liked it even less when I returned to it. It was hard physical work. My father still hadn't found my silver spoon and was expecting me to work hard. Unfortunately, he told that to the labor foreman who delighted in giving me hell. I was a carpenter's tender. Basically, my job was to make sure they didn't run out of material. If I could ever haul enough lumber to last them for a few minutes, I might be able to take a little break. At least that was the theory; I never carried enough to find out.

Job Eight – Live the Dream. I had worked with carpenters long enough to observe pretty much everything they did or so I thought. They cut wood, drove nails, put concrete forms in place and sat on their asses waiting for the materials their laborer couldn't bring fast enough. They made more money than the lowly laborer. I could do that. I told the foreman and later my father, I was going to join the carpenters union and would be a "skilled worker" from that point forward. I'd make my own silver spoon with a hammer and a sixteen penny nail.

Job Nine – If I were a Carpenter. Life as a carpenter wasn't all it was cracked up to be. I soon learned that one of the reasons the carpenters had such an easy life was because they had been served by a slow laborer. Without materials, they could relax and joke around as they waited. The problem was the slow laborer didn't work there anymore; he was one of the carpenters. The laborer that replaced the slow guy was experienced and never let us run out of materials. So much for all the extra breaks. I was working harder and sweating more than I ever did as a laborer. I was sure it was because I was with a lousy company where the foremen were slave drivers under the charge of a despotic emperor who I customarily referred to as "Dad". The solution was to go to work for another company.

One of my father's competitors was hiring. I drove to one of their job sites and was immediately put to work. I had forgotten that I hadn't been to apprentice school and that on a good day I was a lousy carpenter. As the boss's son, one special privilege I did have is that no matter how poorly I performed, I wouldn't be fired. This wasn't the case at the new company. After I had worked there for about a month, some of the other "legitimate" carpenters realized I had bypassed the apprenticeship path and was making the big bucks without having served my time. A couple of them took it upon themselves to remedy the problem. Just before a big concrete pour, they went to a section of the wall where I had worked. They pulled the "hairpins" from the concrete forms in my section of wall. When the concrete was poured, everything was going well until it flowed into my area. The unpinned walls just opened wide and concrete poured everywhere. Heads would roll. Well, at least one head would roll and it did. I walked toward the tool shed to pick up my belongings. Two grinning carpenters stared at me as I grabbed my toolbox and walked away. They didn't say goodbye.

Job Ten – The Factory. Detroit's auto industry was its heart and soul. The Ford Rouge plant alone employed sixty thousand workers. When auto sales were good, jobs were plentiful. The last thing in the world I wanted to do is return with my tail between my legs to my father's construction world. I applied at a General Motors manufacturing plant. They processed my application, liked what they saw and hired me on the spot. I was to report for work the next afternoon for the night shift. I was delighted to have finally escaped the construction world. Even if assembly line work was repetitive and boring, it couldn't be any worse than swinging a hammer all day.

I reported for work only to discover they had seen I had experience as a carpenter. They assigned me to a job building wood pallets to ship the engines they made. This was like going through a dating service only to discover they had paired you on a blind date with your ex-wife. After three days, I ran screaming from that job and looked for another.

Eleven – A Railroad Job. Not far from the General Motors plants where I spent a three day lifetime, Evans Products was building railroad boxcars. The Safety Director for the plant was looking for an assistant to type his decrees and do his bidding around the plant. It was an office job, included a desk and (more importantly) a chair and very little sweat. I'm not sure what Leroy was looking for, but apparently I wasn't providing it. The job lasted about two months.

An Even Dozen – Pulling Pipe. I left the stale air of boxcars and metal welding and moved to South Lyon, Michigan. I took a job in the stale air of metal working at Michigan Seamless Tube. I was a pipe-puller. I ran a machine where I took long cylindrical pieces of steel and pulled them through a precision die. The end result was a length of precisely measured steel pipe used throughout industry. I saw my "calling" in the radio and television industry and had some audition tapes out to a few of the stations in nearby Ann Arbor. I waited and pulled some more pipe.

Baker's Dozen – A Star is Born. Robin Brown, the manager of WOIA radio in Ann Arbor, had heard a tape I had made and decided I needed to go to work for him as an on-the-air "personality". I was about to embark on a career of being a great star. What a life! I could actually sit on my ass, talk and get paid for it. Some people have said I have a great face for radio. I went to work as a reporter, newscaster and jazz show host. Unlike many, if not most, radio and TV "personalities", I truly never thought of myself as a celebrity. However, I did become "known" around Ann Arbor. There are a thousand and one stories from this era involving everything from murder to mischief, but I'll leave them for later chapters.

Success in the broadcast industry is equated with market size. Ann Arbor was a medium sized market at best. If I was to replace Walter Cronkite, I would have to move on. I was offered a position at the number one station in Denver, Colorado, KIMN – The Voice of the Rocky Mountains. It had one of the most famous news operations outside of New York and Los Angeles. So in slightly under three years since Michigan State played the "game of the century" against Notre Dame, I took my thirteenth job. But at least this time, it was on a more normal trajectory (if you consider having breakfast with Ralph Nader, lunch with the Governor of Colorado and covering a murder after dinner as normal). One of my more memorable days in the news room was when I broadcast man's first steps on the moon. After getting crosswise with "Robert E. Lee", a rather famous disc-jockey, Lee exacted his revenge. He knew that preparing the news at one of the nation's premier news operations was a demanding job that called for precise timing. Invariably, the newscaster is sitting at the microphone ready to go live no more than ten or fifteen seconds before the light goes on. It was a weekend and I was the only one in the newsroom.

Every newscast was preceded by a little jingle that served as about a five second warning before going live. When I heard the jingle over the newsroom speaker, it was three minutes before the hour. I was in the rear of the newsroom just beginning to assemble the stories I was to read live at the top of the hour. Some of the stories wouldn't survive the cut and would be discarded, some were not yet in the pile, others still needed some minor editing. Through the glass I saw Lee with a look of "Now what are you going to do sucker?" I ran to the microphone and flipped the switch to go live to Denver's biggest radio audience. The newscast was a disaster. I read stories that shouldn't have been in the news. I missed commercial announcements, public service announcements, major news stories and I read some of the news so poorly that it sounded like I hadn't proofread my copy – which I hadn't. Robert E. Lee may have surrendered at Appomattox in 1865, but he won the war of 1969. It ultimately cost me my job.

Fourteen – Back to the factory floor. It seemed I always had a fallback position, either construction or automobiles. The most expedient income solution was to join the shift workers at the

Ford air conditioning plant. I was actually working on the assembly line for the first time. No pallet building this time. I had always pictured the life of an assembly line worker as boring, uninspiring, monotonous and mundane. I quickly discovered it was boring, uninspiring, monotonous and mundane. In fact, by this time in my illustrious career, I had begun to realize work in general was an unpleasant nuisance and a most inconvenient distraction from life's more enjoyable pursuits.

Fifteen - Ornamental iron magnate. The House of Iron had been purchased out of an estate by a couple of veteran Detroit attorneys. They didn't know a thing about the business of ornamental iron. They found a young attorney, Dick Nimtz, to run the business. He didn't know a damn thing about the business either. He was tasked with the job of finding his assistant. He found me. Like the owners and the company's president, they now had a twenty-three year old vice-president who couldn't find his ass if he was sitting on it. Together, we bumbled and fumbled our way through the day-to-day operation of the business fooling ourselves that we were fooling our employees about our competence, but we survived.

The profit and loss statement didn't exactly give the owners cause for ebullience. (Actually, if they had ebullience, I suspect they'd need diapers.) One day, one of the owners stopped by while President Nimtz was out. Harry Averill began asking questions. "How can we improve the bottom line? What can we do to be more efficient?" The questions went on for a few minutes. I did my best to answer them. I felt like I was making shadow puppets bringing form from darkness. I must have done a good job. I must have done the job too well.

I got a call at home one evening and was told the Mr. Averill and his partner, Mr. Barr would like me to meet them at their office the following evening at seven o'clock. Upon my arrival, I learned I had made such a favorable impression upon Mr. Averill, he wanted me to replace Mr. Nimtz as the company's president. I was there to impress Mr. Barr that I should run the company. I may have been only twenty-one years old, but I had the confidence and pomp of a man twice my age and the maturity of one half my age. Nimtz was fired. I was hired. Oh my.

Sixteen – The Star is Born Again. Despite my abrupt departure from the Denver media market, I did have a fair amount of natural ability and a modicum of talent in the broadcast world. I hoped to return to the exciting world of newscasting and reporting. The call came from one of the principals of Draper-Blore, a national media consulting firm that had heard about my basket of news skills. They wanted me to work for them at their station in Portland, Oregon, KPOK radio. The job was exciting and interesting. I counted the Governor (Tom McCall), a Congresswoman (Edith Green), Senators Mark Hatfield and Bob Packwood and other notables as personal friends. At least one of my good friends did make it big in the business. John Stossel later paired up with Barbara Walters on ABC's 20/20 show and then went on to host his own shows on national TV. He spent plenty of time at our house in Beaverton partying hardy with the rest of us. But where Stossel went on to national fame, I was getting tired of the round-the-clock work (big news stories were rarely scheduled ahead of time). I was actually starting to consider "growing up". After a couple of years in Portland, I decided to return to Michigan and go back to school.

After a year of freshening up the brain at a junior college and playing a little bit of college hockey, I moved on to Michigan State University. I had matured and took my studies seriously. I had been awarded a number of academic scholarships, was admitted into the Honors College and graduated with "High Honors" (MSU's equivalent of *magna cum laude*).

Seventeen – Enter the Scientist. In the summer of 1975, I went to work for Standard Oil of California as a "process engineer". Obviously, this amounted to a major shift in lifestyle from being a college student or a newscaster. Thanks to my extremely strong academic credentials, I was a highly sought after chemical engineer. When I arrived in the San Francisco area, I had a marriage that was disintegrating and a golf game that needed improvement. As a result, I didn't dedicate as much time and effort to my new job as I could have and should have. I did a "passing" job, but my focus was really elsewhere. For the first year, I worked in the Richmond Refinery. I was charged with the responsibility of keeping the "Chemicals Division" running. If a pump, a pipe or a reactor failed, I had to review the cause of the failure, redesign it if necessary and then make sure the job of building and installing the new equipment took place. It was interesting, but frankly, it was too damn close to the construction business to capture my heart. I went to college to get out of that business, not get back into it.

From the refinery, I transferred into Chevron Research. As a Research Engineer, my job amounted to developing a thorough understanding of whatever processes fell under my dominion and then optimizing them such that expenses were minimized and profits were maximized. It called for the application of some good science and engineering and was fun and rewarding. At least it would have been had I not been "distracted" by outside interests. I did win the Sonoma County Golf Championship that year. It was unfortunate that my pay raises hadn't been based upon my golf handicap.

I resigned my job at Chevron after three years. I was to go on my "farewell tour" with Lucy. We went to South America for a month and a half. When we returned, we began divorce proceedings. I had lined up a job with Radian Corporation out of Austin, Texas. Technically, I became a resident of Texas, but actually was part of a travelling research circus studying "fugitive emissions" in refineries up and down the west coast. A team of scientists and technicians spent anywhere from six weeks to three months in any one location. We were scientists by day and party animals by night. We researched the nightlife in Ferndale, Washington, Bakersfield, California, Long Beach, California and coincidentally in the San Francisco area working in the refinery from which I had recently resigned. The job was fun, but the "science" wasn't too deep. When the project was complete, I could have gone with the team back to Texas and worked there, but my heart had taken root in the San Francisco area. I took a job as a process engineer with Union Oil (later Unocal Corporation) at their Rodeo Refinery.

I didn't realize it at the time, but my assignment to the dewaxing unit would open doors that would completely change the course of my life. Paraffin or wax is one of the thousands of classes of compounds contained in petroleum. Wax is great for candles, but it doesn't cause anything but trouble with a car's engine. It must be removed. I became somewhat of an expert on the process of dewaxing intermediate petroleum. Union Oil had a well-known research scientist named Dr. Ted Pullen. He was an expert on the chemistry of the process, but tended to overlook the kinetics. At this point, I'm aware that most anyone reading this document doesn't have the slightest clue as to what I'm talking about. Sadly, Dr. Pullen was also in that class.

Here's what this all boils down to. Union Oil had licensed Dr. Pullen's process around the world for many tens of millions of dollars. The process worked fine in the laboratory, but failed dismally when it was scaled up to the industrial level. Union Oil was in the hot seat when I applied what I thought was some pretty fundamental science to the problem. The solutions I came up with saved the day for Union Oil, Dr. Pullen and a lot of investors. My work ended up in a number of patents and was valued in the tens of millions of dollars. I got only my regular paycheck. That was fair. That's why I was hired and Union Oil owned the fruits of my labors.

However, as my name became heard with greater and greater frequency in that small world of crystallization, I ended up with an offer to head up a research project at the University of Arizona working under the world's foremost expert in the field, Dr. Alan Randolph. I left Union Oil and entered a Ph.D. program in Tucson, Arizona. The joy of studying for a doctorate was a short lived pleasure. When I had to beg a department secretary for a stapler for my lab, I'd had enough. I left the program after less than a year.

Number Twenty – Rocket scientist. The next entry on my resume was that of bomb maker at the dynamite factory. Ok, perhaps that's not exactly what I was doing, but that's not too far from it. I became the Superintendent of Engineering and Maintenance at Apache Powder Company in Benson, Arizona. In many respects, this would be the most interesting job I would ever have. We made prilled ammonium nitrate, probably the most common explosive in the world today. We also produced gelatin explosives and detonating cord. But not everything we did was quite so forward looking. We were one of the last two companies in the nation that made good old fashioned dynamite. We manufactured nitroglycerine by the vat load.

The plant was built shortly after the end of World War I and much of the equipment was from that era. As you might imagine, sparks and high explosives don't mix well. In many areas of the plant, we permitted no electric motors. Some equipment was still driven by leather belts coming from shafts that extended outside the buildings so the chance of a spark was close to zero. Where we did use electricity, we generated it ourselves. Telephones were not even allowed down the "powder line" where the dynamite was packed. Old fashioned hand-cranked magneto phones were the order of the day. I had dominion over all maintenance, construction, engineering, design, the fire department, the security force, truck traffic, railroad equipment, the power plant and even a herd of cattle whose job it was to eat anything on the grounds that could grow and ultimately become a fire hazard. They turned fuel into flop with great efficacy.

Twenty-One – Pulp fiction. In 1983, I received a call from someone who wanted me to trade my job for a similar one at a paper mill in Snowflake, Arizona. I wasn't interested until I heard the salary offer of more than double my current one. I took the job. I hated the job. It wasn't worth ten times the money they paid. After I married Liz, I knew I wasn't going to stay with the dismal and unfulfilling position at the paper mill. She had just started a real estate company. "What the hell?" I thought. I've sold things before. I could probably sell real estate.

Twenty-Two – Land baron. I got my real estate license and went into the business with Liz. In real estate, I discovered I had fooled myself again. The logical, deductive mindset of an engineer was no match for some home buyer who was willing to walk away from fifty-thousand dollars because five-hundred dollars' worth of carpet was the wrong color. "What kind of stupid shit are you?" is not a question that endears a salesman to a prospective buyer. Nonetheless, I did what I could to help; some of my skills had value in running a real estate business, it's just that my sales skill wasn't one of them.

Twenty-Three - My Last Job – Forever. Liz had many of the challenges inherent in running any business, record keeping, production analysis, personnel management, customer contact, marketing and the like. As I watched her struggle with some of these tasks, it was obvious to me that most of these jobs could be made trivial if she had computer software to do the job. The IBM PC had just been put on the market. I thought that much of the drudgery could be eliminated by software that unfortunately didn't exist. I had worked in a field where I had written extremely complex and sophisticated computer programs to manage everything from explosive reactors to energy optimization. Her needs were child's play in comparison. We bought one of the early PCs and I wrote her a simplistic program to keep track of her contracts. She loved it.

I soon discovered a couple of Liz's great management skills, trickery and manipulation. It seemed that every two to three weeks, Liz would approach me and start burying my ego with abundant expressions of praise.

"That is such a fantastically wonderful program you've written. I can't thank you enough" she would say through a broad smile. She let me wallow around in the words like a pig in a mud bath.

As she walked away, she would turn and say "It would even be better if it would do one more little thing". She'd then mention something about that one little feature that would make it complete. She'd smile, turn and begin to walk toward her office. From over her should I could hear her one last utterance. "But you probably can't make it do that."

In a matter of a minute she had filled the sails of my ship named "Ego", reminded me the sails could be bigger and finally, sucked all of the air from the sails leaving me in "the irons" of a windless sea. Needless to say, she always had the new feature within a couple of days. The program grew in size and power. She would occasionally suggest the program should be marketed. I assured her it was a silly idea because any twelve year old kid could write such simple code. I just assumed she was trying to fill up my sails again with some ulterior motive.

As Liz worked day and night to grow the business, we aligned ourselves with one of the nation's major real estate franchises, Coldwell Banker. We had franchise reporting requirements so I wrote those features into the program. Coldwell Banker also sent a management "consultant" to the office every four weeks. On his first visit, he started to explain to Liz how it would be valuable to track some real estate metric that he assumed she knew nothing about. As he continued to "enlighten" her with his vast real estate knowledge, Liz turned around and pressed a button on her computer. Her printer buzzed and she handed a report to the consultant. It contained detailed information on his metric as well as a few more.

"This is incredible" he bubbled. "Wow. It would be even better if it would tell you about . . ." and he would throw out another esoteric metric that no real estate commoner like Liz would ever have known about. She hit another button and handed the consultant another report. His eyes widened further.

"Where did you get this?" he asked. "It's incredible."

Liz displayed more than a little pride as she responded, "My husband wrote it."

The consultant glanced down at the reports in his hand. "You should sell this" he said. "There's nothing in the marketplace like it."

The program continued to grow as Liz prodded me onward with her "you probably can't do it" taunts. I continued to get increasingly less subtle pressure to market the program. I thought about it a little bit and truly thought the programming was so trivial that it wasn't worth the effort. If I wanted to waste time, I could do that on the golf course. My handicap was down to a seven.

After probably a year of nagging from Liz, the business consultant and a few others that had seen the software, I said "Look. Just to shut you guys up, I'll make it available to the Coldwell Banker offices in the Western Region of the company. If I get a ten percent response rate, I'll go ahead and market it further." I knew it was a nonsensical idea. If this was what I had to do to silence the din, I'd gladly do it so I could go on with my life.

I put together the list of about three hundred fifty offices and started to compose my letter. I had to come up with a price for the product. I had no idea how to do that. As the author, I knew where the flaws were hiding. I hadn't set out to write the world's most eloquent piece of software. I just wanted it to work for Liz. With the knowledge of all the dirty software laundry that was buried in the code, I couldn't justify a price of more than a hundred dollars. I set it at ninety-nine.

One other thought haunted me as I composed the letter. Although I was truly confident no sane person would buy this thing, what if I was wrong? What if someone actually ordered the damn thing? I couldn't deliver a piece of software with Liz's company's name embedded in every report. I couldn't force everyone to buy the same printer we used; I had to change the program so they could pick their own printers. The more I thought about it, it seemed like there were a thousand and one things that needed to be addressed before the product could be shipped. Just in case some fool decided to buy the program, I wrote the following line at the bottom of the letter: "Please allow four weeks for delivery."

My worst fears came true. About four days after my letter went out, the day's mail was laid on my desk. I opened the first envelope and found a check for ninety-nine dollars. Someone had just screwed up my plan. I had a month to make a shippable program. I opened another letter – another ninety-nine dollars. Then another and another and yet another. On the first day, I received orders from seven different companies. Hey, you don't suppose Liz was right?

I wasted no time and set to work. I had four weeks to make the program generic. It turned out the job was substantially bigger than I had estimated. For four weeks, I worked roughly sixteen hours per day, seven days per week to complete the task to which I had committed. In the course of doing so, I also had to open more envelopes. Before my first program was ready to ship, I had received orders from approximately one hundred companies.

I had collected nearly ten thousand dollars and no one other than Liz, her consultant and a couple of other people had any proof the program existed. I tried to keep my optimism is check, but it soon became apparent Liz and the consultant had been right; I had been wrong. I had to eat crow. What I discovered is that crow is a delightful and savory dish when properly prepared. In fact, I've never had anything better.

Four weeks almost to the minute from the receipt of my first order, I shipped a hundred programs and Lucero Research Inc. was in business. For the next year, Lucero was a one-man show. I would focus on a marketing push and the orders would pour in. I quickly raised the price to $129, but the orders didn't slow down. After a nominal marketing effort, I would dedicate my time to programming enhancements. I was having a ball. I was essentially "playing" for a living.

For the first year, I alternated between a month of marketing and two months of programming. That seemed to produce a natural rhythm. I'd market – orders shot up. I'd enhance the program – orders would slowly diminish. I would then market the "new and improved" program and orders shot up all over again. By the end of the first year, between three and four hundred companies were using Lucero as their management centerpiece. I had increased the price to about $350 per program. I wasn't on easy street, but the bills were more than getting paid.

With jumps and starts and an occasional step backward, the company became increasingly successful. I hired an assistant to deal with billing, shipping and the business end of Lucero. I managed to handle all the programming the technical support. I finally had to add a support technician, then another and another. A business manager and clerical staff followed. A marketing director led to the creation of a fifteen man marketing team headquartered in Florida. A small programming office was opened in Toronto, Canada. Then another in Melbourne, Australia. More support people and someone to manage the technical support department. New and bigger offices. A training center was built. By now, the retail price on the program started at approximately $2,000 while the average sale was just north of $4,000.

As you might imagine, the bills were not only getting paid, we could afford lots of things we never dreamed we'd have. Against my better judgment, Liz and I had a house designed and built. It didn't dawn on me we could afford to make payments on a half million dollar house when the average home price was less than $100,000. My mind was somehow still living in the days of the $99 program. When I took a step back and looked at our situation, Liz had recognized the level of our success before I had. We wrote a check for the house. There were no payments.

For over twenty years, we worked our asses off developing and marketing a software program that ultimately became the biggest and most successful product of its kind in the world. Almost every minute of the effort was fun. It took us all over the world. It introduced us to a great many people, many of whom became good friends. It gave us a yacht, a home in the desert and a home in the mountains. It was the source of countless memories, the vast majority of which still bring warmth when we reminisce about those great old days.

Then one day, I came home to find a voice message on the answering machine. I listened to it with Liz standing close by. It was someone I had known for nearly twenty-five years who had taken a position in upper management with First American Corporation. He said he would like to get together and talk about doing some joint marketing. First American owned the world's largest multiple listing system for real estate. As the message came to an end, I thought there were a number of possibilities. It was certainly worth talking to him. Liz's first words were, "They want to buy your company."

"Are you crazy?" I laughed out loud. She was delusional.

"I'm serious" she said. "That's exactly what they want to do."

I was thinking she was suffering from a hyper-active imagination. I hadn't heard something that silly since she tried to get me to sell the program itself nearly twenty-five years earlier. "What's for dinner?" I asked. I thought I smelled a faint odor of roast crow.

When I spoke with Mike Lancaster, I came away convinced I was being more realistic than Liz. But I did agree to fly to Los Angeles to talk about the possibilities. Before leaving for the airport, I thought I'd at least be prepared for all possible outcomes. What if Liz was right? I reviewed the company's numbers for the past couple of years and came up with what I thought could be justified if someone wanted to buy Lucero. When Liz and I left for L.A., I had a small piece of paper folded up in my pocket. On that piece of paper, I had written the number.

Our meeting went well. It was cordial, but focused and efficient. Perhaps thirty minutes into the meeting when we were at the point of trying to get a better handle on what these synergistic marketing activities might look like, Mike outlined some possibilities and then said, "We would even consider purchasing your company if that would be of interest to you."

Frankly, I was ready. Life's circumstances were such that I was ready, if not anxious, to get out from under the load of running a substantial company. I told him I would give serious consideration to selling the company outright. For the next hour or so, we talked about the numbers. How many installations? Software pricing? Expenses? We talked about all things that had a bearing on the value of the company. We ultimately took a little break and Mike conferred with a couple of other people in his organization. When we reconvened, Mike said they had come to a decision as to how much they would be willing to pay for the company.

Mike took a pad of paper and a pen and began to write. He turned the pad around so that it faced me. I looked at the number. I said, "I've given a lot of thought to what I would consider the fair market value of my company." I reached in my pocket and pulled out my little piece of paper and unfolded it. I then laid it on the table in front of him.

Despite the fact that it was a substantial multiple of a seven figure number, everyone was pleasantly shocked to discover that the two numbers matched to the penny. We shook hands. The deal was made.

After a couple of months of due diligence on the part of First American and the exchange of what at times seemed to be a never ending succession of legal documents, Liz and I sat in the office of our house in Scottsdale, Arizona. We called our bank's software to the screen and we stared at the balance of one of our accounts. We chatted and waited. I hit the "refresh" key on the keyboard every thirty or so seconds to keep the bank software from timing out and logging us off and more importantly to see if the balance in the account would change. With one magical press of the refresh key, the balance changed by millions of dollars.

I honestly don't remember who said or did what, but I'm certain we celebrated with great joy. And that is how I lost my last job.

Chapter Four – Home Bitter/Sweet Home

You can learn a lot about someone by looking at his home. Everything from culture to economic status is reflected in the appearance of the house and home. I'm anxious to see what it says about me. Remember, just like you, I've yet to read this book.

Freeland Avenue – Detroit. I still have vivid memories of my first home. My father was in college after World War II. He was to become the first member of his family to ever graduate from college. The G.I. Bill paid for his tuition, but money was still tight. My grandparents had a house on Freeland Avenue in Detroit. I'm sure it had less than a thousand square feet of living area. A room had been carved out of the attic area and served as a third bedroom. My parents lived in that room while my father went to college. They were living there when I was born.

I lived in that house until I was four years old. The five of us shared one bathroom, a small kitchen, a little dining room and a living room that was big enough to hold a couch and two comfy chairs in front of the fireplace. There was an unfinished basement that held the washing machine and laundry tubs. The second bedroom was barely big enough for a single bed, a little chair and small dresser or as my grandmother called it, a chifforobe. A black, heavy telephone sat on a little table next to the chair. My earliest memories of my grandmother were of her sitting in that chair talking with her sisters for hours on end. For four or five minutes, her end of the conversation went "Uh huh, un huh, un huh" as she listened to whatever story or gossip her sister was selling that day. Then it was her turn. This went on every day.

I remember that if I walked to the geographic center of the house, I had a door on each side. One opened into the tiny little bathroom. The other opened to a set of stairs that led to the long, narrow bedroom that was my home. One of my earliest memories of my life is of me lying in a crib near the top of those steps as I threw an outrageous tantrum because I was not being allowed to get out of it. I recall screaming and carrying on in a manner worthy of a burlap sack and a rock. I was on my back and would bring my legs into a tight tuck position and then thrust them skyward with such force that it lifted my body from my shoulders down completely off the mattress. Seventeen years later, I would use that exact same skill as an intercollegiate diver.

I recall my grandfather sitting at the dinner table when mashed potatoes, gravy and peas were served. He blanketed them all with ground pepper to the point you could barely recognize them and would thoroughly mix them altogether. I learned to love the combination and to this day, if I were to be served them on silver platters in the finest of restaurants, the wait staff would look on in horror as I duplicated my grandfather's delightful blend. He also loved hot peppers, the hotter the better. He would stand in the kitchen and sweat would run down his forehead, but he would have yet another.

After he had had a couple of beers, he would sit on the couch in the living room, light an unfiltered Chesterfield and fall asleep. He'd hold the cigarette in his right hand as his eyes slowly fell shut. As the ash on the end of the cigarette would get longer and longer, his head would slowly drift backwards until it finally fell on the decorative piece of wood on the couch top behind him. His eyes would explode open and his head would pop up with the sudden motion knocking the ashes off the cigarette and the cycle would begin again. My cousin, Prudy and I would sit and watch without end betting on whether or not the ash would fall before his head hit the wood. If the couch hadn't had the wood back, we probably would have all died in the fire that engulfed us as we laughed and watched him doze off.

Moss Street – Highland Park (Detroit). After graduation from the University of Detroit, my father went to work in the Water Department for the City of Detroit. With a paycheck and a wife, a four year old son and another child on the way, it was time for him to make his own way. He rented a flat in the winter of 1951. We had the lower level of an old two story brick house. This was the home where I tried to remove a finger with a pocketknife in the coal bin. The knife incident wasn't my only bout with mischief. I had more than a reasonable share of curiosity for a boy my age.

The house (our half of it), like so many homes in blue collar neighborhoods in Detroit, had the entryway or vestibule, the living room, a dining room, a kitchen, two bedrooms and one bathroom. In the winter months, it wasn't uncommon for temperatures to fall well below zero outside. That in of itself wasn't a big problem. The big problem would be if the temperatures inside the house fell below zero. With an old fashioned coal fired furnace, there were not thermostatic controls. You didn't set the temperature to seventy and turn in for the night. The furnace had two settings – got coal and don't got coal. So on cold winter nights just before going to bed, my father would go downstairs and shovel enough coal into the furnace to hopefully get us through the night without burning down the house. We had a furnace with room for about six hours' worth of coal. But we had nights with about twelve hours' worth of cold.

On those frigid winter mornings, I would get out of bed and go into the dining room where there was one of the old fashioned heating vents leading up from the furnace. The vent was nearly the size of a four year boy tightly tucked into the fetal position. I curled up on the floor and let the last warm breaths from the dying embers below warm me.

We had electricity. Thomas Edison had roots there. We probably had it before most of the nation. However, the "all electric home" of 1951 meant there were electric lights and rudimentary outlets on the walls for the burgeoning supply of household appliances that were coming into being. We didn't have an electric refrigerator; we had an icebox. It looked almost like a nice piece of oak furniture. We had to buy blocks of ice to handle our refrigeration needs.

The latent engineer in me must have showed signs of restlessness when I was four. I remember one morning as I emerged from my daily winter thaw by the heating vent, I noticed an electric wall outlet and a standing lamp with a large, black plug on the end of its cord. "I'll bet the light would come on if I plugged it into the outlet", I thought. "Let's give it a try." This was my first attempt at applying electricity rather than just seeing the light. I firmly grabbed the plug and thrust it into the wall outlet. Everything would have been fine if only someone had told me that you shouldn't keep your index finger between the two prongs of the plug when inserting them into the wall. It was then that the light really came on.

A half block away was Hamilton Avenue, one of Detroit's main streets. It still had the old electric street cars in 1951. My mother and I would walk up the block, jump on a street car and take it a mile or so south to go shopping. The street cars had metal arms that reached above them to the wires that provided the electricity. I can still hear the sound and see the sparks as the arms jumped across the cross connectors. Occasionally, the arms would jump off the wires and the operator would have to get out and reset the arm before continuing on his way.

A few other significant events took place while I lived on Moss Street. I started school at Liberty School a couple blocks away. My brother Brian was born. And I established my first ever close friendship with a boy named Terry Zeitz. But the flat on Moss was only a bridge to the future. We lived there for about a year.

Griggs Avenue – Detroit. My father was moving forward with his career and left his job with the City of Detroit to join Perron Construction. He had more responsibility and more money. He didn't have any savings of significance so when the opportunity presented itself to purchase a small, new home, he borrowed the down payment from my mother's father. In the winter of 1953, we moved into our new home at 16573 Griggs in Detroit. It was a new two story, brick home with three bedrooms, one and a half baths, a living room, dining room, kitchen and a full basement below. The house had about eleven hundred square feet of living area. Even though it was a humble home in a working class neighborhood, we felt like we'd just moved into Beverly Hills. We were "uptown".

We were living in the lap of luxury with modern appurtenances like an electric refrigerator, a fireplace and even three doors – front, back and side. Wow. As a new home, it didn't yet have a lawn. My father took the pride of a civil engineer to prepare the front yard for grass seed. He made certain the soil was perfect. He leveled it with an eye of perfection. He planted the seed. He watered and cared for that lawn as if it was to become the south lawn of the White House. The back yard received a similar treatment. He bought a little push mower and kept the lawn in an

absolutely immaculate condition. He cut it in a north-south pattern and then cut it again with an east-west motion. The grounds keepers at Briggs Stadium where the Tigers played could only dream of such quality turf.

A year after moving into the Griggs house, the third and final (known) boy arrived.

The Griggs house fifty years later

Jeff was born February 19, 1954. As the oldest child, I had seniority and rank. I had my own bedroom. Brian and Jeff would share one. My room was in the front corner of the second floor. It had a built-in desk; at least, that's what I was told. It was more like a table and existed only because the stairs leading to the upper floor were directly below and wouldn't have had head room for anyone over four feet tall if they hadn't built my "custom table" into the corner.

My bedroom closet contained the hatch that allowed access into the attic area. Over the next eight years, the attic became a part of my bedroom and little boy's empire. I would climb up into the attic and crawl around the rafters "exploring" much as Magellan had done centuries before me. It also served as a great hiding place when necessary, both for toys, play money and for me when I was trying to hide from threats like household chores that were about to be assigned. I was probably nine years old when I tried to extend my scientific knowledge of electricity beyond what I had learned in the Moss house. In my attic explorations, I had observed that all of the lights for the rooms on the second floor were readily accessible. The wiring and their workings intrigued me. Enter "the scientist". I rounded up some wire and a couple of additional light fixtures. I took them along with some tools up to my hideout and started experimenting. I discovered the difference in what later turned out to be series and parallel wiring. Lights wired in series burned much dimmer than those wired in parallel. At that time, I had no clue as to why, but who could argue with the empirical results of my experimentation? One thing I have yet to figure out is how I managed to do all of this wiring and testing without either electrocuting myself or burning down the house.

My brothers' bedroom wasn't big enough for two beds so they had bunk beds. The living room faced the front of the house and was where most of the family "action" took place. It was in that room that my father aroused my passion for reading and literature when he read aloud to me from a collection of the works of Edgar Allen Poe. I hung on every word and saw a side of him I'd never seen before and never saw again as he dramatically presented the story of *The Cask of Amontillado*. Christmas was always centered in that room, but invariably overflowed into the adjacent dining room. In 1956 we got our first television and it became the focal point of the living room. Just like most of life's challenges at that point, it was black and white.

The room that had the next greatest impact on my years in the Griggs house was actually a non-room. It was the basement. About twenty-two feet square, it had a concrete floor with a couple of steel pillars supporting the beams overhead. On one side of the basement were our washing machine, the laundry tubs and the fuse box. Against the wall and underneath the staircase was the cellar. I speak of these things not so much to give you the lay of the land, more to give you some important reference points for the events of my youth.

The laundry tubs were big enough and deep enough to contain a young boy who had been out playing football in the mud, but that now needed to be placed in the tub while his father hosed him down and scrubbed his hair until it hurt. It was also in the laundry area that all three of the boys were subjected to the haircuts of my mother. To save money, she had invested in a barber's kit and routinely harvested our pelts for as long as we lived on Griggs.

The fuse box was the origin of another one of my early lessons in electricity. When a new appliance was plugged into a wall outlet and dangerously overloaded an electric circuit, a fuse performed its function as a safety device and "blew". It was in this laboratory that I learned that (1) copper – in the form of a penny – was a great conductor of electricity and that (2) by inserting pennies behind a blown fuse, you could bypass all of these unnecessary safety devices and overload any circuit in the house with reckless abandon and a complete disregard for the safety and welfare of the occupants.

The cellar was perhaps four feet by six feet. It had walls and a door of wood. The door had a hasp and lock that was used only around Christmas time. Thanks to that cellar door, I taught myself how to use a number of tools with which I could remove hasp, hinges or whatever other impediments to entry my mother had installed. By Christmas Eve, I usually had a more complete inventory of Santa's Bill of Lading than did Santa himself. During the non-Christmas season, the cellar served as a storage room and a mushroom farm for my father.

The other major function of the basement for me was as an ice arena, but without the ice. My father had given me my first ice skates back when we lived on Moss. By the time we lived on Griggs, I was a pretty enthusiastic young hockey player. When it was cold enough for ice outside, I was usually playing hockey. If the streets were covered in snow, we played street hockey. In the summer months, there was "roller" hockey. We'd put on rollerskates, grab the hockey stick and a tennis ball and game on. With such a smooth finished concrete surface, the basement was a great rink for roller hockey. I spent countless hours learning to stick-handle with a tennis ball when it was too dark to play outside.

It was outside in either the front or back yard that did more to shape me than anything else. The backyard wasn't big, but it was big enough so that when winter set in, I shoveled the snow into banks that formed a rectangular area taking as much of the yard as possible. The garden hose was used to wet the banks so they would turn to ice and to flood the area in the middle. I had my own ice rink from around the first of December until mid-March. My closest friend throughout the years on Griggs was a Canadian immigrant and school classmate named Don Moffat. Don lived to play hockey. If it was cold enough for ice to form, there was a good chance Don and I were skating on it. We tried to put up barriers and to control our blossoming slap shots, but we invariably had to replace two or three windows every season.

Summer months turned to baseball. When I first moved to Griggs, my father took me out in front of the house to play catch. I had feelings of ambivalence. It was sort of fun, but it seemed every session ended with me catching one somewhere between the eyes at which time I retreated to the house with tears in my eyes. But my father persisted. He knew his father had been a fairly accomplished baseball player as had been my mother's father. He knew my genes harbored magnificent potential to be a baseball star and he was going to make sure I realized my potential whether I wanted to or not. I'm not going to say I was forced to play baseball, but for the first year or so, it was all his idea, not mine.

As my baseball skills strengthened, I truly became the top dog on the diamond in my neighborhood and at my school. Incumbent upon anyone intent on excelling at anything is the need to engage in incessant practice. With my love for the game I was constantly playing it with friends or if I was alone, swinging a bat or most often throwing a ball. A young baseball player's best friend when alone is a wall or a set of steps. I can't begin to imagine how many tens of thousands of times I threw a rubber ball or tennis ball against a wall or the step in front of the house. The problem was that the top step had a rounded top edge. If I threw the ball and it happened to hit the top half of that edge, it would bounce back toward the front door. The front door had a window. The window was made of glass. Scissors cut paper, rock breaks scissors, ball breaks glass. I broke that window at least a half dozen times. Our glass replacement expenses on Griggs were non-trivial.

In the winter of 1960 as I approached high school age, I was enrolled at Cass Technical High School in downtown Detroit. It was an honor to be allowed to attend Cass Tech. It was dedicated to the "gifted" students. One of my classmates was to be a bright young girl named Lily Tomlin. Her gift turned out to be comedy. But there were other "problems" on the horizon. In those days of racial segregation, "block busting" was when a family broke ranks with the neighbors and sold their house to a black family. Once a black family lived on a block, it was only a matter of time before there was another and another. In a blue collar neighborhood in 1960, integration was not warmly received. A black family had purchased the house directly behind us on Birwood Street. It was an ugly situation. Neighbors threw paint at the house, rocks, trash and an endless stream of vitriol. It was an eye opening experience for me. I had never witnessed such hate and bigotry.

I had never known my father to harbor ill feelings toward blacks. He had his faults and imperfections, but bigotry was not one of them. However, he was concerned about the potential financial impact the situation might have on the family. The sad reality in 1960 was home values fell when a neighborhood became integrated. He didn't want to be left holding the bag and immediately put the house on the market. His income had grown and he could now afford a much nicer home. I graduated from grade school in the first week of June 1961. In the second week of June, we were moving into our new home in Northville, Michigan, far out into the suburbs.

46930 S. Chigwidden Drive – Northville, Michigan. For the first time in my life, I now lived in a neighborhood that definitely wasn't "blue collar". Our new home was in an upscale development in an upscale community. There were fewer than 4,000 residents and the high school had barely 700 students. Our house sat on a big lot with three or four mature, highly productive apple trees in the yard. Just as he did more than eight years earlier, job number one for my father was to put in a beautiful lawn. I didn't think to ask the question, "Who's going to cut the lawn?"

The house was a split-level ranch style with nearly three times the living area of the Griggs house. A large garage was attached to the house and made it look even bigger than it was. With two

The Chigwidden house fifty years after it was built

and a half baths, a nice kitchen, separate eating area, a formal dining room, living room, a laundry room and a huge family room, we were in hog heaven. Again there were only three bedrooms and again, the eldest boy pulled rank and got the private quarters. Brian and Jeff shared a bedroom.

Just as it did on Griggs, the yard played a key role in my life over the four years I lived in Northville. I played on the football and baseball teams throughout my high school years and our backyard became my biggest practice field. As football season approached, I would spend hours and hours punting footballs in the backyard. With over an acre to play on, I had all the room I needed to practice. I soon became the punter on the high school team. When baseball was in the air, I now had lots of room to practice and play. I also had two younger brothers that I could coerce into playing. Brian played but didn't have the toolset to compete on my level. Jeff was younger, but was more of a natural ball player. We spent countless hours playing baseball in that big yard.

The house was in a development called "Northville Estates". It had been cut out of an old apple orchard. We were surrounded by miles and miles of heavily wooded farms. It was a dream world for a fourteen year old boy. I spent countless hours wandering through the woods. Wildlife was plentiful. As fall approached, the colors were indescribably brilliant and beautiful. As I walked through the woods, I noted the location of any substantial lakes or ponds. Winter was coming and it would soon be time to strap on the hockey skates.

On the basis of appearance, we were part of Northville's upper-crust. The big house, the long driveway, the nicer cars, all pointed to an upper-middle class family. But despite our best efforts to decorate ourselves as such, we were still close to our roots in the world of working America. Even in the dead of winter, I frequently walked to school. Northville High School was a little more than a mile away and as you might expect, it was up hill both ways. There was school bus service, but I rode the bus only during the times Kris Deibert was my steady girlfriend (about half the time over the four years in high school). She lived five miles west of our house. If I caught the bus early, I could ride it out to where she was normally the first person to be picked up. We could then sit snugly in a seat for the entire duration of the trip.

Green Lake House – Not long after moving into the house on Griggs, my maternal grandparents purchased a building lot on Green Lake twenty miles northwest of their home in Detroit. My grandfather Radcliffe built a small, two bedroom house near the end of a secluded private drive at the far end of the lake. He did it all, the carpentry, plumbing, electrical, tile work, the whole thing pretty much by himself.

With the exception of two summers when I was living on my aunt's farm in Ohio, I lived at the lake house with my grandparents and two cousins, R.J. and Douglas. The three of us were close in age and inseparable friends. I'd guess the house had no more than six or seven hundred square feet. There were two little bedrooms, one bathroom, a small kitchen, a small living room and an enclosed front porch. The porch ran the width of the house and faced the lake. There were four chaise lounge style chairs with reclining backs. They made perfect beds for young boys and the front porch was our bedroom for the summer.

For two months every summer, we played baseball, went swimming, turtle hunting and frog hunting. Green Lake was spring fed and outboard motors were outlawed. As a result, it teamed with fish, turtles and all things that young boys love. There was a ten foot square wood raft that the neighbors had built. It floated on a group of fifty-five gallon drums and was anchored about two hundred feet offshore directly in front of our house. A day never passed when we didn't spend at least an hour swimming and diving from the raft.

My grandfather built a wood dock that served as home to our twelve foot aluminum rowboat. We fished from the dock often, but more often jumped into the boat and rowed to the "special" fishing spots that only we knew. Between baseball, fishing and swimming, I have accounted for nearly all of the daylight hours of every summer day for many years of my youth. However, there was one more activity and it was the "big one", the one that made us great bwanas and hunters extraordinaire. We were the great turtle hunters.

My grandfather had a number of white, fiberglass square containers about a foot and a half square and a foot and a half high. For two months each year they became turtle bins. Our catch for the day would be brought in, sorted by breed and put into the appropriate container. We gave the turtles everything they needed to survive happily (assuming turtles can be happy) and we treated them as pets. They didn't always return the favor. I remember one time when I held a good sized diamond back turtle up in front of my face. He reached out and latched on to the end of my nose. It took a fair amount of coaxing to convince him to let it go.

We actually became quite expert in the lives and habits of the turtles of Michigan's lakes. We caught countless painted turtles, diamond back, musk and snapping turtles. My grandfather used to give us twenty-five cents for each snapper we caught. He "disposed" of them because they ate fish and the fingers of little boys. There was one other that was the real trophy for young turtle hunters. The Michigan soft-shell turtle was extremely difficult to catch and even more difficult to handle once he was caught. Turtle hunting took two boys working together. One sat at the front of the boat with a long handled fisherman's net and scanned the waters for signs of little turtle heads sticking up or for turtles sunning themselves on lily pads. The other was the oarsman. He was the key to the catch. He had to be able to direct the boat slowly and as absolutely silently as possible. Oarlocks were oiled so they wouldn't squeak. The boat bottom had to be clean so our prey wouldn't hear the sound of our bare feet rubbing sand on the metal bottom.

Once a turtle was spotted, it was the oarsman's job to stealthily get the boat as close as possible before the turtle panicked and dove for the deep and muddy lake bottom. The moment the turtle dove, the netter hollered at the oarsman who in turn put the pedal to the metal and frantically rowed toward the target. The netter's skill then determined success or failure. The Michigan softshell was such a prize because it could swim at easily double the speed of the others. It was much more skittish and tended to dive much earlier than the others. There were times when the netter would actually dive into the water with net extended in an attempt catch the elusive prey. Our success rate on all other turtles was probably about seventy-five percent. With softshells, it was less than ten percent. When the more common turtles were caught, they generally went into their defensive postures and pulled everything safely into the confines of their shells. When the softshell was caught, its initial impulse was to immediately bite the hell out of the first thing it could find – which was either my cousin or me. Unfortunately for the hunters, softshell turtles had much longer necks than the other turtles. They could quickly reach around and bite anyone who was trying to hold them even if by the tail. The trick became a rapid left-hand/right-hand switching maneuver where the slightest hesitation resulted in a bloody finger and a turtle escape.

Nights at the lake house usually included hot dogs and marshmallow roasting. Maybe a game of Chutes and Ladders and whenever he was on, "The Lawrence Welk Show". My grandmother wouldn't miss an episode on the old (then new) 17" black and white TV. Sometimes, our cousins Willard and Clyde (I'm not making those names up) would come to the lake house and join us. Their interests were very different than ours and we got along only because we were forced to. Unquestionably one of the week's highlights came on Saturday night. We were all allowed to stay up late and watch "Shock Theater". It was then and there that we learned about all the movies of the 1930's starring the likes of Lon Chaney, Boris Karloff, Bela Lugosi, Peter Lorre and other great stars from the early days of

Howard (front) with the cousins watching Shock Theater

horror movies.

The lake house came into play in the ensuing years of my life, but its greatest impact occurred during my time in grade school. It was a home for grandparents, cousins, water and marshmallows. It was the Fourth of July fireworks. It was blue gill, bass and gar pike. It was hitting small rocks into the lake with an old baseball bat. It was porridge, white biscuits and gravy. It was my childhood.

How are you going to keep him down on the farm? For the summers of my seventh and eleventh years, I lived with my mother's sister Virginia, her husband Lloyd and my cousins on their farm in Canal Winchester a few miles southeast of Columbus, Ohio. My parents thought it would be an education for me and it was that and more. It was a working dairy farm and when I arrived, I was part of the crew and expected to do my jobs. On the old "family farms", everybody worked no matter how old or how young. The house was built in the 1840s and is now on Ohio's list of historic sites. It had two stories and looked exactly like a classic farm house should look.

On the covered porch just outside the kitchen was a butter churn. We used it to (drum roll please) make butter. Old fashioned glass pitchers were filled with "blue" milk with the cream on top all straight from the barn. On the lawn outside was an old fashion hand water pump where we got (more music) our water. There were lots of "out-buildings" one of the most popular of which was the "out-house". A bucket of lime sat next to the wooden seat. A trip to the out-house in the middle of the night or during a storm could turn into quite an adventure.

We had a hay barn where I would join my cousins and jump from a platform high above the hay pile below. One of the neighbors ended up with a pretty significant cut one day when he landed on a pitch fork that wasn't visible from above. We had a dairy barn into which we brought the cows for the daily milking. We had an equipment barn where we kept our Case, Massey-Ferguson and Ford tractors when they weren't in use. It was actually the equipment barn to which I was first sent to gather goose eggs as a joke. When I approached her nest, I didn't realize she was prepared to defend her eggs to the death. My cousins did and they thought it was great fun for me to learn. We had a chicken coup and dozens of laying hens. It was great fun to chase them all around the coup until my uncle caught me and gave me another of my life lessons on the farm. In addition to the chickens, we had sheep, goats, horses, cats, dogs, a bull (another lesson there) and plenty of milk cows.

My day on the farm began at 4:30 a.m. when I went with my cousins to round up the cows. We mounted horses and rode them bareback up the hill to bring in the cows. Actually, most of the work was done by Major, our collie. He lived to round up the cattle. He was an absolute master at it. If one so much as looked like she wanted to break away from the herd, Major would run as fast as he could to get her back in line barking all the way.

I was sent to the farm to learn. From that standpoint, my summers there were immensely successful. I learned that cows kick, horses buck, geese grab, snakes bite, goats butt, cats scratch and skunks spray. I also learned wasps sting. We had a tornado one summer. Fortunately it missed the house, but it did do some damage to some of the out-buildings. One small shed remained perfectly intact, but had been turned upside down. The next morning, my cousin Douglas and I went for a little tour to see what had been damaged. We spotted the shed standing with its feet in the air. Doug went first and opened the shed door. He stepped into the shed and as I entered, he instantly turned and sprinted in the other direction. As he flew past me, he shouted something. I couldn't tell what he said. However, it didn't take me long to figure it out. It seems the shed had been home to a bee hive. With their lives upended, they probably couldn't explain the causes, but they did know the next person they saw was going to be held responsible. They descended upon me in mass. They stung my face, my head, my shoulders, back, arms and anything else they could find. I turned and ran as fast as I could directly back toward the house. The next problem arose when I found that a straight line from the upended shed and the house happened to pass directly through a rose hedge. I was going full tilt when I ran through the hedge. That evening at the dinner table I was a sight to behold. My eyes were nearly swollen shut. Nearly every part of my body was either swollen from bee stings or sliced from rose thorns. Many body parts were both.

Life on the farm also came with one obligation that didn't exactly thrill me. I was expected to go to church. If I was given the choice between suiting up and sitting through another boring church lecture and risking another bout with the bees and roses, I'm not sure I wouldn't have opted for the bees. My Aunt Virginia quickly came to realize church attendance wasn't high on my list of priorities, but if I was to be part of the family, I wasn't given the option of opting out. One Sunday morning, I somehow managed to get ready ahead of the other boys. I went outside and waited with a sense of dread. I looked over at the pond near the house and saw the little row boat we used to fish when time permitted. I figured I had time for a little spin around the pond. I put one foot in the boat, but before I could get my second foot in, the boat broke loose from the shore. I used every little bit of strength I could muster to bring the boat back to shore, but in painfully slow motion, the boat continued to glide outward. Finally, as my body reached the "make a wish" position, I had no place to go but face down into the muddy water. I got back up to the house at about the time the others were coming outside. My cousins doubled over with laughter. My aunt wasn't nearly as amused. That was the one and only time I did manage to get out of going to church on Sunday, but my aunt made sure that I knew going to church was the most pleasant alternative should I ever think about boating before church in the future. My feeling was that if God wanted me in church, he wouldn't have let me fall into the muddy pond in the first place. Poor planning on his part.

Kalamazoo – On my own. In the fall of 1966, I moved into a dormitory at Western Michigan University. I was a freshman and in my mind at least, I was now an adult living on my own. When I walked into my new home on the third floor of Bigelow Hall, I saw two single beds, two small dressers and two desks side-by-side built into the wall. My roommate, Dick Balser was waiting there. As it turned out, he was most appropriately named. We weren't destined to become closest of friends. I took the bed by the window.

Life in a dormitory was certainly an awakening. We had a large community bathroom that was shared by everyone living on that floor. Two payphones were in little closets in the hallway. Calls cost ten cents, but one of the first tricks I learned in the dorm was to hold a penny in the quarter slot, drop it and with a precisely timed fist to the phone, it fooled it into thinking it was a dime and the dial tone magically appeared. Girls weren't allowed in the rooms or even on the floor. One of the newer dorms out in "the valley" was experimenting with the concept of co-ed dorms, but we still lived under the old rules. If a girl did come to the dorm, she had to go to the desk in the lobby and ask the attendant to contact me. The intercom in the room would come alive. "Howard Jones, you have a guest in the lobby."

Some meals were a part of the dorm package. They were served in a large cafeteria on the first floor. On Wednesdays and Sundays evenings, residents were expected to wear a coat and tie to the dinner meal. That wasn't my style so I had different plans on those evenings, usually a "peanut burger" at the Student Union. I had the joy of doing my own laundry; maybe that should have been in the chapter on trauma. The machines were in the basement

It was while living in the dorm that I learned about things that eighteen year old men are obligated to discover, things like slow gin, Southern Comfort, guitar playing and a variety of other new things - everything that is except how to study. With so many new and exciting things, the books weren't at the top of my priority list. One thing I recall learning was how to "penny" someone in his room. The doors to the rooms in the dorm were metal as were the door frames. I mentioned that my roommate and I didn't exactly see things eye-to-eye. He wasn't terribly popular with many of the other guys on the floor either. One of those guys taught me the "penny" trick. If you lean heavily against the door so that you're putting extreme pressure on the dead bolt lock, you can then wedge a small stack of pennies between the door frame and the door itself. The result is that the dead bolt stays under extreme pressure and it becomes virtually impossible to unlock the door from the inside. It was hours before the "resident assistant" on the floor heard Balser's calls for help. If we had pennyed the R.A. in his room, there would have been a good chance we could have starved them to death before help arrived. But sadly, Balser escaped.

After the first semester, I switched rooms and moved in with a senior in a corner room on the first floor. When Bruce Zylstra was out of town, it was easy to sneak a girl into the room through the window. I was never a big fan of the rules.

Off campus like the big boys. By the dawn of my sophomore year, I was no longer obliged to live in a dormitory. A high school friend, Kent Kipfer and I decided we would rent a place off campus, someplace we could drink, play music and generally be misbehaved college students. We found a big old Victorian house a few blocks from campus. The owner had purchased it as an investment and closed off a small section of it for his own residence. The rest of the majestic old home would be ours. We had three or maybe four bedrooms, a substantial kitchen, a big formal dining room and an even bigger living room. Below was a big basement full of old books in boxes from the previous owners who had no doubt abandoned them there.

This was the first time we had ever been "tenants" and frankly, we didn't have a clue as to how to act with consideration or responsibility. We were oblivious to most everything. After all, we were now "adults". I had all night sessions with a bluegrass group most weekends. The poor owner had to enjoy the sound of guitars, fiddles, banjos and mandolins until sunrise.

Kent and I decided that no respectable college sophomore should live anywhere without a keg of beer. We purchased a cheap, but functional refrigerator and put it in one of the unused rooms upstairs. We removed the shelves and were pleased to discover a keg of beer would fit perfectly. Using my newly acquired "fake

ID", we ordered a keg from the I.G.A. grocery store around the corner. When it arrived, we brought it into the living room and prepared to "tap" the keg, something neither of us had ever done. The tap had a long metal pipe that obviously had to be put into the keg and a locking device that would clamp the whole assembly in place. The keg was agitated after being clumsily carted a block and had built up enough pressure to launch a V-1 rocket from France to London. The only thing we could see to do was quickly plunge the pipe through the sealed hole on the top of the keg and lock it into place as quickly as possible. On the count of three, bang, there it went. There was a small amount of froth that escaped, but by and large, we were successful. After pausing for a couple seconds to make sure all was well, I released my hold on the locking mechanism. I guess I had just barely set the lock and it instantly broke free. The tap assembly was fired upward with such force that it put a hole through the ceiling. As beer spewed skyward, we scrambled to get the tap and reset it into the keg. This time we were successful, but the mess would take some time to clean up.

The beer ultimately lubricated the fingers of a lot of musicians playing into the wee hours. It also served another purpose a month or so later. For the first time in our lives, both Kent and I were on budgets (whatever the hell that was). As it turned out, our budgeting skills weren't yet completely developed. We ran completely out of money in early October. We didn't have enough to buy a quart of milk. It was time to go to class (yes, we were still pretending to be students). The only thing in the house that was edible was a box of corn flakes. I filled a bowl with the corn flakes. It then hit me the only liquid other than water that I had available was keg beer. Flat beer and corn flakes. Now there's a gourmet meal.

There was another small problem living in the house. There was only one heating system. On those cold winter nights, we needed to turn the heat up high to warm the big, drafty, two story section of the house in which we lived. We had the thermostat so we kept it to our liking. Unfortunately for the owner who was holed up in the little three room corner of the house, it turned his partitioned apartment into a sauna. He asked us to not turn the heat up so high. He might as well have been talking to a tree stump. We were intent on being warm. He solved his problem by coming into our part of the house and installing a locking box around the thermostat. He knew we could no longer change the temperature setting.

Although I had no intention of studying engineering at that time (hell, I had no intention of studying anything), the engineer's mind within stirred. I knew the thermostat had to sense the temperature in order to turn the furnace on and off. I concluded I could still control the heating system by fooling the thermostat. I took a washrag and wrapped it around a couple of ice cubes and placed it on top of the security box. As the ice cubes melted, drops of ice water slowly dripped down upon the thermostat. We kept the house warm enough to bake bread simply by leaving dough in front of the heat registers. We didn't get along with the landlord very well after that.

Begin the procession. I left Western Michigan University and the big Victorian to get married. For the next few years, we moved rather frequently. If you read the chapter on jobs, I'm sure this comes as no great surprise. At first we rented a series of little dinky places. As often as not, they were cut out of someone's existing house. A small upstairs area that was converted into a little apartment seemed to be the rule of the day. They were always little and limited, but on the wages of a shoe salesman or golf ball diver, luxury wasn't an option. We were living in just such a place in South Lyon, Michigan when I moved into the world of broadcast news. What made that place special was the fact the house sat immediately adjacent to a railroad track. I wasn't sure which side of the track was the "right side", but I can assure you both sides were equally loud when the train passed. It was on that track that I saw for the last time in my life a train pulled by an old fashioned steam engine. Black smoke poured from its boiler stack and the whistle was powered by the steam it generated. And the sound of the old steam engines was romantic in its own way as the choo-choo-choo echoed from an era long past.

As my career in broadcasting advanced, so too did the quality of our living quarters. Now we were living in apartments, but they were the nicer ones. In Denver, we rented a nice place in the southeast part of the city. Each building on the street had four separate units, two upstairs and two down. The buildings were staggered such that every other one was closer to the street. The end result was that every other one looked exactly alike. I remember coming home one evening and absent mindedly parking in front of the wrong unit. I walked into what I thought was my apartment. I could smell dinner cooking. "I'm home" I said as I closed the door behind me.

"Hi. How was your day?" came the voice from the kitchen. She rounded the corner to greet me just as I entered the kitchen. I'm not sure who was more surprised. Maybe I should have stayed; she was kind of cute and a good cook on top of that.

Homecoming – Back to school. When I left Portland, Oregon to return to college, I rented an old house in Northville. It was conveniently located relative to the college I would attend for the next year and to the construction sites at which I'd be working. It was a good sized house on about an acre of land. It was 1971 and The Beatles, the Rolling Stones, The Moody Blues, Pink Floyd and a host of others provided the beat and the flower children led the way. Vietnam was a curse. Panama Red and Columbian Gold were delights and the back door to the universe was unlocked with Purple Haze and Window Pane. We were living in the midst of a cultural revolution and we were in the middle of the movement.

When I moved back to Michigan, word got around that a former pro-quality baseball player was back in town. Don Thompson was a wealthy local business man with more money than sense. He was a respectable athlete in his time, but never drank from the champion's cup. He decided he would put together a team that would win the slow pitch softball state championship. In order to recruit the best ball players, he had a softball stadium designed and built. He then tracked down and recruited the best baseball players he could find. When I got the knock on my door, I was flattered and immediately accepted. Of the players on the team, the only ones that hadn't played pro baseball, had played either pro football or lettered at a major college. It was a true powerhouse team. The team did win the state championship that year and suffered only one loss the entire season. The loss came to a team of semi-talented pot heads who just put together their miracle game while we hit everything directly into their gloves as they flinched to avoid death by screaming softball. The team had only a couple of high quality ball players, the best of which was my youngest brother Jeff. After more than forty years, he still brings up that game and makes me relive the nightmare.

So what's this got to do with a house in Northville you ask. I'm getting there. Just calm down. I'm getting there.

At one practice session at the new ball park, I was at my usual position at third base. We were working on bunt situations. I charged a slow roller, fielded it and turned quickly to throw to first base. Although the new field had been conditioned, the infield was still "tight". When I wheeled around toward first base, my entire body turned. Well, it was almost my entire body. My right leg from the knee down disobeyed my orders. My spikes hung up in the tight soil. My right foot was pointed directly behind me while the rest of me was looking forward. Ouch!!! Howard was hospital bound. My anterior cruciate ligament and medial meniscus were catastrophically destroyed. I spent a week in traction and then another six or eight weeks in a full length leg cast. It was soon painted with full psychedelic flair. Most of my time was spent at the house. (See, I told you we'd get there.)

A couple of weeks into my rehabilitation, I was coming into the house through the backdoor. It was one of those doors full of glass panes perhaps six by eight inches each. I didn't realize that Lucy was right on my heels with a laundry basket full of clothes she had just plucked from the clothes line. Without looking behind me, I swung the door shut with enough force to make sure it closed. When Lucy saw the door coming, she reflexively put her knee out to keep it from slamming shut. Her knee was squarely aligned with the center of one of the glass panes. After it had passed a couple inches through the pane, she reflexively jerked it out. That move served to drive the pointed pieces of glass deep into her leg. She was cut very deeply and was bleeding profusely.

With my right leg in a full length cast, I was unable to safely drive our stick shift car. I hobbled as fast as I could out to the street and tried to flag down a passing car to take us to the hospital. The first two drivers looked at me as if I'd escaped from the cracker factory. I was shouting something about a seriously injured woman that needed to get to the hospital. They probably thought I was a murderer and drove right on past me. I soon decided I was going to have to drive her to the emergency room. I had to operate the accelerator, the brake and the clutch all with my left foot while my right leg was wedged under the dash on the passenger's side of the car all while Lucy was doing her best to bleed to death. Somehow, we made it and a few hours later, Lucy was home sporting her own full length leg cast. We were a pair to draw to.

The following day, there was a knock on the door. It was a police officer. He was very polite and friendly as he explained one of the cars I attempted to stop had reported the incident to the police. They arrived at the house after I had left for the hospital. They saw puddles of fresh blood. When no one responded to their knocks or calls, they feared someone was unconscious or dead in the house. They had entered and searched the house. He said they just wanted to confirm that everyone was alright and get the full story.

My explanation seemed to satiate his curiosity. He politely thanked me and started to walk away. He stopped suddenly and slowly turned around and looked at me. "Oh, one other thing" he said. "You should probably get rid of all that stuff you've got in the room there in the middle of the house."

Egad! They'd found it. I had turned a ten foot square room into an experimental laboratory where I had dozens of marijuana plants growing under florescent lights. I had been experimenting with varying soil conditions, nutrients, light levels and more to scientifically determine prime conditions for growing the plant that was a de facto currency for members of the counter-culture. He'd discovered the pot and all of the experimental records. He and his partner had made the decision to turn their heads as long as I made it all disappear. And true to my word, the next day, it was gone. I took it all out into "neutral territory" and replanted it. I had a bumper crop that year. I should have shared it with the police officer.

Back to the house; it had a living room, dining room, kitchen laundry room (bloodied), three bedrooms, a bath and a half and a pot farm.

Back to the Campus – East Lansing, Michigan. After a year at Oakland Community College refreshing myself in mathematics and chemistry, I was ready for the big school. I had graduated number one in a class of seven thousand students. I was offered academic scholarships at both Michigan State University and the University of Michigan. MSU was the more generous of the two and we left for East Lansing. It was back to student housing, but this time it would be in the married housing complex called Cherry Lane.

We ended up with an upper floor, two bedroom unit in one of the two-story buildings. Student housing wasn't designed to be luxurious and it wasn't. While standing in the kitchen, I could touch the opposing walls at the same time and that was in the widest direction. The bathroom was so small, I came to appreciate my slightly below average height. The big bedroom was tiny. The little bedroom was far smaller than the closet I currently have in my home in Scottsdale. A little dining table sat just off the kitchen in what was in reality a part of the living room. The living room could seat four people as long as they weren't wearing heavy sweaters. In was definitely a Spartan existence.

Life in married housing was interesting. Our neighbors were from all over the world. Many of them had never lived in such modern facilities. One woman from central Africa had never seen let alone used a washing machine. Until told otherwise, she had no idea that baby diapers should be rinsed before putting them into the washing machine itself. Another free spirit from the back woods of South Carolina was studying for his Ph.D. in psychology. He didn't believe kids needed any guidance in a lot of areas such as how to eat or dress. I can remember his kids running barefoot out into the snow in sub-zero temperatures wearing nothing but underwear. He believed that if a child was cold, he had the innate sense to do something to get warm, something like put on more clothes. In the three years we spent in Cherry Lane, we had good friends from such foreign lands as the Netherlands, Peru, China, Czechoslovakia, Kenya, Scotland, Japan, India, Libya, Brazil, Israel, Australia and even Memphis, Tennessee. It was truly a potpourri of humanity and culture.

It should come as no surprise that with a high population density and such diverse concepts of sanitation, cockroaches were a never ending challenge. Residents could call the university and someone would come out to treat the problem. Borax powder would be spread in the areas known to appeal to the cockroaches, e.g., under the refrigerator, dark areas, and pool halls. That seemed to take care of the problem for a while, but there was a lot of anecdotal evidence that although the Borax may have knocked a few of them out, others just packed their bags and headed to the adjacent units. Those of us that had lived there long enough kept our ears to the walls to find out who was going to be treating for cockroaches. The trick was to schedule your treatment shortly after your adjacent neighbors. It became somewhat of a game of cockroach herding rather than extermination. If a few neighbors plotted together, we could usually get them run off and into the units of people we didn't like such as those who would pound on the ceiling below, also known as our floor, while you were trying to study on a Saturday night.

The Michigan weather made life in married housing slightly more difficult. There were nights it would get so cold that a car battery stood no chance of surviving until dawn. I had to go to the car, remove the battery and bring it into our apartment for the night. There were some good things (other than ice skating) that came from Michigan's insanely cold winters.

In my third and final year at MSU, the nation went on daylight saving time in the dead of winter in an effort to conserve energy in the wake of an oil embargo in the Middle East. As an underclassman, I dreamed of being a senior so I could finally get first crack at classes. Underclassmen were usually stuck with the lousy class times because the upperclassmen got to register first and filled the better time slots. What I didn't understand was that as a senior in engineering, I did get first pick of classes, but there were so few chemical engineering seniors, the required classes were only offered at crappy hours. I had a class at 8:00 a.m. every day of the week. With the daylight saving time nonsense, the class was technically an hour earlier. Worse yet, the path I had to walk to get to class led a mile across a huge open area that was an athletic practice field. Any winds were funneled into the open area and the effects of the frigid weather were made substantially worse. I so vividly recall three consecutive mornings when on the warmest of the three, the temperature was twenty-two degrees below zero. With the cutting twenty-five mile per hour wind, I suspect the wind chill temperature was close to minus fifty.

I was completely miserable. I still remember the fur of my survival jacket plummeting from side-to-side as I peeked out the tiny opening I had left so I could see. I had exceptionally high grades. I was in the Honors College. Chemical engineers were in extremely high demand. I could basically write my own ticket and go anywhere I wished. On the third morning, the temperature was minus twenty-three. I vowed to myself that I would consider no job offer if it wasn't someplace warm. That led me to my next home.

California, here I come. It was duplex rental time again. We found a small, but very nice rental in northern Marin County across the Golden Gate Bridge from San Francisco. It was nestled back in the Indian Valley a couple miles west of the 101 freeway. The duplex was nice, but nondescript. I have hardly any memories of the inside of the unit. I do remember sitting outside in the little backyard on our first New Year's Day in California. We sat amid the flowers and took a photograph to send back to friends and family still suffering Michigan winters.

There are a couple of memories of our time on Ignacio Boulevard in Novato that are worthy of mention. We had lived there for perhaps a month and Lucy went shopping in San Rafael four or so miles to the south. As she approached the exit to Ignacio, she glanced in her rearview mirror to see a rather grizzly looking fellow on a motorcycle. Upon closer scrutiny, she realized the man wore the emblem of the infamous "Hell's Angels". To a young woman from Michigan, this was the substance of legend. She'd heard of them, seen them in movies and television, but somehow, they didn't really exist until now. There he was! She wondered how many rapes and murders he had committed that day. Was she next?

When she veered off the 101, the motorcycle stayed right on her tail. Surely, he's not following me she wondered. When she got to the corner to turn onto Ignacio, he was still there. She made the turn and he remained a few feet behind her. She was actually starting to become a little concerned at this point. What had she done to make him follow her? As she drove the two mile route up the valley, she waited for the Hell's Angel to turn into a driveway or off onto a side street. He didn't. Her pulse quickened. When she finally reached our driveway, she turned in only to see the road pirate turn into the driveway with her. She panicked. She leaned on the horn until I came running outside to see what was happening. As I came running out, I came face-to-face with my first Hell's Angel. He gave me a look as if to say, "Be careful. That woman in the car seems to be a little crazy." He walked past me headed toward the front door of the other unit in the duplex. He knocked on the door and our neighbor let him in. He frequently visited his sister on the weekend. She was our neighbor.

Homeowners at last. With the income of a young chemical engineer, I could finally scrape together enough money to make a house payment. Inflation was picking up and my co-workers suggested getting the maximum mortgage possible. They believed that as inflation continued to rise, I would be smart to use the bank's money to increase net worth. They later proved to be right. We found a house we liked in Rohnert Park just south of Santa Rosa. It would be a long commute, but it beat the hell out of paying Marin County prices.

We paid a $5,000 premium for the house because in fronted the Rohnert Park Golf Course. It seemed like a fortune, but we paid $50,000 for a brand new, 1,800 square foot, three bedroom, two bath, single level house. It was 210 yards off the sixteenth tee. I'd never have to buy a golf ball again. Golfers hit them in my yard all day. I'd watched my father plant lawns in two of his houses; surely, I could easily do the same thing. I over estimated my desire to succeed. I worked at it, but it still looked like hell when I moved out of the house. I was distracted.

Howard's first house purchase in Rohnert Park, California

With a house on the golf course, I could now play golf seven days a week. When I got home in the evening, I grabbed my clubs and headed onto the course. I could usually get at least nine holes in before darkness enveloped the course. When I got up in the morning, I'd grab a bag full of balls, jump the fence and hit sixty to eighty balls to the sixteenth green before leaving for the office. My golf handicap was falling rapidly and I took the game more seriously than ever. There was usually a tournament on Saturday, another one on Sunday and on a few occasions, I played one tournament in the morning and another in the afternoon.

You may be starting to get the picture of why the lawn wasn't looking all that good. Neither was the marriage. But man, could I hit a golf ball! And what's more important?

A year after buying the house for $50,000, I moved out, filed for divorce and quit my job. But I was the Sonoma County golf champion in 1977. So to summarize my first experience with home ownership, it was a very nice house, but it didn't last long. Lucy tried to keep the house. She was kind enough to give the payment book to me. When she soon concluded she couldn't live in the lap of luxury on a bank teller's earnings and whatever she could squeeze out of me, we sold the house for $80,000. I was thrust back into the world of renters.

On the road again. When I worked for Radian Corporation and was travelling as part of the research team, I lived in motels and short term apartment rentals. Lucy had been kind enough to relieve me of the vast majority of my worldly possessions, so it wasn't difficult to move from one place to another. I lived in a succession of rentals as I traveled up and down the west coast. When I returned to the San Francisco area, I moved in with Eleonor in Pinole. I wrote her a check for half the equity in her house and was technically a home owner again. But after I left to go to Arizona to study for my doctorate, I ended up "gifting" my half to her. At the University of Arizona, it was back into student housing. I had a simple, but adequate one bedroom apartment in the foothills of the Catalina Mountains. This was the first time I had lived in the desert. During the summer monsoons season, I spent many evenings sitting or lying outside watching as lightning danced across the sky. It was indescribably beautiful and exhilarating.

Bomb maker's row house. When Apache Powder was first created around the time of World War I, it was built in the middle of nowhere. The residents of metropolitan areas generally frowned upon companies that would occasionally explode when a thousand pounds of nitroglycerine and an errant electrical spark formed an unholy and unexpected alliance. The area remains sparsely populated, but in 1926 it was little more than a stop on the Southern Pacific railroad tracks. It hosted its share of bank robbers, cattle rustlers and con men. Tombstone, the site of the famed "Gunfight at the OK Corral" was only about twenty miles south. Apache Powder needed to hire about 200 workers and without living quarters, it was going to be an impossible task. The company constructed a row of "nicer" homes along a two block section of Benson's West Sixth Street about six miles from the plant. These were for the company's managers. They constructed another set of tiny little houses adjacent to the plant for the dynamite line workers. These were inhabited by the Mexicans that worked at the plant because the company gave them cheap rent. A friend of mine, Salvador Gordillo, lived in one of the little houses when he went to work there around 1930. He was making thirty-three cents per hour at the time.

Fifty years later, management still lived in the Benson houses and the dynamite workers lived close enough to feel the blasts that came from the plant every few years. When I took a job at Apache Powder, I was given a chance to rent one of the manager's houses and took advantage of the offer. It was a single story, wood frame building more than a half century old. There was a one-car garage at the rear of the lot that in reality was a one-car shed. The home was simple and devoid of luxury. In the summer months, it got pretty damn hot in Benson, but a swamp cooler and cold beer was all that existed for cooling.

The house holds some rather interesting memories. Possibly the most unusual involved a family visit. I had just married Roberta when I moved into the house. The Navajo culture is in many respects more different from the Anglo culture than most people could ever imagine. It is a maternal society and one day, the matriarch herself was coming to visit. I left for my office that morning knowing she would be there when I returned later that day. I drove my truck to the plant and left my relatively new Jeep parked in the garage.

When I returned, I expected to find Roberta, the three kids (Kevin, Karen and Kenny) and Roberta's mother in the house. I pulled up by the garage, parked, got out and walked toward the big garage door. Everything appeared to be normal, but appearances can be deceiving. I pushed the door to the side enough for me to walk into the garage and pulled the door closed behind me. When I turned around, chickens went everywhere. There were a dozen chickens sitting in, on and around my Jeep. As I approached, chickens scrambled and flew in all directions clucking and screeching as they went. An egg had been laid on my seat in the Jeep. Another on the floor. Another in the rear of the Jeep. I hadn't left the garage yet, but I knew life was about to get interesting.

I walked out of the side door and glanced to my left. Nailed to the exterior wall was a goat's hide. It had been recently skinned. Oh my! This wasn't the Griggs house was it? I headed for the back door of the house. I opened the door. As I entered, I had to step over what appeared to be the shelves from my refrigerator. I opened the refrigerator door and discovered the shelves had to be removed to accommodate the goat that had been butchered. By then, I had a pretty good idea of what we were having for dinner. As I walked from the kitchen toward the living room, I was given a jovial greeting by Roberta, Kevin, Karen, Kenny, Eva (Roberta's mother) as well as Virgil, Lester, Lisa and a couple of other cousins whose names have slipped my mind. I had ten guests, a dozen chickens and a dead goat. And the visit had just begun. Life was anything but boring.

Upwardly mobile. There was a clear pecking order on "management row". The higher up one rose in the company, the better and bigger the house. As the newest management employee, I had taken the first one that came available. When someone in one of the bigger houses left the company, I was given first choice. I took it. We moved two houses south. The new one was far bigger and more "luxurious" than the previous one, but still lacked air conditioning. I had a two-car garage or shed, living room, dining room, three bedrooms, two baths and an office on a large corner lot. For a town like Benson, this was like the main house on a southern plantation. In most other places, it was a tear-down.

At about that time, Apache Powder was trying to bring some fiscal sense into its operations. Operating a small "company town" wasn't profitable and the decision was made to sell the homes. The current residents were to be given first choice. The company set what appeared to be very reasonable prices. It would carry the paperwork on the loans. The interest rate was to be very low given the market conditions at the time. It asked for no down payment. The houses would be sold "as is" with no warranties. Although the homes were all more than fifty years old, all the residents bought the homes in which they lived. It seemed like an absolute "no brainer".

The Benson house at nearly 100 years old

As it turned out, it was a no-brainer. Anyone that had a brain or at least used the one they had would have turned tail and beat-feet out of town without looking over his shoulder. Very soon after once again becoming a "homeowner", things started happening. The flat, sun baked roof started leaking. I had to have it reroofed. I learned the electrical system had been put in by dyslexic apprentices from the plant. They had apparently been seeking revenge on management. The plumbing system was prone to performing random acts of violence. But the final straw came in the home office.

One evening, I tried to open the window. The weight of my hand on the wooden window sill caused it to crack. I thought that seemed a little odd. I pushed on it lightly and easily broke off a good sized piece. When I pressed on the remaining surface, my index finger easily penetrated the wood. With two hands, I gave the sill a pull and it came right off exposing the wood below. The wood had been absolutely ravaged by termites. I quickly learned that termites have an organization not unlike a medieval city in a war torn country. When you invade a termite colony, they return fire. The women and children are hustled into the bomb shelters and the warriors are sent to defend the fort. Termite warriors are big, mean assed, ugly dudes with pinchers the size of a small lobster's. They come running out and they're looking to do nothing pleasant to you. They aim to do you hurt!

The following day, I took what remained of the sill itself into the Entomology Department at the University of Arizona. I located their resident termite wizard and asked him for his opinion. When I showed him the sill, he recoiled and said, "My God! I've never seen one that completely destroyed." Before I left, he asked me if he could keep the sill to put it in their little bug museum or display case or whatever. To my knowledge it's still there.

Shortly after the termite war, I received my job offer from the paper mill in the White Mountains. I moved out of the house and gave it back to Apache Powder Company. More than thirty years later, the house still stands. It must be a testimonial to the structural strength of termite tunnels.

The Mountain Man Cometh. When I moved to the White Mountains, I rented a small, two bedroom cabin on the Apache Indian Reservation. It sat in the middle of a gigantic stand of Ponderosa pines and was peaceful, pleasant and priced right. Its elevation was close to 7,500 feet and my Jeep came in handy when heavy winter storms hit (or when I ran out of eggs). The sole source of heat was a wood stove. When temperatures fell too low, pipes froze and I had no water. It was just me and my dog, FatBoy. Despite the minor hardships, it was a little paradise. I was living there when I met Liz. After a lengthy courtship, we decided to set up housekeeping together. My paradise and hers would be merged.

Together we rented a large, three bedroom, two and half bath house in an upscale development in Lakeside. Although there were other homes nearby, we were nestled into the forest and close enough to the Mogollon Rim that wildlife was common. One evening, it was too common.

It was late October and cold outside. We had eaten dinner and Liz had retreated with our five year old daughter, Tempest, to the couch in our large and open living room. Liz was reading a story to her about the three bears. I sat at my desk taking care of some paperwork.

There was still a hint of the aroma from the dinner lingering as I worked. Liz has always been an adventuresome and creative chef, but even the greatest chefs miss the mark from time to time. Liz had prepared shrimp creole. As I ate my meal, I tried to appear grateful and enthusiastic. I had long ago learned that if you bitch about the occasional miss, you'll soon be cooking your own meals. But I will confess, I was somewhat relieved when Liz said, "I can't eat any more of this. It's terrible." She took the contents of our plates and scraped it into the garbage. She then took it out to the garbage can by the garage.

A fire burned behind me as I worked at my desk. The desk sat in an area of the great room that wasn't far from the couch on which Liz was reading, but it faced away from the center of the room. When I looked up, I stared directly at the large double doors that were the main entrance to the house. Both doors had grids of diamond shaped windows exposing the tall pines outside or in this case, the cold, dark night that had descended upon us. As I worked, I suddenly heard a single, loud knock on the door. As I rose from my seat, I saw someone with his face against the glass. With Halloween nearly upon us, this person had gone all out and dressed up like a bear. He was about my height and his costume was so real, I waived my arm at him as if to say, "Alright, get back. You should probably be more careful lest someone not appreciate your joke and shoot you."

As I reached for the door handle, I realized this person's nose which was firmly pressed against the glass was actually fogging the window. It wasn't a costume. It was actually a bear, a real one with real claws and real teeth. As the bear dropped down, he dragged his claw across and severely scratched the door. Liz continued to read until I reached deep into my well of personal creativity and uttered the most eloquent words I could find. "Holy Shit!"

That's all I said, but I must have said it with some emphasis. Liz wheeled around, saw the bear and reacted as if there was a sniper at the door. She grabbed Tempest and both hit the deck. If the bear couldn't see them, he wouldn't eat them. Or so she thought. My immediate reaction was to run to the back of the house and grab a rifle. I had no idea if the bear was coming inside or just going door-to-door trick-or-treating.

FatBoy always knew he wasn't allowed in any of the carpeted areas of the house, but on cold evenings, he was permitted to come into the back areas where the floors were tiled. As I ran past him to get a gun, he immediately sensed that something was seriously wrong. He didn't ask permission; he instinctively came running with me across the carpet and toward the front door. He gave me his best "Don't worry; I'll handle this" look and darted out the front door to confront whatever threatened his family. It was only a matter of seconds before he was at the front door trying to get back in. His demeanor and saucer sized eyes betrayed his feelings. "Hey, I didn't sign up for this crap. There's a bear out there." He was happy, albeit a bit anxious, to return to the back end of the house. I told you he was a smart dog.

A few months later with the bear (hopefully) hibernating, we experienced some more excitement at that house. We had been out and the temperature had fallen to well below zero. When we returned home, we thought we'd build a good fire to warm the house. It was particularly cold. We were going to go to bed and not be awake to add wood to the fire as it burned low, so I stocked it with a little more wood that normal. When we retired to the bedroom, it was burning exceptionally well.

It was a little after midnight when I smelled the smoke. Something wasn't right. I walked throughout the house, but really didn't notice anything wrong. The fireplace still had a good fire going, but it was settling down for the night. The odor persisted. I went outside to see if perhaps it was coming from a neighbor's house. When I turned around and looked at our house, I saw smoke pouring from the roof vents in the attic area. We were ablaze. I called the fire department. It was a volunteer fire department, so they had to come in from their homes, but they were there is a surprisingly short time. Or maybe it just seemed like a short time because we were frantically running hither and fro trying to get things out of the house before it burned to the ground.

By the time the firefighters got into the house with their hoses and axes, there were open flames breaking loose in the attic area, but none yet in the living area. The greatest damage we experienced in the living areas of the house (other than smoke damage) occurred when a firefighter missed a step while walking through the attic. He literally fell through the ceiling and landed in the toilet. Fortunately, he wasn't seriously injured, but he had to live thereafter known as the toilet diving fireman of Lakeside.

As you can imagine, the excitement associated with having your home burn is memorable. But what we remember most involves the neighbors. As the excitement was winding down around 2:30 in the morning, one neighbor from four or five houses down walked up to me. "I know we've never met before" he said, "but I suspect you're probably unsure about what you're going to do at this point." He was right. "We'd be more than happy to have you, your wife and daughter come down to our house and stay with us until you can get your feet back on the ground."

It was a touching and heart-warming offer that to this day gives us some faith in humanity. We thanked him deeply, but chose to stay in the house with no heat and the windows wide open to let the smoke dissipate the rest of night. But wait . . . before you go running off convinced that mankind is inherently good and that evil vanishes in hard times like the smoke that rose from our house that night, let me give a shout out to our fine next door neighbor.

Dennis Meyer had been brought to the White Mountains to be the President of Contel, a regional telephone company headquartered there. We had met him briefly when he moved in a couple months before. It was a bit of an effort for him to tolerate common people like us, but he did what he had to do without tarnishing his crown. When a battery of fire engines comes roaring into your neighborhood, you'll hear sirens, bells, pumps, men shouting and myriad other noises. There will be red flashing lights, white flashing lights and spotlights bright enough to see from outer space. There will be smoke and flames. This is how the first neighbor noticed we were having some difficulty.

As I stood outside our house, freezing my ass off watching all the activity, I glanced toward Mr. Meyer's house. It was then I saw a hand reach out and lift the blind in the bedroom window. We had rudely awakened the guy and he was clearly annoyed, but he did seem to experience some relief when he realized it was only his next door neighbor's house on fire. It's not like it was anything important. The blind slowly came back down and Meyers went back to sleep. He never acknowledged that a fire had occurred, never expressed any sympathy, never said hello, never an offer of help or goodwill. So much for building faith in humankind; this clown was an asshole. Hopefully, the bear came back and ate his kids after we moved away.

The last move for twelve years. As the house underwent repairs, it was uninhabitable. We were forced to find another place. Hal and Peggy Butler were family friends and had a house on seven acres of land on a hilltop in Show Low. A long, curving drive led to this somewhat dated four bedroom, three bath house on the edge of the forest. We moved in when Tempest began first grade. We lived there when she was ready for her senior year in high school.

The Butler house was a waystation in our professional lives. It was there we worked to build our businesses and raise our daughter. The house was ample, but far from posh. Its greatest attributes were its seclusion in the forest and its spaciousness, more than adequate for two adults, a young daughter, a dog and a cat. It had some nice views and was conveniently located to our work and Tempest's school.

It was during the years our workloads were heaviest that we thought it would be beneficial to have a live-in housekeeper and cook. Through a network of friends, we found Angelina, a woman of Tarascan Indian heritage from Morelia, Mexico. She didn't speak a word of English and was completely without legal documentation to be in this country. Great! She'd fit right in. Not only would we get a housekeeper and cook, we'd have a Spanish teacher for Tempest.

Angelina lived with us for about three years. She was there when Tempest would come home from school. Dinner was prepared when we came home from the office. She had her own room and we tried to afford her all the privacy and personal time she needed, but she did join us for dinner. Things generally went very well, but the tranquil seas failed to foretell the pending storm.

Angelina missed "her people" as she called them. Life in the mountains of Arizona was different in many ways from the life she knew growing up in her Tarascan village in central Mexico. Her inability to speak English compounded the stress she felt being estranged from her home. What we failed to recognize was that Tempest became a source of jealousy. Tempest wasn't a materially spoiled child, but she did have some toys and other things Angelina had never been able to enjoy. We discovered Angelina had "taken" a couple of Tempest's dolls and hidden them in her room. Angelina's envy slowly evolved into a competition with Tempest and that competition wasn't always healthy.

It began to take on the airs of an Alfred Hitchcock movie. On one occasion, Angelina murdered every fish in a small aquarium in Tempest's room. When Tempest was at school, Angelina went into her room and turned the heater on the tank to its maximum setting. Tempest came home to discover a fish soup reeking in her room. On another occasion, Angelina used a vacuum cleaner to remove the contents of the fireplace. This wouldn't have been a problem had it not been for the fact that the fire was burning at the time. She damn near burned the house down. It seemed to be one thing after another and the events were coming with an increasing frequency.

We knew we had to cut Angelina loose one day when Liz came home from the office a couple hours earlier than normal. It was the dead of winter and temperatures hovered in the high teens. Angelina was outside the front door. She was cold and shivering. An hour earlier, she had gone outside to get some additional firewood. Tempest closed the door and locked her outside. Tempest was surprised to see Liz and said, "What are you doing here?"

Liz pointed out that she lived there. Tempest was "counseled" and Angelina came in to thaw. Conditions didn't improve. When I discovered that Angelina was preparing wonderful meals, but was "salting" them with foreign substances like metal shavings and nail clippings, it was time for her to leave.

Obviously, we had our share of exciting times in the Butler house, but for the most part, it harbors nothing but fond memories. As our business success continued to grow, Liz tried to convince me we could afford to build a nice, new home of our own. I guess I was more cautious financially; maybe more fearful is a better term. Regardless, she convinced me we should buy a lot and build the house of our dreams.

Pine Oaks - The last house we would ever live in. For some reason, it was more important to Liz than it was for me, so I told her to pick out whatever lot she wanted. There was a new development near the office. It was gated with a guard house at the entrance. It was cut from a dense stand of ponderosa pines and rose up the side of the mountain to reach the highest point in Show Low. Liz came into my office one day and said she had it narrowed down to one of two lots. She wanted me to come and pick one of them. I told her to select the one she liked best and buy it. She did. It was nearly an acre and sat on the peak of this little mountain. We owned it before I had ever seen it.

Liz paid an architect a few thousand dollars and had a set of plans drawn up for a massive post-and-beam home. We didn't like it so we started all over. She really wanted my input, but frankly, I just wanted her to be happy. If this was to be the last home we ever lived in, she had to be completely satisfied. I finally told her I'd like it to have a nice view from my office and that it be warm. She finally picked a plan that gave me all I wanted and everything she had dreamed about. Construction began at 860 Pine Oaks. It took almost a year to build, but when it was complete, it was indeed our dream house.

Our dream house – Castle Hoth – Show Low, Arizona

We had recently spent time in Ireland and fell in love with the countryside. Every home was indeed a castle even if it was only a small bungalow. For reasons I'll save for a later time, we felt compelled to name our new home. It became "Castle Hoth". It sounded rather Irish, but simply stood for "house on the hill" or Hoth.

The views from Hoth were absolutely breathtaking. To take advantage of those views, we had glass seemingly everywhere in the house. There were large picture windows throughout including in our bathroom where we could relax in the Jacuzzi tub and look out on our little pond and waterfall where a never ending parade of wildlife came to drink, fish and rest. We had eleven foot ceilings throughout the house and dark cherry hardware floors everywhere. The kitchen was fabulous. The library was reminiscent of the castles of seventeenth century Great Britain. A fire place in the great room, another in the library and another in the master bedroom added more charm than warmth. We had two completely independent heating and cooling systems. In the event one ever failed, a button opened a series of ducts overhead and the remaining system could handle the entire house. Even our driveway was heated. Whenever it snowed, we flipped a switch and the snow on the driveway was melted by the embedded heating system. The house was the shape of a boomerang and in the rear, we enjoyed a huge covered deck complete with a summer kitchen and seating for two dozen people. Throughout much of the house, we had windows at about the nine foot level. They proved to be delightful additions in that we could watch the moon and stars on cloudless nights. The house was truly our dream house. We intended on living there for the rest of our lives. We had "arrived".

With countless miles of undeveloped forest behind us, it was as if we lived in a wildlife dream world. Deer, elk, coyotes, raccoons, fox, skunks, bobcats, hawks, eagles and many other animals paid us regular visits. We became so familiar with a group of javalina, they would eat from my hand. If it was cold and I wasn't there to feed them, they would climb up on the back deck and rattle our door. The little pond seemed to beckon the animals in from all directions. By far and away, the most memorable of those encounters involved bear and mountain lions.

I can't begin to remember every time we were visited by a bear. When we first realized how common it would be, we thought it would be in our best interest to learn a little bit more about them. The Arizona Department of Fish and Game was to give a seminar on bears, their habits and behaviors. Liz and I enrolled. Our eyes widened somewhat when the uniformed instructor said, "Sightings are very rare. I have been with Game and Fish for seventeen years and I have never seen one in the wild."

We were stunned and suggested he might want to come by our house because we saw them on an average of once a week. I wondered if perhaps we should be the ones giving the seminar, but we listened politely until its end.

There was one time in the mid-spring of the first year we lived at the house that a bear definitely got our heart rates well above normal. I was working in my office. The warm mountain air felt good so I had raised my windows to allow the breeze to pass across my desk. I had three large bay windows and a view that spanned more than two hundred degrees of the panorama. The window to my left overlooked a large covered front porch. Liz had a question about something and came into my office. She stood between me and the porch side window. As she spoke and not two feet behind her, a black bear rose up on his hind legs and stood looking inward with his paws up against the screen. Once again, my great command of the English language became evident as I again uttered the phrase, "Holy Shit!"

I bolted from my chair. There was no need for Liz to ask for instructions. If she had done so, she would have been talking to herself because I was gone. So was she. I wasn't used to seeing bears stand up and face me from a distance of less than five feet especially when I sat comfortably in the safety of my own home. The bear gently dropped down without so much as scratching the screen and lumbered away. Or so we thought. We soon saw him standing in front of another window, then another. He was slowly working his way around the house looking in every single window. In a couple of cases, he inadvertently left his paw prints on the glass, but never severely damaged any of our screens. He was actually doing a complete loop of the house without skipping a single window. The fact that he wouldn't leave was frankly starting to concern us a little.

When he completed his first lap, he was back on the front porch and looking in the front door. I didn't want to harm the bear, but neither did I want him to harm me. Somehow, I had to encourage him to leave. I retrieved an old 22 caliber rifle from my closet and went to the door. He was standing there on all fours. I opened the door just wide enough for me to put my rifle clutching hand outside. I aimed just over his head and pulled the triggered. The noise was deafening. Surely, the bear would turn tail and run. He took one step back, then stood up on his hind legs and looked directly at me with an expression that seemed to say, "What the hell are you doing? That was loud and obnoxious." But I saw no sign of fear on the bear's face. Liz's face was another story altogether.

The bear that came for breakfast

The bear ended up slowly completing three revolutions of the house deliberately looking in every window as he reached it. It took hours. Finally, he seemed to be gone. It was approaching midnight. We went to bed. It was a warm and beautiful night. There were two massive doors in our bedroom leading out to the back deck. Eight foot high screen doors kept the bugs out and let the mountain air and the sounds of the forest in. We felt secure enough to open those doors before retiring for the evening. Sleep was a little uneasy that night.

As the light of dawn began to seep into our room, I heard or sensed something. I opened my eyes to see the bear up on the deck and walking directly toward the door. I flew out of bed and dashed toward the doors and slammed them. The bear took a couple of steps backward and again stood up on his hind legs. He stared at me. Even as I look at the photograph, I still believe I can see a hint of hurt feelings on his face. He dropped down and walked off in a bit of a funk, but it wasn't the last we'd see of him. Over the course of the next few weeks, he provided more entertainment than anyone can use. We finally had to trap him and have him hauled off to a forested arear nearly a hundred miles distant. He was back in a matter of two or three days.

On another occasion, I got out of bed in the middle of the night. With the picture window in the bathroom, it was always interesting to flip on the outside spotlights to see what animals happened to partying at the pond. I was stunned to see a large male mountain lion standing there. I beckoned Liz to come quickly. The lion didn't move. I grabbed the camera. I didn't want to use the flash for fear it would startle the lion. I had no idea if the light would be sufficient to get a photograph. It turned out to be marginal, but at least we could see the lion. We watched in stunned amazement for about five minutes. He finally started to wander away. We felt fortunate to have had such a close encounter with a majestic king of the mountain.

As we returned to the bedroom, we glanced out the window and saw the lion slowly step up onto the deck. He slowly walked along the wall of the house. Our cat liked to lay by a corner window near our bedroom doors and watch any activity that might occur outside. I stood buck naked by the window as the lion approached. Liz was immediately behind wearing a matching outfit. As the big cat walked directly in front of the window, our cat was so startled, she immediately put herself on the opposite side of the room. Cali moved so fast, I don't believe she passed through any points in between. The lion detected movement inside the house and became suspicious or inquisitive or whatever lions become when they decide to investigate further.

After taking one additional step, the lion stood directly in front of me and put his nose against the glass in the door. We were separated by no more than two inches. I whispered to Liz, "Hold perfectly still." I didn't want the lion to decide we were delectable appetizers. As I looked at his large, incredibly muscular legs and shoulders, it was apparent that a pane of glass wouldn't slow him down had he wanted to come inside. I honestly feared that the sound of my rapidly pounding heart would betray my presence. After a few seconds of staring directly through me, the lion turned his head and continued to slowly walk along the exterior wall. We were exhilarated, but relieved.

Mountain lion six feet head to tail

In 2002, an air-headed woman who became disoriented in the forest about twenty miles west of our house had the brilliant thought that if she lit a small fire, someone would see the smoke and come to rescue her. She had unwittingly and dimwittedly ignited what would become at that time the second largest forest fire in the nation's history. We didn't feel threatened until authorities started evacuating small communities to our west. As the plumes of smoke grew closer, we started to take matters more seriously. After about a week, the unchecked fire caused authorities to issue an order to evacuate everyone from the towns of Show Low, Lakeside and Pinetop. Thirty-five thousand people abandoned the mountain, some going to Phoenix or Tucson, others to emergency shelters in Holbrook fifty miles to the north. We stayed. I decided that I would do what I could to protect our dream home. I tried to convince Liz to leave, but she insisted that if I was going to stay, she was too. The events of the next two weeks would fill a book by themselves. Abandoned communities were turned into piles of white ash. Friends and employees lost their homes and everything in them. Incredibly, we never lost our electric power, but there were no stores open so whatever we had in the house would have to last for the duration. The only times we saw fellow human beings was a couple times each day when a National Guard Humvee drove within sight of Castle Hoth. As the fire approached Show Low, we lived in a heavy, thick cloud of smoke. It was so dense, we never saw the sun. The light from the approaching flames at night combined with the lack of sunlight made it difficult for us to know whether it was day or night. We listened to the radio where emergency alerts were nearly constant and fire status updates were broadcast.

A photograph taken on our rear deck as the fire raged toward us

One Sunday afternoon, we heard the miserable, raspy beep that preceded an emergency alert. To this day, that sound brings back the haunting days of the fire. This time the alert changed our lives. The Forest Service spokesman said the flames were on the western edge of Show Low headed directly toward our home. They would move at a rate that meant our house would burn at 4:00 p.m. Monday afternoon – not 3:30 p.m., not 4:30 p.m.; our house would be reduced to ashes at 4:00 p.m.

Liz and I sat down on the couch in our great-room. After spending nearly two weeks clearing brush and small trees from around our house, we sat with our blistered hands and looked at each other. A wound that I had incurred while removing one tree colored my forehead. We were dirty and tired, but strangely accepting and resigned to our fate. After a brief respite, we went back to work. With extension ladders and hammers and nails, we mounted three or four garden hoses high on the twenty foot exterior walls and turned them on. People would later laugh at us saying that a garden hose wouldn't stop a two hundred foot high wall of flame. We knew that, but we also knew that when you fight for your life, you fight with your heart and soul. Who could know if the hoses could have knocked down the single spark that was to be the difference? We fought on. If we were to lose the fight, it was not going to be because we quit. The fire marched on.

Phoenix papers didn't paint a rosy picture of our chances

By this time, we had pretty much run out of food. Liz scrambled and found a box of old, stale saltine crackers. In the back of the freezer in the garage, she found a small package of old, freezer-burned ground beef. That was it; we had nothing more. Her presentation was excellent. The beef had a smoky flavor. It was one of the most memorable and oddly delightful meals of my life. Before we ate, I looked over at our wine refrigerator and realized we had a couple of bottles of wine valued at about five hundred dollars each. I'd be damned if those bottles were going to boil away in a fire. With fine linens on the table and our best china, we sipped one of France's finest wines and dined on exquisite beef laden crackers. We looked around the room at some of the beautiful artwork hanging on the walls. We took in the richness of the cherry hardwood floors. We felt fortunate to have lived in a magnificent castle that in less than twenty-four hours would cease to exist.

After dinner, we moved out of the house. It wasn't a physical move; it was an exodus that occurred only in our minds. We wondered about our future. What would we do? Where would we go? In less than twenty-four hours, we had a decision that had to be made. What we didn't know was that night, near the base of our little mountain, a man named Rick Lúpe was going to violate the order he had been given by the man who commanded the fire crews for the U.S. Forest Service. Lúpe led a team of elite Apache firefighters. Because of the level of risk to the firefighters, the decision had been made to let the fire burn up the mountain side. After all, it had a four o'clock appointment with my house. Lúpe was an experienced hotshot and believed that with an impassioned defense, the line could be held. He took his team out and established that line. He saved our house. Although the fire burned for another two to three weeks, Lúpe had diverted it from its chosen path of destruction. As a sad aside, Lúpe made a similar decision in a fire a year later and died in his attempt. A statue of Rick Lúpe stands today in the heart of Lakeside, Arizona where his memory is strong and honored by people like us who kept their homes because of his heroic efforts.

We were delighted Monday evening when we still had a home and another bottle of fine French Bordeaux. However, it may come as a surprise to learn we also had a sense of disappointment, of "letdown". We had gone to such great efforts to reconcile the impending doom in our minds the night before, we had moved on in our minds. Liz's mother, grandmother and great-grandmother were born in the White Mountains. I never dreamed Liz would consider going elsewhere. For many years, I would have moved in a heartbeat, but I knew the White

Mountains were in her blood and heart. When she said she wanted to move on, I didn't ask her what she had said for fear she might change her mind.

Scottsdale, here we come. We still had our real estate company and our software company in the White Mountains so we couldn't just pack up and move. But we could buy a second home somewhere and frankly, just to get out of there, it could have been anywhere and I would have been ready to go. We first made an offer on a home in Flagstaff, Arizona. Fortunately, it wasn't accepted. In retrospect, it wouldn't have been the smartest move. Flagstaff wasn't unlike Show Low. It had the same climate, same elevation and the same big pines that had a bad habit of burning.

We ultimately stumbled on a two story townhouse in Scottsdale that made nothing but good sense to us. It could serve as a second home and a hotel room. The previous year, we had spent thousands of dollars at the Ritz-Carlton when we needed a hotel room before and after our frequent trips to the airport. The home is in Old Town Scottsdale within walking distance of museums, art galleries, performance venues, fine dining and world class shopping. We never actually "lived" in the house, but we used it for extended periods of time. We've loaned it to friends and family in times of needs and in times of pleasure. The house harbors many great memories and by virtue of the fact that we still own it, we'll no doubt create a few more there. It also served as the bridge to our next house.

Our mobile home. She was the sweetest mobile home imaginable. Her name was "Tempest". She had three bedrooms, two baths, a kitchen, living room, dining area, office and plenty of storage. She generated all of her own electricity. She had a great communications system, waste management system, heating and cooling systems. With a seven foot keel and a fifty-one foot mast, she pretty much had it all. Tempest was a forty-seven foot sailing yacht.

When we purchased sailing vessel Tempest, she was in San Diego. However, due to California tax laws, we soon moved to Ensenada, Mexico. In effect, the tax code gave us more than $25,000 to move the boat to a foreign country for a few months. I may not be the brightest bulb in the marquis, but I'm not totally burned out. I get to save twenty-five grand if I spend a few months on a yacht in a vacation paradise where we can buy lobster dinners for twelve dollars. We weren't expert sailors when we first bought the yacht, but we could do the math. ¡Bienvenido a México!

Over the next couple of years, the yacht became the home in which we spent most of our time. With high-speed internet, I ran the software company from the boat. We could be

Sailing Vessel Tempest at anchor in Pelican Bay

at sea for weeks at a time and have all the luxuries we could ask for and the traffic congestion wasn't nearly as bad. When we were in port in San Diego, we would sit out on the deck and look at the lights glowing on the ridge called Point Loma. It was almost magical. I looked at Liz and said, "I wonder what house prices are like up there."

"It can't hurt to look" she said. That leads us to our next house. And just like the Show Low dream house, it would be the last house we ever owned.

Armada Terrace in San Diego. We had just sold the real estate company. We were involved in discussions to sell the software company. We found a house that with a little remodeling could become our next dream house. It had four levels, a living room with a view to die for, four bedrooms, two and half baths, a little den with a fireplace, a hobby room, two car garage and a roof top deck. We could walk to our yacht in the marina. If we woke up one morning and decided we wanted to have dinner a hundred miles away on Catalina Island, we could walk out of the house, board the Tempest and be in Avalon by dinner time.

After dropping a half million dollars into the remodel, one bedroom became Liz's office. Another was incorporated into my office and library that was nothing short of spectacular. A small couch sat in front of a beautiful fireplace framed in travertine tile. The hardwood floors complimented the dark, European style library designed and built by a master woodworker. My desk was built such that it was wrapped by bay windows that faced a twelve foot high wall of thick, red flowers that encased the secluded front yard. The third level and part of the second glowed from the travertine tile floors. A crane put the finishing touches on the remodel by gently lifting the new hot tub over the fourth level and lowered it into its new home in the back yard amongst the giant Peruvian pepper trees that hosted the local parrot population.

But all of this paled in comparison to the new kitchen that was built for Liz. It was huge and had every imaginable tool and toy that a chef could ever want. Had she chosen to do so, Liz could have put as many as eleven prep-cooks to work at their own stations. The granite areas were massive

Liz's kitchen was spectacular

and beautiful. She had a little cooking library, a separate area for cleaning crystal ware, a wine refrigerator, a built-in coffee center, warming drawers, pot-fillers, extreme appliances and a host of other cooking accoutrements that I'm still unable to identify.

The views from the house were incredible. Sitting in the living room, the signature skyline of downtown San Diego was clearly visible with its lights twinkling on the San Diego Bay. To the south, the classic red roofs of the Hotel Del Coronado sat above the homes and naval base on Coronado Island. The lights of Tijuana, Mexico danced across the bay's waters. Slightly west of that the open ocean disappeared into the horizon beyond the Coronado Islands off the coast of Mexico.

The view from the living room was of the city and the bay

Back in Scottsdale, a new, ultra-modern, very high end condo project was under construction. As it came out of the ground, we began to realize it would end up blocking much of our previously unrestricted view of Camelback Mountain. We sold the Show Low dream house and bought a beautiful new condo in the Optima Camelview project. From our previous Scottsdale home, if we looked directly at what used to be our view of Camelback Mountain, we were now looking into the living room of our new condo. Optima's condos were floor-to-ceiling glass and even on the upper floors, they were beautifully landscaped with flowering plants and even full sized trees. The Optima home was very nicely appointed and had what we had come to expect in a residence, incredible views.

With the house in Show Low, two in Scottsdale, one in San Diego and a yacht, we had reached our house limit. When the Show Low house sold, we were down to four. Aside from the cost associated with having so many homes, there are other problems. Having a roof leak in two homes at once, neither of which is in the same state, can be an aggravation. We also found that one of nature's laws has something to do with your favorite shoes or coat or whatever; it's always at the other house. We attempted to beat nature by purchasing complete wardrobes, tool sets, music, etc., for each house. We discovered that nature's laws are inviolate. Both of your favorite coats will now be at "the other" house.

After many discussions, Liz and I finally concluded life would be simpler if we settled on one location and sold all the others. The question became, "Which location?" We did an old fashioned "Franklin close" on ourselves. That's where you list all the pros and cons of each of your choices and make your decision accordingly. The first challenge was deciding on San Diego versus Scottsdale. Both places are wonderful in so many ways; it was a tough choice. We kicked around things like culture, dining, views, cost of living, golf and a variety of other issues. It seemed that Scottsdale offered a lot that San Diego couldn't match, but there was one major unknown. Although Liz is a fifth generation Arizonan, she had never spent a summer where temperatures can approach 120°F. And I certainly hadn't. We decided we would select Scottsdale if and only if we could survive a full summer living there. In 2011, we endured the entire summer in Scottsdale. We were pleasantly surprised to discover that it wasn't nearly as tough as we had anticipated. We decided Scottsdale would become our only home. Show Low had sold, we sold our yacht and we put our San Diego house on the market. We moved into our Optima Camelview condo.

The condo was a delight in most ways. There were a couple of drawbacks, but now that it was our primary home, it was proving to be too small for our needs. It had 1,800 square feet of living area and a large, covered terrace area surrounded by garden, but we still felt cramped. Our first solution was to make an offer on one of the huge penthouse units on the top floor. We came close to buying it, but the owners didn't completely agree with our estimate as to its value. A year later, they did sell it for the same price we offered, but by then we were on to other things.

Having joined a country club, I was golfing three or four days each week. I later learned that Liz would go out casually looking at houses while I was on the course. One day after a round of golf, Liz said, "I'm moving. Would you like to come with me?"

It quickly dawned on me that I had decided to buy a house. I say all this slightly tongue-in-cheek, but that has become the accepted version of history to tell people when they ask. The truth is we talked about the prospect of buying one more "this is our final" house. We agreed that it was starting to look like that was the most reasonable option. We found a neighborhood we liked – close to the club and close to Old Town Scottsdale. We found a house we liked and made an offer. We were surprised to learn that the market was heating up so fast that our offer was only one of four that were submitted on the house that day. And ours wasn't the best. We kept looking.

Via Linda – the beautiful way. When we spotted this property, it had just been placed on the market. In fact, we later learned the owners were in the midst of an acrimonious divorce and the husband hadn't yet agreed to sell the house. Nonetheless, we toured the house and concluded it would serve our needs perfectly after a near complete remodel. We immediately made a full price, cash offer and demanded a rapid response. We didn't want to end up in a bidding war again. The wife accepted. The husband was strongly encouraged with threats of lawyers, thugs and baseball bats and finally acquiesced. On March 12th 2012 we once again owned the last house we'll ever buy. It was our third one.

No house would ever offer perfection. To us, the biggest drawback with the house was that it had a swimming pool. Liz had always agreed with me that the last thing in the world we would ever want was a house with a pool. Between maintenance costs, legal liability and general nuisance considerations, the pool would be filled in. After hiring a contractor to perform the big remodel, we anticipated four or so months of construction and confusion. I rounded up a couple of bids on pool removal, but before I placed the order, the temperature hit 105°. I jumped into the pool. I was suddenly cool. I got out of the pool and was cool. When my clothes dried and I started to warm up again, I jumped in the pool. After doing this a number of times, I tore up the bids. Liz and I are now in full agreement that a swimming pool is a rather nice feature to have when owning a house in a hot climate.

With 3,000 square feet of living area on a single level, the home is big enough for the two of us. After the remodel, we ended up with many of the same features we had in our previous two houses, an office and library for me, a nice new kitchen for Liz

Our Scottsdale home is a delight

(and me if you consider who eats the product), an office and music room for Liz. In addition to the master bedroom, there's a dedicated guest bedroom, a sitting room that serves as a second guest bedroom. If the guest list is deep enough, Liz's office can be converted into a third guest bedroom for a short time. A good sized putting green was built in the back. The yards, both front and back, are large and nicely landscaped. There's even a workshop that doubles as an exercise room. We get fresh produce from "McCarty Farms", a raised bed garden in which we have everything from tomatoes, eggplant and onions to peppers, hot peppers, hotter peppers and hottest peppers. Citrus trees provide us with a good supply of grapefruit, lemons, limes and numerous varieties of oranges. The walls are decorated with a significant and eclectic collection of pieces that comfort us and serve to remind us of the footprints we've left around the world over the past thirty plus years.

The Via Linda house is the last house we'll ever have. No, really.

Chapter Five – School Daze

Maybe I'm flattering myself in thinking that education in "my day" was superior to the education of today. On the other hand, maybe I had the good fortune of growing up where education truly was a priority. I remember wondering why I was studying things like how to diagram an English sentence. Surely, it was something I would never use. However, later on in life when I was learning foreign languages (including English), the knowledge gained in those seemingly futile exercises has proven to be more than beneficial. Are there kids today that have a clue what it even means to diagram a sentence? Let's take a look back in time to get an idea of what education was like back in the early 1950s.

Liberty School – Highland Park, Michigan. My mother walked me to my first day of kindergarten. Unsurprisingly, I don't have a lot of vivid recollections about my time at Liberty. We had milk and cookies every afternoon. I don't remember if it was just before or just after our little afternoon nap. I do remember laying on a little cot obediently keeping my eyes closed and thinking, "This seems to be silly. I could have done this at home." Otherwise, the principle function of kindergarten was to finger-paint, walk – don't run – with scissors and to learn how to interact with other five year olds without pulling their hair and stabbing them with the scissors. I guess I passed. I made it to first grade and I still don't run with scissors.

Schulze Elementary – Detroit, Michigan. I attended first through eighth grade there entering when I was six and graduating after I turned fourteen. The majority of my formative years were spent at Schulze. It sat in the heart of a predominately Jewish neighborhood that was ringed by us goyim. The student body was slightly more than ninety percent Jewish. In addition to learning Chanukah songs, dreidels and circumcision, I recall learning a great many things while at Schulze.

In the first grade, I learned that when Jane watched Dick run, he had Spot. I also learned that it wasn't nice to put a thumbtack on Paul Fisher's seat, but I never did understand why he found it necessary to cry and carry on like he did. He was another Dick. Mrs. House taught us how to print. The small letters came up to the middle line and the capital letters stretched all the way to the top line. We also dove headlong into advanced addition and subtraction, but I don't think we carried the ones just yet. I also learned that girls used a different bathroom and laughed differently than boys; more on that later.

By the time Mrs. Kerr got her bony hands around our necks in second grade, we were seasoned pros. We started learning advanced topics like writing in cursive and adding numbers whose totals were into the double digits. I believe it was second grade when we got to write with ink, not the ball-point pen kind, the real deal where you dipped the pen into the ink well and then spilled it all over your desk and clothes. We also learned the classic pigtail in the inkwell trick. Girls with pigtails learned not to sit directly in front of mischievous boys. Mrs. Kerr was nice enough, but she didn't show up every day wondering which child she was going to coddle. I don't think she was ever in the Army, but if she was, she was a sergeant.

Third grade made a lasting impression on me, but apparently not a long one. I don't even remember the teacher's name. I'm confident I remember what she taught though. I had to in order to get into the fourth grade.

My fourth grade teacher was more memorable, so memorable in fact that I still have an occasional nightmare with her in the starring role. Miss Van Otten had probably been Joseph Mengele's nurse in Nazi Germany, but showed no targeted animosity toward the Jewish kids in class. She pummeled the non-Jews with just as much vigor and sadistic delight as she did the Jews. In truth, she was probably one of the best teacher's I ever had. She was a pusher. Even though her standards were demanding and set very high, no one failed her class. The fear of having to spend another year in her class was a motivator greater than threats of electro-shock and public hanging.

There is one special story involving Miss Van Otten that warrants retelling. We always jumped into the math section of the class shortly after lunch. I hated it, not because I didn't have the aptitude – quite the contrary. I hated it because she made us work our little asses off. One day, Iris Blatt developed a headache. I frankly didn't know there was such a thing, but I discovered that Iris was sent to the principal's office who in turn called her mother to come and get her. I had a plan. The next day about the time the arithmetic book was coming out, I had a headache. I was sent to the principal's office. My mother came to get me. An hour later, the headache was gone and I was playing baseball.

The next day, I'll be damned if I didn't end up with another headache. I got one the following day as well. Obviously, there was a medical problem that had to be addressed. My mother took me to Dr. Alpern's office and waited outside the examination room while the doctor questioned me and looked for signs of disease or maybe for signs of bullshit. I remember being concerned that I was about to be busted for faking headaches, but I couldn't figure out how to get around the problem. Dr. Alpern called my mother into the room and I prepared myself for the trouble I was in.

He looked at my mother and said, "I'm afraid I can't see any specific signs of illness or disease, but I can only be certain of one thing at this point. He is definitely having the headaches."

It scared the holy hell out of me. I thought "Faking headaches must be the cause of headaches. This could be serious. I've got to stop this nonsense or I'm going to end up with . . . headaches!"

I have no idea if he knew the truth or was just playing with my head. I can say that I never had another headache and that I did my long division and calculated my square roots every day without fail from that time on. It was quite the miracle cure. He must have been a great doctor.

Fifth grade brought me into a new and exciting world. Up until fifth grade, I spent the entire school day in a cage with whichever lion tamer I had been assigned for the year. Now, the format of the school day changed where only a half day was spent with the main teacher. The other half was broken into four equal periods of about forty-five minutes each. From fifth through eighth grades I spent time in Mrs. Jacobstein's music class, Mr. Cooney's wood shop, Mrs. Rubin's art class, Mr. Gunn's gym class, Mrs. Goodman's auditorium class where we worked on speech and theater, Mr. Fleichman's civics and history classes, Mrs. Brown's library, Mr. Kazanowski's health and first aid class and Miss Conoboy's science class. There were probably a few others, but if I still can't remember my third grade teacher's name, don't expect me to remember the other classes.

I suspect every kid tried cheating at least once. I was no exception. I was in the sixth grade and we were studying world history. By the end of the school year, we had to write a report on some significant person or event in history. I had been rummaging through an old army chest in which my father had kept some of his memorabilia from the past. I stumbled upon a paper he had written in high school. It had the grade written atop of it – "A+". His teacher had written "Excellent Job" next to the grade. I read through the paper and found it was about General Pershing, the Commander of the American Expeditionary Forces in World War I. Problem solved! Why work my tail off to research and write about something when I already had a proven commodity in hand? I would just copy my father's paper.

Unfortunately, there were a couple of problems I wasn't equipped to overcome. The first was that the very last page of my father's paper had been lost. I had no idea what he had written. Not having a hint as to what it might have said (remember, I was trying to avoid work), I obviously couldn't fill in the last few paragraphs by myself. My solution to the problem was ingenious, but ineffective. I exercised extreme care in copying the report so that my handwriting matched my father's with respect to spacing. I finished the next to the last page with the words spaced exactly as found in the original document. I turned in the paper with the last page missing. When the teacher tried to grade the paper and discovered the omission, I just told her she must have lost the last page. It never dawned on me she might ask me to rewrite it.

She didn't ask me to rewrite it. She concluded that wouldn't be necessary. It seems I had left another bit of incriminating evidence that made it quite clear that something was amiss. In 1958, World War II was still fresh in the minds of everyone. They knew about World War I too. The problem was that prior to 1940, there was no such thing as "World War II". Without the existence of World War II, it would have seemed silly to call the previous war "World War I". Prior to 1940, World War I was known as "The Great War", the war to end all wars. The fact that my report never referenced the First World War, only "The Great War" clearly pointed to not only an act of plagiarism, but to one where the source document was written prior to 1940. I was busted. I learned that more often than not, it's easier just to do things right. Sometimes shortcuts take you to the wrong destination.

It was in the years between fifth and eighth grade that we thought about and then entered puberty. It's a given that those years presented some of life's most interesting encounters. It was a time when young men were trying to imitate adult males. Young girls were training their bras. We weren't sure what we were supposed to be doing, but somehow we knew we wanted to do whatever it was.

It was in gym class that I was first taught to dance. And Liz would assure you they did a damn lousy job of it. I don't think dancing is in the Jones gene pool, but Mr. Gunn had no way of knowing that. The first dance we learned was the waltz. Diagrammatically, it was pretty simple. I mean how tough can one-two-three-four, one-two-three-four be? With twenty-twenty hindsight and a Jones boy to work with, it was difficult. Nonetheless, it was time for our first test flight. A line of boys faced the line of girls. We paired up and did our best imitation of dancing. The first girl I ever danced with was in that gym class. Her name was Alta Willis. Alta later changed her name to Allee Willis and became a Grammy Award winning song writer with her songs selling more than fifty million copies. I sometimes wonder if she felt that having survived a dance with me, she could do anything involving rhythm.

My inability to dance didn't prevent me from being one of the alpha-males at Schulze Elementary. At that age, athletic ability seemed to be one of the dominating factors of "popularity" or at least it seemed to correlate well with it. There were four of us. Along with me were Don Moffat, Dave Disner and Stuart Lester. We were popular socially and the school's best athletes. We were strong academically. And we were the least "manageable".

On the first day of the school year in about seventh grade, we entered the art classroom. There were a number of tables each of which hosted eight students. There was one table in the rear of the room that accommodated only four students. Those four seats were taken by me, Moffat, Disner and Lester. When the teacher walked to the front of the room, her eyes immediately went to our table. She made an announcement to the class that was clearly directed at us.

"I see one table where there is a problem. I'm going to turn around and when I look again, if they're smart, these boys will have taken different seats." She then began writing some material on the blackboard. We got the message loud and clear and rapidly moved to comply. All four of us stood up and rotated clockwise one seat and sat back down. She turned around and knew it was going to be a long year.

As a non-Jew in a predominately Jewish school, I had the good fortune of learning a great deal about Jewish culture and heritage that I otherwise would not have learned in another school. I'm certain it had a dramatic impact upon my personality development. I sometimes say I am at least to a significant extent, "culturally Jewish". I know how to solve all of the world's problems sitting in a deli over matzo ball soup or bagels and lox. I can argue vehemently on a subject and despite outward appearances still like and respect my opponent. I can use guilt like a surgeon's tool. I treasure education. I grew up in a world that was rich in many ways. I was given a currency of the heart and mind that could never be spent – only invested.

During the holiday season, like all other schools in Detroit, ours was obligated to present a "Christmas" program. Mrs. Jacobstein worked with us hour after hour and when the day came, we were on stage singing enthusiastically. Mrs. Jacobstein sat at the piano just below the stage and played as we sang Christmas favorites like "Silent Night", "Oh Little Town of Bethlehem", "Jingle Bells", "Oh Hanukkah" and my personal favorite, "Oh Dreidel, Dreidel, Dreidel – I made it out of clay." We spent a fair amount of time throughout the year playing "dreidel". It's a little top you spin. Depending upon which of the four sides finished on top, you won or lost money, candy or whatever we were gambling at the time.

On the Jewish high holidays like Rosh Hashanah and Yom Kippur, none of the Jews came to school. That left two or three students per class. There was nothing the teacher (usually a substitute for the Jewish teacher who also took the day off) could do. So classes were combined and we usually spent the day on the playground with ball and bat in hand. Although I soon learned about all of the Jewish holidays, their history and significance, to the typical non-Jew at Schulze, "Rosh Hashanah" was a Hebrew term meaning "Play Ball".

The Jewish demographic at Schulze was a great asset for me as a student, but once a month, it made my mother feel a little self-conscious. She attended the PTA meetings in the school auditorium and they called the roll of its members. As they worked their way towards my mother's name, it sounded as you might expect. "Goldman, Goldstein, Gornbein, Greenberg, Grossman" and into the "H" names, "Heinman, Hersch, Horowitz, Isaacson, Jacobson, Jesselman" and finally "Jones"!

The room invariably went silent for a few seconds as heads turned to stare at the goy in their midst. My mother would smile and the roll would resume. "Kahn, Kaplin, Kleinman, Lederman, Lipman . . ." and onward.

Much of my education in the Schulze years came while I was in transit to or from school. Don Moffat and I without question had the strongest throwing arms in the school. We were inclined to use them from time-to-time, not always with the best results. On one occasion, Don and I were walking home from school. We would challenge each other. "I'll bet I can hit that telephone pole," I'd say to Don. The pole was a couple hundred feet distant. I grabbed a nice throwing rock and let it fly. Sometimes, I hit it; sometimes I didn't. One particular afternoon, Don said, "I'll bet I can hit that car." It was just over a city block away. We were standing on the corner of Birwood and Santa Maria. The car was parked just west of the corner of Mendoza and Santa Maria. I recently used Google Earth to measure the throw; it was 340 feet. Don grabbed a fine throwing stone and proceeded to put it in the front seat of the car. Unfortunately, the windshield was between Don and the seat, but fortunately Don and I were also two of the fastest runners in the school. And we already had a one block head start. To my knowledge, this is the first official confession of this crime. Don passed away a couple years ago and is not here to defend himself. You'll have to be the judge as to whether or not Don threw the stone or if his pal did the deed. I'm sure it was Don.

We didn't fare as well one other time. Again we were on our way home from school, but this time during a heavy winter storm. When it came to making snowballs, no one was better than Don and me. We walked in an alley that ran parallel to Six Mile Road in Detroit. It was behind a row of businesses between Griggs and Ilene where Don lived. For some inexplicable reason, we concluded it would be entertaining to make snowballs with a good throwing rock in the center. We then lofted them skyward with such strength, they would arch over the buildings and come raining down almost vertically onto Six Mile Road. We couldn't see over the buildings so we couldn't see what, if anything, was hit. Somehow, we were exhilarated simply by the randomness of the act. We never thought about the damage we could be doing; we were just having fun being mischievous. The only thing of which we were certain was that we couldn't be caught. If someone's car was hit, he would have absolutely no idea from where the snowball had come. And who would have guessed that the car we hit and shattered its windshield would have been driven by someone with the ability to think like a mischievous twelve year old? Apparently, the man pulled off to the side of the road. He saw no kids throwing snowballs, but he could clearly see them being launched from behind Berman's Dry Cleaners. He drove around the block and headed for the alley. We didn't see him until he almost had us in his grasp. He took us home and introduced himself to our parents. It wasn't a good night for Don or Howard.

We weren't the best little criminals in the world. I'm going to guess I was eleven. It was around Halloween. We had equipped ourselves with the weapons that all naughty eleven year olds carried at that time of year – a bar of soap. Don and I set off on our walk home from school. We liked to mix up the routes for variation. This time, we'd walked south on Pinehurst to Grove Street, then turned east and walked the three blocks to Griggs where I lived. At the corner of Grove and Mendoza there was a garage that had two rows of small, rectangular glass windows. We could have a field day by rapidly scribbling on each in succession. We could soap two dozen windows in less than a minute and triumphantly run on our merry ways. I started with the first. Bam! Done! The second like lightening. A third; I was flying now. I had probably soaped ten windows when as I put the soap to the eleventh, staring right at me through the window was the face of the owner. Don turned in his best sprint time of the season as he streaked down Grove. I was transfixed like a deer in headlights. I froze with my hand holding the soap which still rested on the glass. The man came from behind the door. He had a bucket in his hand. It was full of water. He taught me how to wash windows. It wasn't all that hard. There was plenty of soap. But it sure was embarrassing.

I was a student at Schulze when I first kissed a girl. Edna Diedrich was a redhead who had grown hooters. She invited me to her house one Saturday so we could listen to Elvis Pressley, dance and play a new game called "Spin-the-Bottle". I'm not sure I'd call Edna my first girlfriend. At that age, she was more of a curiosity.

Schulze teachers and my fellow students went a long way to making me who I am today. For that I am eternally grateful. But after eight years, I graduated and it was time to move on to high school. The puberty train was pulling out of the station and I was onboard for the next stop.

Northville High, Northville High – V-I-C-T-O-R-Y. My four years of high school were spent in Northville, Michigan. Well, actually that's not completely true. By the end of my sixth grade year, I had been identified as having an unusually high aptitude for mathematics. Maybe it was only a manifestation of a subconscious fear of Miss Van Otten. Better to excel in math without headaches than face Van Otten's math wrath. Regardless of the source, I was enrolled as a twelve year old at Mumford High School in Detroit to take algebra during the summer of 1959. I remember it was tough on me, but I passed the course and now had a big edge over the other students in my seventh grade year.

I never actually attended my second high school. Again I had been singled out as a "special" student and invited to attend Cass Technical Institute in Detroit. Cass Tech was not for your run-of-the-mill student. It was intended to help those with special "gifts" to realize their full potential. Lily Tomlin had just graduated from Cass Tech. Toward the end of my eighth grade year, I enrolled at Cass Tech and actually went through the orientation classes where I was to spend my next four years in downtown Detroit.

My third high school was my first and only high school. (I guess you have to be "gifted" to figure that one out.) In the summer of 1961, my family moved to Northville about twenty miles west of

Detroit. New house, new community, new school and I knew no one.

Northville had about four thousand residents. Northville High School had about 725 students. I was one of about 200 in the freshman class. Before school started, the football team began its workouts. I signed up and quickly made the team. I began meeting other students and soon began making friends. The coaches at our mid-sized school were tickled to see they had a new player with big city skills. I was immediately placed in a starting position on the junior varsity team. It was all great except … when permanent lockers were assigned to those who had made the team, Coach Longridge went from locker to locker putting a piece of white adhesive tape with the player's name on the locker. On mine he wrote "Howie Jones". Suddenly, all the other players and coaches knew me as "Howie". I didn't like it, but didn't complain. After all, I'd have four years to get used to it.

When classes finally began, I was again in the advanced placement classes as a result of my test taking skills. With an average amount of effort, I was supposed to be an exceptionally high achiever. I also discovered that I could be an average achiever with no effort. Actually, I was delighted to learn I could perform at a level quite a bit above average with next to no effort. Think of all the extra time that left me for more enjoyable pursuits like Janice Butler and Kris Deibert.

After a few weeks of school, I was getting along well. I had moved up to the varsity football team, a rarity for a freshman. I had been voted onto the "Student Council" by my fellow students. The school was going to hold an "Open House" for the parents so they could get a glimpse of the day-to-day lives of their teenagers. In Miss Dorian's English class, we were told to write our name on an index card and leave it on the corner of our desk. In that way, the parents would sit in the same seat as their high school student. When my mother arrived that evening, she had no trouble finding my desk and taking a seat. (Pretty sharp herself, eh?) When everyone was seated, Miss Dorian closed the door, went to the front of the room and began addressing the parents.

"Welcome" she said. "I'm Pat Dorian and I'm the teacher for freshman English for the gifted students. Now just because these kids have been identified as having special abilities, I take nothing for granted other than the fact that they can spell their names."

At that moment, my mother glanced downward at the card I left on the corner of my desk. It said "Howard Jons"! I had misspelled my name. It seems Miss Dorian had given her brilliant students a little too much credit. My mother never let me forget that. It was a source of humor until her dying days. It also served as a subterfuge for her to tell whoever would listen that her son was in the "gifted" class. She was always proud of that even if I couldn't spell Jons or Jones or Jonez or whatever the hell it was.

For the next four years, I had a great time. I was popular. I was a multi-year starter on the football and baseball teams. I was even on the wrestling team one year; that was a stupid idea. I regularly dated two or three of the cheerleaders. I got respectable grades. They were outstanding when you consider the fact that I put forth almost no effort. One area in which I apparently excelled was speech and theater. I say apparently because I truly don't remember doing that much in it. I recall winning a "humorous reading" competition in my freshman or sophomore year. I did well in oratory where I had to take the stage and give a compelling talk. I must have been involved in a few other related activities or events because at the end of my junior year, I was inducted into the International Thespian Society. Believe it or not, I hadn't even heard of this organization. It is the equivalent of the National Honor Society for theater. Invites are supposedly only offered to those who have performed admirably in the field. After the induction ceremony, I went home and told my mother about the honor. She too had never heard of the Thespians. The following day, she went to her office at Consumer's Power Company and proudly told everyone she could find that her son was a lesbian. Obviously she didn't know what that was either. She picked up a few stares, but her pride was undiminished.

My classes followed the prescribed "college prep" curriculum. The sciences included biology, chemistry and physics. I took Latin and French, four years of English and four years of math. By my senior year, the school had identified me and a couple other students with high math aptitudes and concluded the conventional teaching methods were holding us back. A special class was created and labeled "Advanced Math". Although we were expected to spend the scheduled time in the regular math class for seniors, we were actually separated in the rear corner of the room. We were given the book at the beginning of the year and told we were expected to complete it on our own by the end of the semester. We were to alert the teacher whenever we were ready to take the test at the end of each chapter. If we passed the test, we went on to the next chapter. I finished the book half way through the semester and spent the second half trying to fly below the teacher's radar. My attendance record was not exemplary.

Speaking of attendance, I was smart enough to know that learning things the easy way tended to be better than learning things the hard way. I was more than willing to listen to the advice of anyone who had already been down the road I was facing. At the end of my junior year, I was at a party with Terry Winter who had just graduated. "If you knew then what you know now, what would you have done differently?" I asked my friend.

He didn't hesitate. "I would have skipped class more often" he responded.

I trusted his judgment and took it to heart. I skipped more classes in my senior year than I had missed in my previous three years combined. One morning, I was sleeping in at the house. My parents had already left for work when the phone rang in my room. I was still half asleep when I put the receiver to my ear and issued a groggy greeting. No one spoke. I could clearly hear the sounds of the school "office" in the background, yet the caller said nothing. Finally the caller hung up. It pissed me off. I concluded it had to be Mr. Quay, the assistant principal calling; he normally had that task. I assumed he had hoped to talk with a parent and when I answered the phone, he was at a loss as to how he should report me to myself. I immediately dialed the school office and told him I didn't appreciate being awakened and not to do that again. I may not have been the smartest tie on the rack, but I had balls.

One event in high school undoubtedly changed my life's path more than any other. By my junior year, I had become a pretty accomplished baseball player. The pro scouts were hovering, collecting data on my performances and I was looking forward to an opportunity to play professionally after successful junior and senior years on the diamond. In the winter of my junior year, I was in a gym class playing volleyball. A fellow student kept infringing upon my area of the court (which I defined as most of it). After he ignored my warning, I did what any red blooded boy would do. I hammered him and did it with authority. Unfortunately, he was about nine inches taller than I was and as I wheeled around do decapitate him, my fist landed solidly on his upper chest area. I succeeded in keeping him out of my court area. In fact, I think he ended up at the clinic. But my wrist hurt. By the time I got home that evening, there was some swelling and plenty of additional pain. I told my father about it and I got the standard Jones response, "It's probably nothing. You'll get over it."

I didn't get over it and although the continuous pain eased somewhat, it didn't quit hurting. After about two weeks, my father came into my room after I'd fallen asleep. He took my hand and moved it. I woke up with a scream. Maybe there was something wrong. We'd give it another couple weeks to heal. The pain gradually diminished, but I didn't have full movement. We finally made an appointment with a doctor. Nearly six weeks after the injury, x-rays revealed a break of the "carpal navicular" or scaphoid bone in the wrist. Because of the delay in treatment, it would have to be set in a cast for a lengthy period of time if there was to be any hope of the bone mending. I was only a week away from the beginning of baseball's spring training. If I had the bone set, I'd miss my junior year of ball and might lose my chance to play professionally or so I thought. With twenty-twenty hindsight, I can safely say I made an imbecilic decision to play my junior year with a broken wrist and deal with it medically after the season.

My greatest asset on the ball field was my throwing arm. When I was fifteen, I finished third in the Michigan Junior Olympics for throwing a ball. I was surprised to learn that even with a broken wrist, I didn't seem to lose any velocity on my throws. I was in the ninety-plus mile per hour range when I cut loose. The problem became one for the people sitting in the stands. My throwing accuracy went to hell. I still remember one throw from third base to first base that had some extra zing on it. Maybe I shouldn't say "to first base" although that was the original target. I watched with fear and amazement as the ball sailed into about the tenth row of the stands narrowly missing a woman's head. Needless to say, the pro scouts now had a little comment by my name on their scouting sheets, "Extremely strong arm, but unfortunately, he's prone to random ball launches into many directions." I'd pretty well taken care of my pro aspirations with my own stupidity. After the season, the arm was placed in a plaster cast for four months. The bone ends had died and refused to heal. To this day, I can only bend my right wrist slightly past parallel. Oh well.

My foolishness with the wrist killed my baseball hopes even with college recruiters. However, I did get a scholarship offer from Dennison University in Ohio for of all things, football. If I ended the story right there, you might conclude I was a superstar on the gridiron too. The truth was I was a four year starter on defense, but only because I could be vicious when attacking anyone carrying a football. I was also the team's punter. I did a pretty good job kicking the ball and maintained a punting average of about forty yards. That's more than respectable for a high school punter. I suspect I still hold my high school's record for the longest punt; never mind that I kicked the ball with a thirty-five mile per hour wind to my back and that it bounced until it lost all its air. Meanwhile, back at Dennison. Dave Kerr was a talented center on our football team with extremely high grades. He was recruited not only by Dennison, but Dartmouth and a number of other "heady" schools with football teams. When they realized his best friend was a proficient punter, they thought that if they offered scholarships to both Dave and me, they might land Dave and they could tolerate me. So in truth, my football scholarship was flattering, but had it not been for Dave, I seriously doubt I would have been of much interest to them.

I was a "good boy" in high school. I chased the girls like a man on a mission, but I neither smoked nor drank beer with the boys. Well, at least until half way through my senior year. The night after the final football game, some of my teammates were going to pitch a big tent somewhere in the woods of Northville and have a party. I was asked to join my teammates and didn't hesitate. There was plenty of that nasty tasting stuff called Pabst Blue Ribbon beer. Not that Pabst was particularly nasty; to someone that wasn't a beer drinker, it was all nasty tasting. I learned a number of things that night. I learned that a 240 pound tackle on a football team could climb a tree and imitate an airport beacon by lighting farts with a match. No, it wasn't Jerry Burns, the guy that farted in Miss Dorian's English class; it was the other tackle on the team. I learned that nature has a way of saying, "Don't drink any more beer." It involves regurgitation and a most unpleasant physical sensation. The following day, I learned what it was like to have a hangover. I'd rather regurgitate - which I did.

I managed to survive the rest of my senior year and graduate with grades good enough to get me into college. I applied to the University of Miami. It seemed like a dream place to live where I had dreams of the girls coming to class in bikinis. I applied to LSU in Baton Rouge, Louisiana. Looking back on it, I don't have the slightest clue what appealed to me about LSU. I also applied to Western Michigan University in Kalamazoo. It had recently been rated as the nation's Number Two Party School behind Arizona State by Playboy Magazine. When it came time to make a decision, I selected Western Michigan over Miami and

LSU. A number of factors came into play. One of the more convincing was when my father discovered that out-of-state tuition at Miami and LSU was many times the in-state tuition at Western, he said I could go to any school I wanted as long as it was Western Michigan.

Bronco Burgers rule. So in the first week in September of 1965, I jumped into my 63 Ford Galaxie 500 convertible and drove off to Kalamazoo. I became a resident of Bigelow Hall and a college student. It may be a bit of a semantic issue, but I was only a "college student" because that's what they called someone who lived in a dorm and occasionally attended classes at the university. My principal goals were girls, beer and parties. Class attendance was merely a necessary evil for the attainment of these goals. After all, I got pretty respectable grades in high school with close to no effort. Why should college be any different?

As a freshman with little sense of direction, but a firm erection, I enrolled in Sociology 101 and German. A course called "freshman reading" was mandatory; it was part of the basic English curriculum. I'm sure there was one other course in which I enrolled, some science type course if I recall. But apparently, it didn't make a big impression on me because I don't remember it. I also signed up for R.O.T.C. because I could waive the phys-ed requirement. I got a free uniform and they taught me some really cool things like how to shine shoes and polish brass. They also tried to teach me how to take orders, but that didn't work out as well as any of us hoped.

Nonetheless, in the first week or so of school, I went to the campus swimming pool just for the fun of it. I spent some time diving while I was there. As I was leaving the pool area, I was approached by someone who identified himself as the assistant swimming coach at the university. He said he had watched me on the board and wanted to offer me an athletic scholarship if I would join the swimming team. He said it would be a relatively small scholarship, but would help pay for books and expenses. I read the offer as books and beer. I took him up on it and earned an intercollegiate letter on what turned out to be one of the nation's finest swimming teams. Now I had something else to occupy my time when there was nothing else to do but study. A wonderful side benefit of being on the swimming team was that it counted as satisfying the phys-ed requirement. I quit R.O.T.C. at the end of my first semester. Colonel Marsh said I was toast and that I'd be drafted and wake up in Vietnam before my brass had tarnished.

When grades came out at the end of my first semester, I had a rather rude awakening. I logged a less than outstanding grade-point average of one-point-eight on a four point scale. This was my first award at Western Michigan University. I made the dean's list. Well, not "The Dean's List"; that was a different thing altogether. This list came with a letter which said I had earned the honor of being placed on "academic probation". It was their way of saying "Get the grades up or get your ass out." I discovered that the no-effort approach worked in high school, but it wasn't going to cut the mustard in college.

In my second semester I again majored in girls, beer, swimming, but this time, I busted my ass studying. OK, maybe I'm stretching a bit. At that time, I thought busting my ass meant I'd actually crack a book from time-to-time. My intense efforts paid off. By the end of the school year, I had raised my G.P.A. all the way up to a two-point-one. I was off academic probation and in my mind, I had learned almost everything that could be taught at the university level. But I did return for my sophomore year.

I still had my swimming scholarship and tried not to let my studies interfere too much with my frequent travel to swimming meets all over the mid-west. I remember being enrolled in a second year sociology course on criminology. I was also in an English literature class where the professor thought I was supposed to be interested in the religious subtleties described in books written long before I could ever care about by authors I didn't know and didn't want to know in places I'd never been and never intended on going. Two months into my second year at Western Michigan University, I created an opening for a student who would appreciate having my place. I dropped out.

Forgive me professor for I have sinned. Four years passed while I pretended to be an adult. I worked, played, traveled and made a baby. I also had what amounted to a little epiphany. As I matured, the importance of education became apparent. Despite numerous obstacles, I decided I was going back to college, only this time I was going to take it seriously. This time, I didn't have the generous financial support of my parents. The athletic scholarship wasn't there. I had a wife and daughter that had to be cared for, but I was bound and determined to succeed.

I knew it would take some effort to blow out the dust that had settled between my ears over the previous four years. I enrolled at Oakland Community College in Farmington Hills, Michigan. I had a full time job and I took a full load of course work at night. For the first time in my life, I applied myself academically. I enrolled in chemistry, history, math and music courses. I finally found out what I could do with serious effort. At the end of the year, I graduated as the number one student in a class of seven thousand.

It paid off. My high grades got me academic scholarships to the University of Michigan and to Michigan State University. Both schools were outstanding institutions and the decision wasn't easy. Michigan State's offer was better financially and included enrollment in the prestigious "Honors College". In the fall of 1972, I became a Spartan. I'm still a Spartan.

Initially, I selected a major of biochemistry and plant physiology. Why plant physiology? Remember this was the early seventies and most college students had a personal relationship with an agricultural product euphemistically referred to as "pot". I was intrigued by the plant from a scientific standpoint (seriously) and thought that if I couldn't earn a legitimate living with that knowledge, what the hell? I could still grow radishes.

As an Honors College student, I could waive any and every "required" course if I saw fit. I tossed aside all required courses in English, philosophy, history and anything else that didn't have a direct impact on the Kreb's Cycle or photosynthesis. I dove headlong into the toughest science courses they offered. My first inorganic chemistry class was taught by a world renowned professor with a take-no-prisoners approach to teaching. I wasted little time in jumping into the high level calculus classes - physics, thermodynamics, statistical mechanics and more courses of the same ilk. They were brutal, but I was more than up for the task.

At the end of my first year at Michigan State, there was a little social function in my university housing complex. Neighbors grabbed a glass of wine or whatever was their pleasure and mingled. I met Bob Brace. He was a Ph.D. student who lived two doors down from me in Cherry Lane. After some perfunctory dialogue, Bob asked me what I was studying. "Biochemistry and plant physiology" I told him.

"Oh really? What are you going to do when you graduate?" he asked. I really hadn't given it much thought.

"I don't know" I replied.

"You should consider changing your major into Chemical Engineering" said Bob. "I think you'd like it and there are things you can get as a ChemE that you can't get in your field, like a job."

I thought it over that evening, did a little research and concluded that with my logical mindset, it would suit me much better than the world of tumbling carbohydrates. I changed my major the next day and for the first time in my life, I actually had a real sense of direction.

Michigan State's grading system was based upon the common four-point system, but half grades were common place. By the time I entered my third quarter, I had received nothing less than a perfect four-point-zero in each and every class I'd taken. In a particularly grueling class on biochemistry and plant physiology, I was awarded a grade of three-point-five, a half point below perfect. I remember being devastated, but I vowed to work even harder. I attended none of the sporting events on campus. I remember hearing the roar of the crowd from Spartan Stadium on Saturday afternoons while I sequestered myself in my little apartment and studied. Physics formulas were taped to the inside of my bathroom door so that anytime I was seated, there would be no time wasted thinking about anything but my studies.

When I graduated from MSU in 1975, I was ranked third in my class. I would have finished higher but I suffered a major knee injury in my last year there and some of my classwork suffered while I was hospitalized. And don't forget that miserable bastard that gave me the less than perfect grade in the biochemistry class. I was invited into Phi Beta Kappa, Tau Beta Pi and Phi Kappa Phi, all honorary societies for only the highest academic achievers. My diploma from Michigan State is inscribed with "High Honors". This all may sound like I'm doing nothing other than tooting my own horn. Although there may be an element of that going on, I have another motive. Read on.

Many people jump to the conclusion that when someone has academic credentials as high as mine, that person must be incredibly intelligent. I wish I could say – with a straight face – that they're right. But the reality is it doesn't mean the person is brilliant. I'm probably not the dumbest person on the planet (although you couldn't prove it with some of the exploits I've discussed in this book), but I assure you, there are countless others that are far brighter than I will ever be or have ever been. My exceptionally high grades say nothing more than "I worked my ass off." I would read, re-read and read again my books. I would do twice as much work outside the classroom as was expected. This stuff didn't come easy; I fought hard for it. An ounce of hard work is worth far more than a pound of brilliance any day of the week. Consider an example or two.

At the end of the second week of my calculus class, I was extremely close to dropping out of college. The first chapter of the book (Calculus and Analytic Geometry by George B. Thomas) was just a rehash of some pretty basic concepts.

However, the second chapter dealt with "Limits". For those of you unfamiliar with the mathematical concept of a "limit", consider the phrase "at any point in time". For example, if you dropped a ball from three feet above the ground, the velocity of the ball when it hits the ground is its instantaneous velocity at the time. It's the change in position as the increment of time approaches a "limit" of zero time, i.e., at an instant. The concept of "limits" is essential to understanding calculus; that's why it's covered in chapter two.

Nonetheless, I somehow had it in my head that this was supposed to be a complex and challenging class so I subconsciously made the whole discussion of limits far, far more complex than it really was. I was getting increasingly frustrated because I wasn't even beginning to grasp what I thought they were trying to tell me. I made an appointment with one of the graduate assistants in the math department in the hope that he or she could pound it through my thick skull. I was truly getting frustrated. If I couldn't handle the stuff in chapter two, I'd be suicidal by the time I got to chapter five or six. With twenty chapters in the book, I was planning my own funeral.

"I'm not getting this" I said and then I begged for help. The T.A. would ask me some simple question and I would give him a simple answer. "But what do I do now?"

"Nothing. Go on to the next question." He seemed confused now. After about fifteen minutes where I felt like crying, it finally sunk in. There was nothing more. The obvious WAS the answer. I was looking for something that wasn't there. I was overcomplicating a simple concept. I felt embarrassed, but relieved. When it finally dawned on me that I was the problem, life got a whole lot better. Obviously, I stayed in school. In the subsequent years and taking probably another hundred credits of heavy math or math related classes, I never received less than a perfect grade. It wasn't because I was particularly bright. It was because I didn't quit even when I thought I was beat. My first lesson of Calculus 201 was "Persist".

I can remember at least two other classes that were supposedly easy compared to the bulk of my work. Introductory computer programming where I learned to code in the computer language called Fortran and "Quantitative Analysis", a chemistry laboratory class are the two that come to mind. Both of these courses brutalized me and made me question the wisdom of even pursuing a degree.

The introductory computer programming course necessitated a minor restructuring of my thought process. A Fortran programmer has to learn to think "procedurally". Every line of code had to have a purpose and had to fall in a logical sequence that gave the desired result. It wasn't hard; it was different. We had to write out programs and then have Fortran cards "punched" before submitting them to the operator of the big mainframe computer. If one card was out of order or mispunched, the job was trash. Heaven help the poor guy that accidentally dropped his deck of 500 punch cards. It was easier just to start from scratch rather than try and sort them into the correct order. Turnaround time on the mainframe might be two or three hours so there was a high premium on getting it right the first time, something I don't remember anyone ever doing. Looking back on that class, especially after spending forty years working with computer programs, the work we were doing was pathetically basic (no pun intended) and trivial. When first immersed into a new way of thinking, someone can find a seemingly unclimbable wall of frustration. But when someone finally gets to the top, he is humbled. My first lesson of programming was "Persist".

Quantitative Analysis wasn't unlike taking a semester long cooking class, but instead of sugar and flour turning into chocolate chip cookies, you've got poisons and flammable liquids that turn into explosions. There was an element of charm associated with wearing the white "mad scientist" lab coat and staring into an Erlenmeyer flask bubbling on the bench, but for me, the reality wasn't nearly as enchanting as the picture. It also tends to lose a lot of its charm when after trying to "improve" on a long accepted procedure, a gaggle of grad students come running to your work area with fire extinguishers blanketing your bench while they try to get the raging flames under control. I'm sure to some people, this would be more fun than home economics in high school, but I wasn't one of them. Washing dishes isn't my idea of a picnic. But I persisted.

In the two previous examples, there were examples of simple classes that were extremely difficult for me. That wasn't always the case. In my senior year, I was scheduled to take two classes that had to have been MSU's answer to water-boarding. Advanced organic chemistry and quantum mechanics gave me everything I could handle and more.

Quantum mechanics is the branch of physics that deals with the stuff of Albert Einstein, Steven Hawking, Erwin Schrödinger, Niels Bohr and a number of other scientists who's I.Q.s defy measurement. The mathematics in quant is so advanced and complex that I spent an entire year studying one equation. I still recall walking into my first day of class and seeing a tall, bearded, distinguished looking professor who addressed the class. His talk quickly devolved into a realm that I would have previously classified as pure science fiction, but this guy was looking serious. He started talking about time reversal as if it was a real thing. The longer he talked the more I waited for the punchline. It slowly started to hit me that this guy wasn't joking. Oh man! If time reversal was really possible, maybe I could figure out how to back out to the registration desk and not sign up for this class. For my final year at Michigan State, I sat in this lecture hall three days per week. It was the intellectual equivalent of being the ball in a four dimensional pinball machine. Students would leave his lecture literally sweating and with fear in their eyes. Trying to grasp some of the concepts was like playing chess with a grand master in a dark room. Understanding the lectures was a challenge that was like working all the way around and behind the magic orb and meeting the world of metaphysics. I was getting cranial hernias just thinking about this stuff and Einstein thought a lot of it up in his spare time. Holy crap! If you survived this course, you shouldn't get a grade. You should get a Purple Heart.

With that said, I'm proud to say I received perfect four-point-ohs in quantum mechanics. But again, it wasn't mental horsepower that got me through. It was unreasonable stubbornness. I worked as hard or harder in that class than any I've ever taken. The lessons I learned from quant were (1) up isn't necessary up, (2) three grams weigh more than three grams unless they weigh less and (3) there are an infinite number of questions, but only one answer. But above all else, I learned to "Persist".

I need to mention one other academic experience at MSU that proves my bus doesn't hold any more passengers than other people's buses. It's just that everybody's bus runs a different route. As I have unhumbly stated, I earned pretty high grades when at MSU. I fully expected to ace every course in which I enrolled. There was a series of advanced classes in organic chemistry that were taken only by chemistry or chemical engineering majors. They were requirements for graduation in my field. I took them in my junior year. The first of the sequence I aced. The second was also aced. The third class was taught by a professor I'd never had. On the first day of class he announced that he would not be following the material in the text book. We would be expected to read the book, but that all examinations would be based upon his lectures. I knew right then and there that I was about to have a problem. My approach to learning was to read the book before ever listening to the lecture. The lecture then served to clarify any questions or areas of confusion I might have on the material. Finally, I would fully read the material in the textbook again after already having a solid understanding. The second reading locked my knowledge and understanding in place. I never took notes in a lecture class. Aside from the fact that my broken wrist prevented (and still prevents) me from writing legibly, I also found that taking notes and listening simultaneously prevented me from fully grasping everything the lecturer had to say. This guy's exams were going to be based upon my notes? Trouble in River City!

I was rock solid in every subject where the material was logical. I never memorized calculus. When it came time for an exam, I deduced the answers. Organic chemistry has elements of logic, but they're generally pretty well hidden. To succeed, memorization was required. More trouble brewing! At the end of the class, I struggled and labored over the final exam unlike any I've ever taken. I anxiously awaited publication of the grades. With a cumulative G.P.A. of 3.96 out of four, I nearly fell over when I looked and saw my final grade in the class – a nice, round zero-point-zero! I had flunked the class. To me a failing grade would have been a "B" or 3.0, but I had achieved the honor of flunking, crash, zilch, zero, nada, a dirt bag failure. Aside from my pride and self-esteem taking a direct hit, I also had to face the fact that it was required for graduation. The course was offered only once a year so I would get to repeat the class in the last quarter of my senior year with my diploma hanging in the balance.

The following year, the same professor made the same announcement I'd heard the previous year. I scrambled, studied and scrambled some more. I even took notes, although I couldn't read them. The final exam rolled around and again I suffered for two hours as I dug deep to retrieve facts from a memory box that was half empty. I waited for grades again, this time with a greater sense of dread than ever before. When grades were posted on the wall in the chemistry building, I saw that I had managed to escape with a fine 2.0, the equivalent of a "C" grade. It replaced the failing grade on my transcript. It was the only "C" I'd received in all my years at Michigan State. I'm not proud of it, but it certainly proved I was human when it comes to learning.

When all was said and done in 1975, my grades and experiences at MSU were good enough to get me a lengthy list of job offers. I packed the car and headed toward San Francisco and Chevron Research. With the exception of a number of educational seminars and a couple of classes at Cal-Berkley, I was finished with the classroom until 1979.

Dr. Jones I presume. After doing some fairly creative work and research in the field of crystallization at Union Oil, I was recruited to study for my Ph.D. at the University of Arizona in Tucson. The world's foremost expert in the field of crystallization, Dr. Alan Randolph, was looking for a Ph.D. student to head up a research project funded by the National Science Foundation. I was to be that guy. Fresh from the corporate world, I became Howard Jones, Ph.D. candidate. I handled the classwork pretty much as I did at Michigan State, i.e., with an expectation of high grades. I didn't let myself down. I did my research work reliably and well. After about a year, I'd had enough of the classroom and the research lab. I left the University of Arizona. Since that time, I've taken countless classes and seminars to enhance my computer skills and my skills as a photographer. But my life as a full time student came to a quiet close in Tucson, Arizona in 1980.

Chapter Six – Travels to the Under Side of the World

Some say we're born with either the "adventure gene" or the "nesting gene". Societies survive generation after generation in part because some are programmed to "stay at home". They become the core of a society, its anchors. They build its institutions, plant its farms, raise its families and preserve its traditions. Others are born with the "adventure" gene and are destined to explore the frontiers, to push the boundaries, to discover new worlds and defend its limits. Where would Western civilization be without Sir Francis Drake, Columbus, Cabrillo or its Lewis's and Clarks? Anyone that has ever spent time observing a new litter of pups has seen that at birth. Even before their eyes are opened, some of the pups are rambunctious and aggressive while others are docile and quiet. Our roles in life are to some extent programmed long before we're able to stand on our own two feet.

Looking back over the past seven decades, it would be hard to argue that I got anything but the "adventure" gene. I'm delighted that I did. I've seen much of the world. I've had so many interesting and varied experiences, I could write a book. It's been an exciting and wild ride and I wouldn't trade any of it for a more sedate life style. It has been a joyous life and with continued luck, I'm not done yet.

I held travel and exposure to other cultures and worlds in such high esteem, I made sure I exposed my daughters to travel and world experiences few of their friends ever had. I wonder if they were too young to fully appreciate them, but I wasn't going to use that as an excuse to deny them those opportunities. I would be curious to hear them reflect on the values of the lessons learned on some of those trips. But even if they didn't glean all they could from the experiences, if they are richer for any of them, I glad. I'm sure that like them, I was too young to fully grasp some of my opportunities, but I remember them all with great favor and gratitude.

¡Viva Cuba! I wasn't yet two years old when I first arrived in Havana, Cuba. My mother and I had accompanied my grandparents on a trip to Florida. Cuba had become a popular tourist attraction and we climbed aboard a DC-3 in Key West for the short trip to Havana. You might think that I'd have few memories of a trip taken more than sixty-five years ago when I was two years old and you're right. However, I do recall some things. I remember the beach, the palm trees and the police officer that was so nice to me. I remember walking down a street that was too narrow to allow cars. There were open air stores on both sides of the street selling vegetables, fruit and meat. And I remember standing behind a tall fence as the plane came rolling up. When it spun around, the wash from its twin propellers stripped the hats from all who wore them and launched them into the air. I wonder how much of my future wanderlust came from this early experience with international travel. Even at two, I came away with a realization that there were places where things were different, very, very different from the way they were at home.

Howard in Havana 1949

Throughout my grade school years, I periodically traveled. With only one exception, my father never went along. I'm sure he was "working". We made a few trips to the farm in Ohio and a couple of trips to my mother's old family home in Tennessee. But for the most part, travel involved visiting family and wasn't particularly valuable from the standpoint of building an expansive thought process. It was fun, but it was family.

International travel was restricted to an occasional trip across the river into Windsor or Sarnia Ontario to play hockey. It was technically "international", but the truth is there was no significant difference between the countries. Many families, mine included, had roots on both sides of the border. The Jones wing of my family had actually migrated to Port Huron, Michigan from the Georgian Bay in central Ontario about a hundred years earlier.

Oh, that's a big mountain. My first travel awakening since Cuba took place in December of 1957. My uncle Frank Ubel, the husband of my father's sister Jackie Lou, had lost a lung in a battle with the Germans in World War II. Supposedly to reduce the risk of respiratory problems, the Ubels decided to move to the arid land of Arizona in 1956. They lobbied hard with my father for him to also make the move. They told him business was booming and life was good in the Phoenix area. The week before Christmas, we piled in our 1957 Buick and my parents, my youngest brother Jeff and I took off on the three day drive to the Valley of the Sun to give it a look. (Brian, the "middle" brother, stayed behind with my mother's parents. Brian was always a little different.)

As we drove across the country, I saw things I couldn't have imagined. We took the famed Route 66 from Chicago and followed it all the way to Flagstaff, Arizona. I still recall gas prices in Tulsa, Oklahoma advertised at nine cents per gallon. As we forged on into the panhandle of Texas, my world began to change. I had never seen such a vast expanse of flat, bare land. We got a motel room in Amarillo, Texas and I remember thinking that you could spot a tennis ball laying on the ground five miles away. As we drove on the next day, we began our rise into the great Rocky Mountains. I was completely awestruck by the majesty of what I thought were big mountains. By the time we got to Tucumcari, New Mexico, four thousand feet in elevation, it began to snow. It snowed all the way to Flagstaff.

As we drove on through Sedillo, New Mexico, we were in blizzard conditions at nearly seven thousand feet. Because of the weather, I didn't have the long range panoramas of the mountains, but couldn't believe the steepness of the mountain walls surrounding us. I had seen the mountains of Tennessee, but these were different. Their sheer scale took my breath away.

A couple hours after passing through Albuquerque, we crossed into Arizona. We were in the high desert as we crossed the Navajo Indian reservation. I could see small six sided cabin-like hogans. I never would have dreamed I would someday live in one. As the snow continued, we saw more and more cars off in the ditches that lined the road. As snow seasoned Michiganders, we roared right on through the storm. We got to Flagstaff as night descended. The storm had finally abated somewhat and I could see Humphries Peak more than 12,000 feet high. There was magic in what I saw. It was love at first sight.

We dropped south onto the road for Phoenix three hours distant. I could see nothing in the darkness except for the headlights of oncoming cars. Finally, we crested a ridge and the faint lights of Phoenix came softly into view over a thousand feet below us. Another magic moment was etched into my memory. My cousin was still up waiting for us when we got in late that night.

On the return trip a week later, another winter storm was blanketing the mountain states with snow and ice. We opted to take the southern route back to Michigan. We drove toward Tucson, Arizona and spent our first night in a motel in Arizona. The following morning, I was up and dressed an hour before my parents were ready to get back on the road. To kill time, I went outside the motel room and walked around taking in the scenery. Directly behind the motel, there was a mountain, a single rocky promontory that in the eyes of a ten year boy from Michigan, reached all the way to the sky. I was captivated by its beauty and mass. Something inside said, "You must go to the top." I can't explain it, but it turned out that wouldn't be the last time I heard that voice.

I had no experience with mountains. I had no way of judging its size or its distance. As far as I could tell, it was right in front of me and getting to the top couldn't be that difficult. I started walking into the desert dodging cactus as I went. After a few minutes, the mountain was no closer. I continued on with my trek. I walked for twenty or thirty minutes and still the mountain stood in front of me no closer than it was when I first left the room. The mountain still called to me, but I finally realized I wasn't going to get there on that day. I turned around and headed back toward the motel. My parents were waiting for me and had begun to worry. In the years since that morning, I've tried to determine where I was and under what circumstances I had set out for my first summit. I'm not certain, but I suspect it wasn't far from Tucson. I also suspect the "mountain" stood no more than five hundred feet above the motel. It was probably four or five miles distant. But to a ten year old from the woods of Michigan, it was Mount Everest. And in the words of George Mallory, I felt like I had to climb it because "It was there." The "adventure gene" had kicked in.

We drove on to El Paso, Texas, then on to Midland-Odessa. We bypassed the heart of the winter storm and headed north to Amarillo and finally back toward Michigan. If a single trip can shape one's future, I suspect that was the one. Forever more, the mountains and the desert held a special place in my psyche. As I write this, I look out my window across the desert and see the beauty of Camelback Mountain towering above me.

Have License – Will Travel. My travel horizon expanded dramatically when I turned sixteen and got my first driver's license. I wanted to see places unknown. I went to the office where I was to take the test for my driver's license, took it and walked out with the license. From the door of that office, I went directly through the door of a 1955 Ford that a friend of mine, Kent Kipfer, had purchased. The two of us immediately followed the hood ornament on that car all the way across the state of Michigan until we arrived in Sagatuck on the sandy shores of Lake Michigan. It was a memorable adventure. Lewis and Clark had nothing on us. We discovered water, sand, girls and other things that had been previously out of reach.

Another friend, Dave Kerr, had a father that was in management at the World Headquarters of the Ford Motor Company in Dearborn. Dave's father frequently came home in cars that hadn't even been released to the general market yet. Dave and I had access to those cars and on a couple of occasions took them to Florida over Christmas and Easter breaks from high school. We were young, foolish and immortal. We drove at high rates of speed and in more than one instance come precariously close to paying the ultimate price, but we somehow got through it all alive. During one drive straight through from Northville, Michigan to Miami, Florida, we drove a 1964 experimental Mustang from Macon to Valdosta, Georgia, a distance of more than one hundred forty miles, where the speedometer never dropped below one hundred miles per hour. We were topping out at speeds greater than one hundred twenty miles per hour.

We had a lot of fun on our Florida trips and we had our eyes opened a few times in the process. It was on these trips I first saw separate restrooms for "whites and coloreds". Some restaurants wouldn't serve blacks. There were even separate drinking fountains for the "coloreds". I had seen open racism and bigotry before; my mother's family was from Tennessee. But I had never seen it so wide spread, so institutionalized. I was shocked and amazed.

I also learned that Mr. Molema, my high school history teacher, had been wrong. He said the civil war had ended in 1865. On one of my trips to Florida, I learned it hadn't yet come to a close. Dave and I were in Miami one time and were introduced to a couple of beautiful young girls. We decided to ask them out on a date, the old fashioned kind where all the lewd and lascivious thoughts were confined strictly to our imaginations. When the time came, we were obliged to pick the girls up at their homes and to meet their fathers before leaving the house. The father of the girl I was taking out discovered I was from Michigan and was therefore a "Yankee". He honestly wasn't real thrilled with the idea that his daughter was going to spend an evening with a boy from the North. It was only after I told him my family was in fact from southeastern Tennessee that I finally got clearance to take his daughter out the door. Oh my. The South is a bit different isn't it?

After I married Lucy and entered the world of radio and television, my travel boundaries widened. Working as a reporter and newscaster on the West Coast and in the Central Rockies helped me expand my world view, especially when I was dealing regularly with politicians, cops and murderers. It was a time of enlightenment for me. Every day held surprises. I was keenly interested in society's nuances. I watched the cultures, sub-cultures and micro-cultures. Dealing with all segments of society made it increasingly apparent to me that this great mass of people we call Americans was made up of a tremendous number of pieces and parts of humanity. And the pieces of that great puzzle didn't always fit together perfectly.

Following Butch Casidy. As my marriage with Lucy disintegrated, we decided to take one more trip together. A friend from Michigan State lived in Peru. Rosa invited us to visit her in Lima and we took her up on her offer. We scheduled a six week visit. It would be my first lengthy international trip and it would change my life.

The Latin culture of Peru was very different from even the most diverse cultures with which I had become familiar in the United States. When I arrived, I didn't expect to learn

Alone in Machu Pichu

so much from it. Looking back, I ended up learning a lot about the people of Peru, but more about America and its people. It was as if I was an astronaut circling the globe looking at planet Earth from space. I stared back at the United States in general and at my life in particular and viewed them through the lens of a South American.

When I stepped off the plane in Lima, I was an ethnocentric, naïve American. Like so many of my countrymen, even today, I assumed we were number one in everything. All other countries in the world couldn't possibly be as developed, as cultured, as prosperous and as wonderful as the good old U.S.A. We were the only nation in the world that refused to lower the flag in the opening ceremonies of the Olympics when our delegation marched past the reviewing stand of the host country. All other nations lowered their banners as a show of respect and gratitude to the hosts. I guess I just assumed that other nations didn't expect the greatest nation to bow to anyone. It never dawned on me it might be a result of unbridled arrogance.

One of my memorable lessons came when Rosa, her friend Jorge, Lucy and I took a drive south of Lima. We were about an hour and a half into the desert. There was everything you could ever want as long as you never wanted anything but sand. There were no towns, no structures and no people. Off in the distance we could see the mountains rise toward the majestic peaks of the Andes. I thought to myself that if anything were to happen out here, we'd probably just die from dehydration.

Then something happened. The engine stopped running. We coasted to a stop on the side of the road. I was in a foreign country with a dead car and no way to get help. The boy from the suburbs of Detroit didn't have a clue what to do. We couldn't call "road service". We couldn't waive down traffic for help; there was none. We were totally and completely screwed. I now knew how I was going to die.

Jorge calmly got out of the car, lifted the hood and tinkered a bit. He then slowly started walking up the road. I saw him bend over and pick up something. He continued walking, crossed the street and began casually walking back toward the car. He stopped and picked up something else. When he got back to the vehicle, he went back under the hood. After a couple minutes he got back in the car and turned the key. The engine started and we were soon on our way. He had found a piece of wire and a piece of metal. He used them to connect a broken carburetor linkage. He used no tools other than his fingers.

It was an epiphany for me. I learned that no matter how dire your straits, you must adapt to the situation and find the best solution to whatever problem you're faced with. There are times in life when you can't lean on others to help. You've got to figure things out on your own. It's a lesson that has served me well for forty years. It caused me to look at life a little differently.

On another occasion, a light went on after getting to know one Lima man. Sidewalk coffee stands were very common in Lima and we spent more than a little time in them relaxing and talking with the locals. There I sat one day enjoying the company of one guy and thinking what wonderful and happy people lived in Lima even though they didn't have the luxury of being from the best and the most wonderful and most enlightened and richest and smartest and blah, blah, blah country in the world. I knew this was true because I had been taught it from an early age. After all, every school day, I had been expected to recite the Pledge of Allegiance where it said we had "liberty and justice for all". In the Star Spangled Banner, I learned we were the "land of the free and the home of the brave". I had pretty much been brainwashed into thinking real civilization had begun with the 1776 Declaration of Independence and we were the only ones that had it.

So you can imagine my surprise when Juan made a comment about our lack of freedom. I thought he was joking or misinformed or both. For a Peruvian to tell me my country lacked freedom was roughly the equivalent of learning your father was your mother. How was this possible? I was stunned and asked for an explanation.

Juan told me he had spent two years going to college in Florida. He learned a lot about America while living there and came home thinking that Americans tended to be slaves to technology. He said, "In the United States, if someone is driving through a small town at three in the morning and comes to a stop light that is red, he stops and waits for it to turn green before proceeding. It doesn't matter if it's obvious no one else is on the road; you sit there and wait until the machine gives you permission to go. In Peru, if we come to a red light and no one else can be seen within miles in any direction, we have the freedom to drive through the intersection. You're slaves to technology."

What I took away from that discussion was not that I should run red lights at three in the morning. I learned the same reality can be viewed from many different perspectives. One isn't necessarily better than another. Juan and I had two different realities, but they were of the same thing. Conflicts and misunderstandings can easily result when realities collide. But if we take a step back and attempt to view things from a different perspective, life can sometimes become easier and more pleasant. But first, you have to acknowledge your view isn't the only one.

I went on to spend a week in Cuzco, Peru, a few days in Quito, Ecuador and some time in Bogota, Columbia. When I returned from South America, I had fallen in love with Latin America, its history, its culture and its people. I worked hard to learn the language, but found the streets of life were the best language classrooms.

I ventured into Mexico, first barely across the border into Nogales and Tijuana. I then booked a two week long trip into the Yucatan. I stayed in Mérida, but rented a car and drove out into the jungle and along the coast. I visited one Mayan ruin after another and with each, my interest in the history of the Western Hemisphere burned brighter.

Another trip took me to Guatemala. Another to Mazatlán, Mexico. Over the course of the next forty years, I spent between two and three years collectively in Mexico, Costa Rica, Peru, Chile, Argentina, Ecuador, Colombia, Honduras, Cuba, the Dominican Republic, Puerto Rico and Nicaragua. Most of that time was spent in Mexico. For periods of a few months, we lived in Ensenada and Mazatlán. We still visit Mexico a couple times per year and were we not so comfortable where we live now, we could easily be convinced to live there permanently. The people tend to live more with their hearts than most of my fellow Americans and that ain't all bad.

Living on the Poop Deck. My travel horizons expanded when our friends, Bob and Janet Quackenbush, urged us time and time again to join them on a short ocean cruise. My image of someone on a cruise ship was not a favorable one. Pretentious, blue-haired old ladies and fat guys in tuxedos smoking cigarettes in ivory holders painted my mental landscape of this seemingly boring pursuit. Of all the things to do in life, passing time on the poop-deck with some boring, pompous ass wasn't high on my list. And oh . . . you get to play "dress-up" and wear a tie to dinner. I'd rather eat potting soil and pluck my nose hairs with a pair of pliers. I have a knack for the performing arts, but I've never been a good enough actor to fake enjoyment with that itinerary.

"Just go on a three day cruise out of Los Angeles with us" Janet pleaded. "Trust me; you'll love it."

"What the hell?" we thought. "We can endure most anything for three days." As we boarded the old Norwegian Cruise Lines ship, Liz and I vowed to do our best to enjoy the experience. We were fairly confident this would be our first and last ocean cruise, so we wanted to experience everything there was to offer. The itinerary included a day in Avalon on Catalina Island and a day in Ensenada, Mexico. At that time, we'd been to neither place so we looked forward to seeing our "port-of-call".

As is the custom with most cruises, it began with the "sail-away party" on the top deck. The music got better with each of the cute little umbrella decorated drinks they gave us. Nearly two thousand people partied, took in the views and had a good time – some too good. The following morning, we awoke to see Avalon harbor, a charming European looking village on the hillside awaited us. We had a wonderful time exploring the island all day and returned to the ship in time for a nice dinner. Like the others aboard, we pretended we were members of the bourgeoisie and ate our seven course meal with our noses pointed skyward. After dinner, there was another party and then a Las Vegas style stage show with some surprisingly professional entertainers. We were up until after midnight, but had actually enjoyed the day immensely. The next morning, we looked through the little port-hole in our cabin to see the harbor of Ensenada, Mexico. We went ashore and explored a city that some years later, we would live in. We had another great day, returned to the ship in time for the fanciest of the dinners and watched as hundreds of revelers joined in the conga dance line as the flaming baked Alaska was brought to the tables. We stuffed ourselves like we belonged in the court of Louis XIII. By the time we had finished dinner, we were close to being completely spent physically. Early mornings and late evenings were taking their tolls. But the night was still young and we had vowed to do it all.

After freshening up a bit, we went to the meet-and-greet event where we met the ship's captain. We thought that must be some kind of big deal; it was only in our later years that we realized this was the maritime equivalent to being introduced to your bus driver, but hey – he had a cute uniform. After having a toddy with the captain, we had an hour or so to waste in the casino or wherever. Then came the show. The final night's Las Vegas spectacular was in fact pretty spectacular. Sadly, Liz didn't get to see much of it. We sat at a table with a flashy New Yorker in a fancy tuxedo that we nicknamed "Mr. Saturday Night". He was engaging, friendly and fun despite the fact that he was on the cruise to celebrate his ninetieth birthday. By eleven o'clock, the show was approaching its crescendo of entertainment and excitement. I looked to my side to see that exhaustion had conquered both Liz and Mr. Saturday Night. Liz was sound asleep with her head on Mr. Saturday Night's shoulder. He too had fallen into a deep sleep and his head rested atop Liz's head. It looked as if Liz was out on the town with her grandfather and neither of them could handle such a level of excitement.

When the show came to an end, everyone woke up and found their way into the bowels of the ship. But we still weren't done. The "Midnight Chocolate Buffet" remained. As a chocolate fiend, there was nothing that would keep Janet Quackenbush from being the first person in line. To honor our commitment to take everything in, we stood directly behind Bob and Janet when the doors opened at the stroke of midnight. It was another show in of itself with beautiful ice carvings and every kind and shape of chocolate imaginable. We did our bests to devastate the chocolate stores of the ship even if others behind us had to go without.

When we returned to Arizona, we had worn ourselves to a frazzle. The trip took its toll on us, but we had honored our commitment and done it all. We also found we had a great time. As a result, we went on numerous cruises in the six and seven years that followed. We did a four day cruise with the same itinerary as our first one, but with a day at sea sandwiched in between Avalon and Ensenada. We moved up to seven day cruises and sailed all over the Caribbean. We probably cruised the Caribbean a half dozen times.

One of the most memorable was when we sailed from San Juan, Puerto Rico to San Juan, Puerto Rico with pretty much nothing in between. It wasn't planned that way; we were supposed to have five exotic ports-of-call. Unfortunately, as we arrived in San Juan, we had the joy of experiencing the tail end of a major hurricane (Luis). Right on the heels of Luis, a bigger and more powerful hurricane (Marilyn) hit. We spent the next six days at sea running from the storm as it demolished villages on the various islands we'd been scheduled to visit. It was an experience neither Liz nor I will ever forget. It seemed half the passengers felt cheated. They threatened to sue the cruise line for selling them tickets for a hurricane. The other half thought it was a great experience and wouldn't have traded it for anything. We were in the latter half. Sure, we missed some great stops, but you haven't lived until you're on a six hundred fifty foot ship that is being tossed around like a cork in a bathtub. As the ship would pitch in one direction, we'd hear the sounds of platters being thrown from shelves and crashing to the floor. As it pitched the other way, all the metal objects would slam the walls in a great cacophony of impromptu metal Caribbean drums.

Across the Big Pond. Between my congenital wanderlust and varied career path, I got to see much of the western hemisphere. I didn't jump across "the pond" until I was fifty. My first European destination was the Emerald Isle, Ireland. With Liz and me both having some of our roots in Ireland, we were anxious to see our ancestral homeland. We booked a flight into Dublin and together with our friends, Bob and Janet Quackenbush, we flew from Los Angeles all the way to Ireland. As the plane began its descent over the west coast of the island, I'd never seen a land so saturated with the color green. Countless old castles dotted the landscape. It truly seemed to be an enchanted place even before we set foot on the ground. For the next week and a half, we drove our rented car all over Ireland. As we travelled, we'd spend one night in a magical town and take in the sites. The following day, we were off to the next enthralling destination. "The pub" proved to be the cultural center of the nation. The locals defined their politics, shared their joys and sorrows in the Irish pub. Some school children even took their lunches in the pubs. It was an eye-opening and wonderful trip and we would return.

The World's Seven Summits. As the twentieth century came to a close, I developed a renewed interest in mountain climbing. I began training in earnest and it wasn't long before my quest for some of the highest peaks began taking me to distant parts of the world. Many people would be surprised to learn the third highest peak in North America is actually in southern Mexico. Pico de Orizaba in the State of Veracruz was my first eighteen thousand foot climb (18,401 feet). Just before the climb, we stood in shocked awe as "Popo", an adjacent volcano blew its top and filled the sky with black ash. Cerro de Aconcagua located in Chile and Argentina was my next big one at a few feet shy of 23,000 feet.

Aconcagua was to become the model for other big climbs. An ascent of that magnitude typically takes three to four weeks. I would fly into the country, perform the climb and then, a few days before we hoped I would be down and alive, Liz would fly in. She toured the area while she waited. After Aconcagua, Liz and I hooked up in Santiago, Chile. We then spent the next couple of weeks relaxing and enjoying our time in the "thin country". We found Santiago so wonderful and "tranquilo", we actually looked at real estate while we were there. When the grim reality of having a twelve hour flight to our second home finally set in, we decided we could remember our time in Chile through our pictures.

Climbers descending in the distance in this photo taken from 22,000 feet on Cerro Aconcagua

The single longest trip we undertook included a climb of two of the world's Seven Summits, i.e., the highest peak on each continent. As you can imagine, such an aggressive itinerary was not to be without its share of excitement. The plan was for me to fly out of Phoenix to Amsterdam in the Netherlands. From there, I would catch a flight to Moscow and a few days later, I would fly a dilapidated 707 with Air Siberia to Mineralnye Vody in southern Russia between the Black Sea and the Caspian Sea near the border of war torn Georgia and Iran. From there, I worked my way into the Caucasus Mountains and finally to the summit of the highest peak on the European continent, Mount Elbrus (18,510 feet).

By the time I began the trek down Mount Elbrus, the trip had hardly begun. I backtracked to Mineralnye Vody, survived another flight on Air Siberia and arrived safely in Moscow. It was here that I experienced the first major snafu of the trip. Liz and her sister Victoria had plane tickets and had intended to fly into St. Petersburg, Russia to spend a few days seeing the sights. I was to meet them in St. Petersburg. In the three weeks since I'd left Arizona, a major forest fire had ravaged the White Mountains. With employees who had lost everything, with a town that had disaster relief teams helping the homeless and thousands of fire fighters battling the blaze, both Liz and Victoria felt there was no way they could leave everything in crisis. I spent a few days in Moscow while Liz and Victoria had bigger mountains to climb back home.

Liz rescheduled her flights and our revised plan was to rendezvous in Amsterdam and proceed with the rest of our original itinerary. I arrived at Schiphol Airport about six hours before Liz was due to land. I could hardly wait to see her, but she didn't arrive. Snafu number two was now in motion. Security personnel were useless and unwilling to help. They would neither deny nor confirm that her plane had landed and wouldn't tell me if she was on it. I was three hours from a scheduled departure for Arusha, Tanzania and my spouse was either still in the U.S. or was lost somewhere in Amsterdam or already in route to Africa or somewhere else. In a nearly frantic state, all I could do was half run throughout the airport hoping to find my bride. If I couldn't find her, I didn't know if the best approach would be to fly to Africa and hope she too could find her way or if I should skip the flight and stay in Amsterdam. If something had happened stateside, I would be returning to New York to catch a flight back to Arizona.

As the hours to the scheduled departure to Tanzania fell to minutes, my fears increased. I was running through the airport calling Liz's name without any response. With fewer than ten minutes remaining, I hurried toward the gate where a dozen lines of travel weary passengers pushed toward the terminal wing for African departures. I fought my way through the middle of the lines in the hope of finding Liz. At a moment of peak frustration, I forcefully exclaimed "God Dammit" with theatrical emphasis.

Not five feet away, a woman wheeled around and said, "I thought I recognized that voice." It was Liz. The end of the world had been averted. She laughs about it to this day. I'm sure I'll be able to laugh about it someday.

When we arrived in Arusha, we were shuttled to a beautiful lodge. Porters cared for our every need. Meals were spectacular. From the decks and windows, we could see wild game everywhere. It was truly as if we had walked into a scene from a Clark Gable movie. When we awoke the next morning, a giraffe had his head at our open window and peered at us with huge, dark eyes. Cape Buffalo grazed a stone's throw from our room. It was a sign of things to come.

I never had an interest in going on a "safari". I had concluded it would be akin to going to the zoo. I expected it would involve driving around and every couple of hours getting a fleeting glimpse of a zebra or monkey. One of the first things I learned after getting to know Liz was that she had always wanted to go on a safari. I had spent twenty years adroitly avoiding the question. With a climb of Mount Kilimanjaro on my itinerary, I thought I might talk Liz into tackling the highest mountain on the African continent. I knew she could do it.

After protracted "bargaining", she said she would be willing to climb Kilimanjaro if and only if I would be willing to go on safari. We did the deal. With less than twenty-four hours in Africa, it was apparent my perceptions of safari were far from the reality. There was wild game everywhere we looked.

We set out that afternoon for our initial camp on Kili. We went to sleep as best we could. Howler monkeys screeched throughout the night. The following day we set out for the summit. If we were successful, it would take us a week to get there. Unlike the climbs of other 19,000 plus foot mountains where life and death hung in the balance, a Kilimanjaro climb was almost luxury. We had nine climbers, but fifty porters carried most of our gear. Four guides led the way. Two chefs accompanied us and prepared great meals at every camp. It still called for some hard physical exertion; not everyone in the group was successful. At each successive camp, not only was the air thinner, the environment

Howard and Liz atop Mount Kilimanjaro at 19,341 feet

changed. Starting in a tropical jungle, we gradually ascended until our last camp was adjacent to the massive glacier barely a thousand feet below the summit. After a week of effort, Liz stood with me at the top of the African continent 19,341 feet above sea level. She had lived up to her end of the bargain; now I had to live up to mine.

After our descent, we spent a day at another marvelous lodge in the jungle. The following day, we boarded a small plane and took off for the Serengeti. It was safari time. I was a bit more optimistic than I had been, but I still couldn't imagine what we were about to see. Although I was never a "licensed" pilot, I had taken flying lessons and had spent many hours at the controls of our family plane. As we began our approach to the little airstrip at our destination, my pulse quickened as we headed for the runway at what I thought was an extremely high speed for a landing. I could see the controls from my seat and wondered if the pilot had fallen asleep, died, or just plane (pun intended) lost his mind. If he tried to land at that speed, we'd be a twisted heap of smoldering metal far from the end of the runway.

Just before we hit the runway, the pilot pulled up on the wheel and rose quickly into the sky again and circled the strip. The wild game was so plentiful, it had covered the runway. The pilot was making a low pass to get antelope, zebra and myriad other four legged visitors running from the runway. On the next approach, the instruments looked much better and we landed safely. I exited the plane and stood on the runway. As I scanned the horizon, it became clear; my expectations of seeing an occasional animal could not have been more erroneous. If I saw one, I saw a thousand.

For the next week, our days were filled from sun-up to sun-down with a constant stream of excitement and awe. We saw nearly every animal we had imagined lived in Africa and many we'd never heard of. We were there for the annual migration of the wildebeest where a line miles long made its way north. One morning, we were awakened when someone came running into our camp to warm us that a lion was stalking us presumably with breakfast in mind. On another morning, I heard a bit of a ruckus and left the tent to investigate. I found two young bull elephants stripping trees about fifty yards away. I grabbed the camera and ever so tentatively approached for a better shot. When I got about twenty yards away, one of the elephants turned and faced me. Although we didn't share a common language, we had no difficulty communicating. "Take one more step in this direction and I convert you into a stain on the bottom of my foot."

I froze in my tracks (except for the shaking), but that didn't seem to please the elephant. His ears flared out wide and he lowered his head and charged. Just as he began his charge, I snapped a picture. It is the only photo I took all week that was blurred. There's just something about holding a camera steady as a twelve thousand pound animal comes after you that is problematic. I later learned it was an elephant's answer to a poker bluff – a false charge. He stopped after a couple of quick steps. I didn't know he had stopped because I

This is what a bull elephant looks like just before he charges

was running at full speed plus twenty percent in the direction of the camp. As I reached the camp boundary, adrenaline was still on the rise. I didn't slow down and darted straight through the camp slowing down only after I reached the jungle on the other side of the guide's tents. If an elephant has a sense of humor, this one had to be rolling on his side convulsed with laughter.

The "safari experience" was the jungle's answer to a luxury hotel. Our tents were almost as nice as student housing at a major university. We had comfortable cots on which we slept and even a little end-table/bookstand for each of us. There was a separate little room for storage and dressing. This led into our shower! Every morning, the guides would heat water and pour it into a tank that fed our shower. Dr. Livingston, I presume, did not enjoy a hot shower every morning when traversing the African continent. This was "up-town" stuff.

The only "convenience" we truly did not like in the least was the "mess tent". The guides prepared our meals every day. With nine Americans on the safari, they knew they'd have to deal with some tender stomachs and picky eaters. They did their best to give us food with which we'd be familiar. A typical lunch spread for example included packaged and sliced cheese, sliced, processed ham, white bread and all the culinary delights we wouldn't consider eating at home even at gun point. We hated it. Liz and I took most of our meals with the guides in their tent. We enjoyed the real staple of east Africa. Most meals included "ugali", a maize flower cooked to a doughy consistency and used somewhat the way traditional Mexicans use a tortilla. We tore off a piece of ugali and used it to grab whatever stew or mixture of local ingredients happened to be in the pot. We loved the food, but even more, we loved the regular interface with the guides who shared stories of their lives and times growing up in Africa.

On the last night of the safari, we gave up our tents in exchange for a wonderful room in a lodge overlooking the Ngorongoro Crater. It was a great time for reflection as we absorbed the fading pink light of in incomparable sunset over the lake. The overall safari experience that I had so long feared and avoided turned out to be one of the most exciting and rewarding weeks of my life. It was truly an awakening. We also passed the halfway point on the trip while in Africa. We weren't even close to being finished.

Once the safari came to an end, we drove on to the Olduvai Gorge where Louis Leakey and other anthropologists made their earth shaking discoveries of man's ancient ancestors including "Lucy" (not my first wife). Mankind's ancestral heritage has been traced back nearly two million years in the Olduvai Gorge. As a former anthropology major in college, I found it a spectacular day.

The following day, we spent our time in a village of Maasai warriors. Two centuries earlier, slave traders did their best to avoid members of this tribe after they discovered their warrior characteristics made them a bit more difficult to manage than other tribes. We passed part of the afternoon as guests in the home of the tribe's patriarch. Together with his most senior wife, we sat in the mud hut, sipped tea and talked at length about life in the Maasai Mara. They were most gracious hosts, but then if we had asked them if they'd consider returning with us as slaves, I suspect the reception may have cooled off some.

Maasai warriors performing a ritual

By nightfall, we found ourselves in an indescribably beautiful lodge on the outskirts of Arusha, Tanzania. Our pillows had been decorated with red flowers and seemed to merge into the lush garden area outside our room. It gave us a peaceful place to relax, wind down and get prepared to get wound back up again for the rest of our trip.

The following day, we boarded a small bus in Arusha and headed north toward Nairobi, Kenya. It turned out to be a near death experience. It soon became clear the driver's number one priority was to get us to Nairobi as soon as possible. He seemed to believe the bus had only two speeds, stopped and full-speed-ahead. As near as I could tell, top-end on the bus was somewhere in the vicinity of ninety miles-per-hour. The road was paved and actually in pretty good condition; that wasn't the issue. The issue was that as we barreled down the road, animals of all kinds were walking across it. At one point, we narrowly missed an adult giraffe. When we got to Nairobi, we checked each other to make sure we were still alive. It was with great delight that we concluded we had survived.

Our hotel in Nairobi seemed to be in an area where an air of caution was warranted. We didn't feel as "comfortable" as we normally did in most other cities. History would prove our concerns to be justified. The conflict between two major cultures was visible everywhere. The atmosphere seemed to offer great fodder for a novelist, but I damn sure wasn't going to stay there long enough to write one. We were on our flight destined for London the following morning. It was another ten to eleven hours in the air. We found it interesting that before we left Kenya, flight attendants walked the aisles of the aircraft with little spray bottles of some kind of bug-spray. Everyone on the plane was sprayed. It seemed like an odd welcome to England – a little sip of insecticide wasn't exactly the "spot-of-tea" we'd seen in the movies.

Nonetheless, a few days in London were fun and educational. We tried to pack as much in as we could. I'm sure we tackled most of the real touristy sites, Big Ben, Hyde Park, the Palace and much more. Perhaps the most pleasant surprise of the visit was the massive department store called Harrods in the Knightsbridge district. If they didn't sell it, it probably didn't exist. It was the closest thing to an amusement park I'd seen without a Ferris wheel. I wouldn't be surprised if they had that too and we just didn't have time to see it.

Our trip had now gone on for about five weeks. We were starting to see the end of the tunnel, but we still had a ways to go. After a few days in London, we jumped on a plane for Switzerland. Geneva was our destination and we took in all the sights, sounds and tastes of the Swiss capitol city. It was beautiful, but oddly sterile. The people were welcoming and nice, but somehow formal and slightly distant. If some cities are completely alive and full of enthusiasm, they probably had it shipped in from Geneva. They didn't leave much for the locals. They seemed to be a little short on it. The highlight of the trip to Switzerland was the trip to France. We took a bus to the skier's paradise of Chamonix, France at the foot of Mount Blanc. We took the lift to the lodge high up on the mountain. After returning to Chamonix, we had our first dinner in France. We felt like we were eating a work of art.

After a couple days, we flew back to Amsterdam to catch another six thousand mile flight, this time to Tokyo, Japan. Keep in mind that by this time, our bodies had become pretty confused as to where they were, what time it was, what day it was and who they were in the first place. I'd gone from Arizona to Minneapolis to New York to Amsterdam to Moscow to the Iranian border to Moscow to Amsterdam to Arusha, Tanzania to the Serengeti to Nairobi, Kenya to London, England, London to Switzerland to France to Amsterdam and my internal clock wasn't running all that well. Try counting the number of time zones we'd been in recently. By the time we arrived in Tokyo, our bodies sent our minds a message. We got to our hotel at about three in the afternoon. We thought about going out and wandering through the city. We sat down on the bed to discuss the plan. We woke up nine hours later. The body had proclaimed that it didn't care where it was or what time it was; it was going to sleep.

We tried to get our diurnal rhythms back on track, but didn't meet with complete success. It proved to be a stroke of luck. The next morning at three, we sat wide eyed talking about what we wanted to do. The Tokyo fish market is the most famous in the world and it was only a few blocks away. It turned into a fantastic experience walking throughout the market when the real work was being done. We stood by and watched as auctioneers collected ten or twelve thousand dollars for one fish. We watched in amazement as tons of fish were off-loaded from trucks. We saw and tasted sea critters that to this day we're not real sure what we ate. The market is huge and we did our best to see every bit of it.

After a few days, we were ready to return to the United States, especially after experiencing one slightly frustrating and tiring aspect of life in Japan. In nearly every country I had ever visited, I could either speak the language or I could discern enough clues from the signs, newspapers and magazines to figure things out. Even in Russia, I knew enough of the Russian language and alphabet to get an idea of whether I was walking into a restaurant or a funeral home. However, the written word in Japan was totally and completely foreign to me. I realized how much I depended upon signage in foreign countries only after standing in one of Tokyo's largest train stations and staring blankly at a map with what appeared to be chicken tracks all over it. We couldn't figure out where we were, where we had been or where we were going. Were it not for a kind Japanese gentleman who happened to speak English, there's a chance we'd still be standing in Tokyo blankly looking at the train map.

As much as we had enjoyed our around-the-world trip, it was now getting close to two months since we'd been home. We were ready and anxious to return. We still had a lot of traveling to do. We were to depart Tokyo for Seattle then fly to Arizona. When we arrived at the airport, the lines seemed to be longer than we'd expected. Apparently, there had been some glitches in the travel world and many flights were delayed. When we finally stood in front of the overly polite Japanese woman who was to help us, she began to apologize profusely. She was very sorry to tell us our Seattle flight was over-booked and asked us if we would consider catching an earlier flight to San Francisco and then on to Phoenix. Liz and I looked at each other in subdued amazement. We thought about it and concluded that for a journey of over six thousand miles, we could probably survive leaving sooner, going to a city we both knew well and loved, getting home earlier and having an hour less time in the air.

"We'll do it," I said. If the truth be known, I probably would have paid

Liz grins from a most welcome upgrade to First Class

a premium for the opportunity. The lady thanked me with such sincerity, I began to feel guilty. And then – the grand prize!

"Because of your inconvenience and your willingness to help us today, we'll be upgrading you to the First Class cabin." I thought about joking with her and saying, "I paid for a crowded and cramped coach seat, dammit. I want to fly coach." I thought better of it realizing that Liz would bloody the back of my head before I could turn around and give her a wink. We enjoyed a relaxing, peaceful and most importantly, a comfortable flight across the great Pacific Ocean. In roughly twenty-four hours, we set foot in Show Low, Arizona for the first time in nearly two months and for the first time in nearly three months since we'd seen it without smoke and flames raging. After nearly thirty-five thousand miles, we had completed the trip of a lifetime. We are also a day younger after crossing the international dateline without backtracking.

Mountain climbing travel accounted for a lot of my miles for the next couple years. Trips to Alaska to climb Denali (Mount McKinley), a couple trips to Mt. Rainier in Washington for training, a pair of climbs of Mt. Whitney in central California, climbs in New Mexico, Colorado and northern Arizona racked up some miles on the travelometer. By the time I climbed Denali, I was beginning to conclude the body had possibly seen enough avalanches and frozen fingers. The nature of my travel was to take on a distinctly different character. Trips would become more diverse and typically longer. We reached a point in our lives where the nuisance associated with traveling wasn't worth the trouble unless the trips were much more substantial.

Back to The Continent. Liz and I returned to Ireland for a couple of weeks, rented a vehicle and drove the most of the island. Tensions were still high between those in Northern Ireland and the Irish Republican Army. We ended up stumbling into a little "planning session" in a pub in Belfast and our lives got pretty interesting for about an hour. Obviously, we're still alive, but for a while, the outcome wasn't guaranteed.

Another trip took us to England, Wales and Scotland for nearly a month and a half. We had planned on spending most of our time in England, but had allocated three days in Wales. When we arrived in Wales, we fell in love with it and ended up spending a couple weeks there. Scotland was beautiful and fun. The trip covered November and December so we ended up seeing more snow and ice than we had learned to enjoy, but it was a memorable and rewarding trip. We spent a week in an old estate castle in Wychnor in the midlands. Another week was spent in Lancashire in "the Lakes" district in northwestern England. Edinburgh, Scotland was an absolute delight. Llandudno was a delight, but our favorite destination in Wales turned out to be Aberystwyth on the western coast a hundred miles across the Irish Sea from Wexford, Ireland. We had the good fortune of having Stonehenge all to ourselves on a cold winter morning. The last week of the trip was spent in Windsor near the castle and in London. The most rewarding aspect of the entire trip was to touch the heart of our heritage. It was interesting to gain a greater understanding of our ancestry. The food, culture, attitudes and so much more seemed to be at the other end of the bridge that was my childhood growing up in the homes of parents and grandparents that were but a generation removed from the midlands of England and the hills of Wales and Ireland.

We had Stonehenge all to ourselves

Over the years, I had heard the horror stories from countless Americans. Two cities in the world were full of rude, aggressive, obnoxious, assholes. I avoided those cities like I had an arrest warrant on my name. They were New York, more specifically Manhattan and Paris, France. Even if I had to fly through New York, I would make it a point to have no overnight stay and hopefully, not even have to change planes. I was led to believe New Yorkers were pushy and abrubt, probably violent and hated anyone from west of the Hudson River. Parisians were haughty, rude, arrogant and unappreciative weaklings that despised Americans. They all spoke English, but pretended they couldn't just so they could ignore Americans in restaurants. These are the stories I had heard.

But as someone with a track record of being open minded and thoughtful, it occurred to me that perhaps I should make up my own mind. Liz was in complete agreement. We planned a trip where we would spend a few days in New York, fly to Paris for a few days, spend a month in Italy and then return to Paris for a few more days. I figured that if I could survive an avalanche on one of the world's highest mountains, surely I could survive New York and Paris. Time would tell.

We booked a hotel a couple blocks away from Times Square. It was a convenient walk to Central Park, restaurants, shopping and many of the sites. We found the subway to be a simple and convenient solution for all of our other transportation needs. We took in a couple of Broadway plays, some great dining, museums and even the Empire State Building.

It was a fabulous city to visit, but what about the people? Were they as bad as we had expected? New York is a big city and there are a lot of people. It goes without saying that with so many people, you can find all kinds. However, we were stunned at how friendly and warm we found the people of New York. Sure, they tended to be "forward" and less than shy; it was New York. But their aggressiveness tended to carry over into everything they did and said. They were aggressive whenever they wanted to help you which they frequently did. After a few days in Manhattan, we concluded most New Yorkers were not so much aggressive as they were enthusiastic. It is a vibrant city and naturally, its people are vibrant people. By the time we were ready to fly to the next stop on our self-abuse tour (Paris), we had fallen completely in love with New York. Liz and I are in complete agreement that we could live there in a New York minute. My only regret is that I listened to the negative comments of meek people who couldn't differentiate between aggressiveness and enthusiasm. As Frank Sinatra said, "These vagabond shoes are longing to stray right through the very heart of it - New York, New York."

After being delightfully surprised by New York, we were in the air headed to the city famous for hating Americans or so we'd been told. We considered our sources. They tended to be a bit ethnocentric and not the most expansive thinkers we'd ever known. One of our acquaintances who had repeated a common American in Paris horror story told us how he was in a restaurant and a rude and condescending waiter pretended to not speak English just to annoy him. He was certain the waiter was fluent in English because he had heard the waiter ask another customer – in English - if he would like a menu. We had suggested to our friend that perhaps the waiter had a very limited English vocabulary associated with common restaurants terms, but our friends was adamant, "No, they just hate Americans over there." We arrived with an open mind.

Almost without exception, we were treated in a most warm and friendly manner. Parisians were delightful and gracious hosts. The city was incredibly beautiful. Outdoor cafés dotted the landscape of a vibrant and exciting world class city. We walked everywhere we went. When the legs tired or the rains became heavy, we sought shelter in one of the countless cafés or restaurants. They had a pretty good selection of French wine in Paris; who would have thought? We hoofed it across the city and saw all the famous attractions, the Eiffel Tower, the Arch de Triumph, the Louvre, the Seine and more. My French skills were sufficient to get by, but I was far from fluent. I barely passed high school French. No one in France tried to pretend he or she didn't speak English. It was just that most of them didn't. But with a little bit of effort and that age old universal language translator, i.e., a smile, we got by handsomely.

As an example of how some of the locals went out of their ways to make our visit pleasant, I'll share the situation in a little restaurant in the heart of the city. It was a small, family run operation. The waitress didn't pretend to speak English. Liz and I were both adventuresome eaters and always liked to try the local fare wherever we went. We spotted an exotic French dish on the menu that would appeal to a small minority of Americans. I don't recall its name, but it consisted in large part of "innards", tripe in one form or another. I didn't hesitate. I ordered it.

As it happened, the waitress became concerned that I may not understand what I had just ordered. She didn't want a visiting American to have a bad experience eating something that he wouldn't normally try in the United States. But she didn't know how to handle the matter. She disappeared into the kitchen. A minute later, the waitress reappeared with the restaurant owner in tow. The woman spoke some English, but I wouldn't call it polished. She smiled at me as she bent over and almost whispered in a beautiful French accent, "You realize you have ordered guts?" I smiled at her and assured her I had indeed requested "guts". She was delighted and pleased. Her smile made the table light up like a French sunrise. Whoever says they are uncaring people who don't like Americans never went to the Paris we know. In our years of traveling, we have found that people tend to mirror the attitudes of those with whom they're dealing. If someone tells you the French are rude and arrogant people, I suspect you might just find they're looking in the mirror.

We left Paris in love with another of the world's great cities. Given the opportunity, we wouldn't hesitate to live in Paris. It is so alive, so vibrant, so beautiful – it is so Paris.

From Paris, we flew to Firenze (Florence), Italy. We rented a car and spent the next month in Tuscany. It was grape harvest time, the "crush". We had rented a villa for two weeks in Cortona, an ancient hilltop city where the movie "Under the Tuscan Sun" was filmed. It was breathtakingly beautiful and we did our best to blend into the "neighborhood". An elderly couple that lived directly across the street from us befriended us and treated us almost like family. They had made their own wine for generations and although my Italian wasn't strong and their English didn't exist, they took us in and showed us the operation of making wine from start to finish. When we left, they called us over to their house. They went deep into a dark cellar and returned with a dust covered bottle of well-aged "vin santo", a traditional Italian dessert wine. They wanted us to have it. It was some of the finest wine we'd ever tasted, perhaps because it came from their hearts.

Police in Florence prevent me from taking this picture

We left Cortona with an open week and no hint of a plan. We just followed the hood of our car. It took us through a number of tiny Italian towns with more charm than we could imagine. We spent a little time in Siena, but elected to drive on until we found another place that seemed "right". That place would be Volterra. It was another medieval fortress city with awesome charm and character. After a few days there, we moved on for a week in a villa we had rented in San Gimignano, the city of towers. Fourteen old stone towers give the city the appearance of a medieval Manhattan.

A week later, we were again on the road with nothing but serendipity to chart our path. We drove along the west coast of Italy from Piombino to Livorno. We slipped into Pisa; the tower was still standing. After a little more sight-seeing, we all but stumbled into the city of Lucca. What a great discovery! It is another walled city, but the architectural style is completely different than most other medieval Italian cities. Atop the walls, a wide, beautifully landscaped walkway surrounds the city. Lucca turned out to be one of our best finds in Italy. We wouldn't hesitate to return.

We did experience one rather odd occurrence in Lucca. As you might imagine, mountain climbers have no choice but to be the most efficient packers in the world. Liz was as good at packing as was I. Her sister normally brings four suitcases on an overnight trip. Liz and I were spending a month and a half in Europe and each of us was carrying only one medium sized suitcase. We knew tricks that allowed us to travel lighter than an astronaut on a spacewalk. One of those tricks was to ship home our dirty laundry. It freed up luggage space for anything we may have purchased on the trip and made life easier. We had a couple more days planned in Florence before departing for Paris. The afternoon before leaving Lucca, we went to DHL and packed dirty clothes and other items no longer necessary for the remaining week of the trip and shipped them back to Arizona. The following day, we arrived in our hotel room in Florence and unpacked. I found no underwear, dirty or clean. "Liz, did you put my underwear in your suitcase?"

She assured me she had not. It was then I realized I had packed every pair of underwear I possessed and shipped it all to Arizona. With a week to go, I could go "free" or go shopping. Shopping won, but it wasn't cheap.

After a couple days in Florence, we flew back for a few more days in Paris. It was the same city, the same people and the same wonderful experience. Our love for Paris only intensified, but we were glad to be heading home soon. It had been a long trip.

Some Trips More Eventful than Others. Another trip that delivered more excitement than planned found us bound for Costa Rica in Central America. It's a country of breathless beauty with jungles full of colorful birds, frogs and a diversity of life that defies description. In addition to the "expected surprises", we ended up with a little more than we could imagine. We spent a few days at the base of Arenal, an active volcano in the northwestern part of the country. We stayed in the Observatory Lodge, an old research facility that was turned into a lodge for tourists. We could lie in our bed at night and take in the view of a volcano as it belched flames and molten rock above us. On the third day, I had an insatiable urge to climb the volcano. I was in my peek climbing condition. I knew there was an element of danger, but I couldn't contain my curiosity as to what conditions were like near the summit of the nearly five and half thousand foot mountain.

I headed out into the jungle and slowly up the mountain. I carried a handheld radio so I could communicate with Liz back at the hotel. It took me about thirty minutes to reach the "forbidden zone". There was a fence and a sign that read "Zona de Alta Peligrosidad". Loosely translated from the Spanish, it means, "Only idiots pass this sign and not all of those return."

Of course I hopped the fence and continued on with my climb. I finally got high enough that the jungle had been reduced to some scrub grasses and a few hardy trees that grew on the ridge lines. Everything else in the valleys had pretty well been beaten into submission by the heat and falling rocks. I stuck to a ridge and continued my ascent. Rocks the size of cars were being spit out of the crater above and came tumbling down the valleys on both sides of the ridge. There was no longer any vegetation, only ash and rock. The higher I climbed, the hotter it got. The rocks upon which I was climbing finally became so hot they began to burn me when I touched them. They heated the soles of my shoes. The air became not only hot, but unpleasant with an odor of sulphur. When I set out, I knew I wasn't going to get all the way to the crater itself – something about sticking your head into a volcano's flaming mouth. I did get within a few hundred feet of

Arenal discourages guests with frequent eruptions

the summit before even crazy people had the good sense to turn around and descend. I took in the scenery and set a path toward the lodge. The sound of massive boulders landing near me and tumbling to their ultimate repose was exuberating. I can still hear it in my memories as if it were yesterday.

Our next stop after Arenal was to be the quaint little mountain town of Monte Verde. Unfortunately, a group of terrorists from Nicaragua had invaded the town while we were at the volcano. They were attempting to withdraw money from a bank without having an account there. Army troops had closed off the roads to Monte Verde and no one was allowed in or out. The terrorists had killed some people and were holed up in the bank in the middle of town. The standoff ended after three days and we were finally allowed to depart for Monte Verde. When we arrived in town, it wasn't exactly "tourist ready". Army troops swarmed the bank where they had killed the terrorists the day before. They were more than a little antsy not knowing if more terrorists were hiding somewhere. As we drove by the bank I raised my camera to snap a picture. As I lifted it, three machine guns were immediately pointed in my direction. I concluded that after surviving the climb of an active volcano, there was no sense in dying in a fusillade of bullets just to snap a picture. Normally, Costa Rica is a wonderful place to visit filled with warm and friendly people. Terrorist attacks aren't the norm; we just happened to pick the wrong day.

Another bout with the "authorities" brought us a big boy's serving of excitement. I had visited the most famous of the Mayan ruins in the Yucatan Peninsula many times. I knew Chichen Itza extremely well. I had been offered a position as a scuba diver when the vast sacrificial cenóte was first excavated in the mid-1960's. I saw Chichen in the mid-1970s while it was still being unearthed, but had been developed enough to accommodate tourists. I was there again in the 1990s after they closed off the road used to traverse the center of the massive site. By the time I returned in 2004, the Mexican government had really commercialized Chichen Itza. I had arrived with my camera gear with the intent of getting some high quality pictures.

Much to my surprise, the entire archeological site had now been closed off to the public except for the hours of 8:00 a.m. until 10:00 p.m.

El Castillo, Chichen Itza's main pyramid

You had to buy tickets to enter and numerous restrictions existed to protect the site and/or maximize the government's income. The problem I faced was that to get some top quality pictures, I had to be at my selected locations before the sun rose in the sky and long before the 8:00 a.m. opening. As you no doubt realized when I passed the "Zona de Alto Peligrosidad", I have not always been one to be hobbled with minutia and trivial rules and regulations. With my knowledge of the lay of the land and Chichen Itza itself, I could run through the jungle before first light and enter Chichen in an unguarded and hopefully unfenced area. I could get my photos and be out long before it was opened to the public. That became my plan.

The following morning, Liz and I were in the jungle at 4:30 a.m. After a brisk twenty minute walk through the darkness, I was inside Chichen at first light. I had entered in the area of the "Temple of the Warriors" and was clicking away as the shadows grew shorter and the magic colors of the early morning slowly lost their magic. We left the way we came and by 7:00 a.m. were back at our little casita in the jungle adjacent to Chichen Itza. We enjoyed breakfast with our friends, Bob and Janet Quackenbush and by the time Chichen opened to the public, we were at the gate with tickets in hand and camera gear in tow.

We wandered for a couple hours snapping a few pictures here and there, but none with the quality I captured early in the morning. All was well until a man in a police uniform tapped me on the shoulder and asked for my permit. "Que licensia?" I asked. He said I was a professional photographer and that as such, I needed a special license to photograph the site.

"No soy profesional" I explained. "Soy tourista." Even though I was technically a professional, in this discussion I was going with pure amateur.

He explained that because I had a tripod strapped to my pack that made me a professional according to their definition. I argued at some length, but to no avail. I asked him how much it cost for the permit; perhaps it would be easier to buy one than to argue with this guy. When he told me it would cost the equivalent of nearly seven hundred dollars, I drew the line. I mean, what could he possibly do? Take me to jail?

He took me to jail! Liz came along with me even though she was free to go. She's such a nice girl. Nonetheless, the nice officer escorted us quite a distance to a complex near the main gate that had everything needed to run the operation including a police department and a jail. We were put in a cell with a nice, cool concrete floor and steel bars to keep us from escaping. We weren't charged formally. It was taking on a bit of an air of a good old fashioned shakedown. Once we paid the $700 for the license, we would be released.

I refused saying I wanted to meet with the commander or whoever was in charge of the entire operation. I was told the chief was in Merida a couple hours away and wouldn't be there until late that afternoon. I said I'd wait. We had a genuine Mexican standoff.

But as I sat on the floor of the cell (we lacked certain amenities, like something to sit on), I had a chilling thought. They had left me with my camera and the memory card contained the images I had captured by entering Chichen Itza illegally early that morning. If one of the guards came over and took the camera and took a look at the images, it would suddenly become a much more serious matter. I wouldn't need a $700 permit; I'd need the American consul and a good attorney. I sat facing the jailer and slipped the camera behind my back. While intently watching the guard sitting across the room, I fiddled with the camera behind my back trying to extricate the memory card that could be our ticket to the Mexican "big house" from the camera. As I struggled, Liz looked over and in a less than subtle voice asked, "What are you doing with the camera?"

The jailer looked our way and I looked Liz's way with eyes wide and an expression that strongly encouraged her to "run silent". I held perfectly still and the guard ultimately looked back down at his magazine. I did get the card out of the camera and hid it in my back pocket.

My ability to speak Spanish came in quite handy as the guy in charge worked on me every thirty or so minutes. With each attempt to strike a deal, the price for the permit and fine came down. With each refusal, I insisted I'd wait for the supreme commander's arrival. With each price reduction, I became increasingly convinced they'd played the game on other foreign visitors before. I also became convinced they were slowly coming to the realization that they had misjudged their target this time. They got one that knew the language, knew the culture and knew the ropes. They gradually seemed to understand their biggest challenge was to get rid of us before the commander arrived late that day. Finally, after a couple hours in the comandancia, the guy in charge threw up his hands in frustration. "Ok, we're going to let you go, but you can never come back to Chichen Itza. You're banned for life." He turned to the man who had originally detained us and told him to escort us back across Chichen Itza to the rear gate and give us the boot.

It was a long walk and as we began the trek, I began telling him a lengthy story. It would be the finest Spanish speech I had ever given. I told him a story about how a Mexican man had been traveling through my home town in Arizona when his car had broken down. I explained that the man didn't have a lot of money, had no place to stay and lacked the tools and parts to repair his car. I went on to tell him how I invited the man and his family into my home and towed his vehicle into my garage and gave him the tools and place to repair his car. I explained how I fed the man and his family for two days until he could finally leave. I explained to him that was how I treated foreign visitors where I lived.

I could see the officer softening. Finally, he stopped and threw his arms up into the air and told me that I could stay, but that I couldn't use my tripod. I thanked him and shook his hand. Unbeknownst to me, my friend, Bob Quackenbush, had waited outside the jail and was now following us as we were escorted out. When the officer turned and saw Bob, he saw that Bob had a backpack and that strapped to it was a tripod. The officer's face turned to one of pure amazement. Bob looked at him sheepishly and said, "I'm with them" as he pointed in our direction. The officer again threw his hands up into the air, hesitated and then briskly walked toward the jail. It was quite a day.

Looking back, I've had great fortune in traveling over much of the world to dozens of countries and cultures. I am much richer for the experiences. I've learned that people are people. I've learned that money doesn't buy happiness. I've seen that mankind generally means well, but that it may not be as equipped to deal with the future as it likes to believe it is. I've learned that every moment passes with no return and that every one of those moments can be used to enrich life. I've learned to try and put as many of those moments as possible into the "happy bucket". Without seeing so much of the world, I'm not sure I could have figured that out on my own.

Chapter Seven – Religion – Everyone's a Believer

Everyone is a believer. The only question is "In what?" There are people who believe the Chicago Cubs will someday win the World Series. That seems a little far-fetched, but I guess it's possible. Another question involving "religion" and "believers" is "Are the two words one-and-the-same?" Can someone have a religion and not be a believer? Can someone be a believer and not be associated with a religion. In my world, the two words are only distantly related. I know avowed atheists who are far more "Christian" than most Christians I know – at least if you judge on the basis of someone's actions rather than words.

Religious Upbringing - My grandfather Radcliffe was an ordained Methodist minister. Following World War I, he worked as a minister in Harlan County, Kentucky. My mother and her sisters were raised in a religious household. They attended church regularly. The older sister, Virginia, was a lifelong believer and raised her kids to be the same. I was extremely close with at least two of her four boys growing up, but now they are rabid, right-wing, evangelical Christians. We have little contact and what little there is quickly becomes fractious and subliminally acrimonious, i.e., we have virtually no respect for each other's world views. The second sister, Marion, was clearly an atheist. She got along with Virginia, but only because they didn't take on the topic of religion. My mother was third in line and was a believer of sorts and went to church in her early years. I suspect her belief system was built on a shaky foundation, but she probably shared Rene Descartes' belief that she'd better accept the preaching just in case. I'm not sure what the fourth sister, Priscilla, believed in other than food. She was rotund and worshipped regularly at the altar of the three layer cake. She could and did go either way – angel's food or devil's food and preferred the extra blessing of two scoops of ice cream.

I never knew anyone on my father's side of the family to attend church. About the strongest indicator in a belief in the supernatural I ever saw on the Jones side of the family was in my grandmother. She believed that if you forgot something, you had to sit down and count to ten and throw salt over your shoulder. I'm not sure what was to happen if you didn't do this, but it seemed to work for her. She also thought black cats were indeed bad luck. A rabbit's foot was good luck. Walking under a ladder was bad luck, especially if there was a sloppy painter on the ladder at the time. Crossing her fingers did truly help her win at bingo. My father believed cheating helped him win in pinochle.

I only brought up the subject of religion with my father once in my life. He believed there had to be something "bigger" out there. I suspect he was referring to my Aunt Priscilla. He said he believed there must be something, a greater power, but he didn't seem to believe it was anything that would be troubled by listening to someone's prayers for the Tigers to win the pennant or anything else for that matter. It was probably the engineer in his personality assuming that if a god did exist, he, she or it would be better off working on improving some of the imperfections in his existing creation rather than listening to the prayers of self-centered fools hoping for World Series tickets.

My grandparents on the Jones side listed their religions on legal documents like marriage licenses as either protestant or catholic, but I suspect it was more for "tribal compliance" than as a result of belief. On the Jones side of the family, Sunday's were dedicated to playing ball and drinking beer or to hunting and drinking beer or to fishing and drinking beer. Sometimes they would just drink beer; it was probably raining.

When I was little, my mother did her best to drag me to church. I went to Sunday school, but when I became older and wiser at the age of twelve or so, she took me into the big chapel with the adults. I'm not going to say it was a waste of time. I gained an appreciation of good quality stained glass work. I learned church music despite hating beyond description the singing of the hymns. I learned a lot about the Bible. I learned the prayers. I learned to tie a tie and put on a suitcoat. I hated it then and I hate it to this day, but I played the game. I listened to the homilies and learned the Ten Commandments. My favorite hymn was the one they always sang just before they adjourned.

To tell you the truth, it struck me as the supreme oxymoron to be old enough to look at Santa Claus with a critical eye and say, "Come on. It's silly to believe a fat dude with eight or nine (depending upon weather conditions) deer lands on your roof, crawls down your chimney with a bag full of goodies, slugs down your cookies and milk and flies off for a year" while at the same time saying with a straight face, "A virgin had a child that magically converted water into wine, died and came out of the cave to see his shadow and everyone lived happily ever after, but only if you fear this god that is love." Such were the teachings of my tribe, so I went along with them. But at that age, I didn't fully understand the concept of metaphor and I was truly having trouble buying this stuff literally. I played along.

When I got into high school, I became active in the Presbyterian Church in Northville. I was a true believer. I believed that Joyce Stoddard had a beautiful smile and monstrous tits. She also went to the Presbyterian Church so I did too. There was a "youth fellowship" group that met on Sunday nights. My mother would drop me off; she was undoubtedly happy that her son was such a good Christian boy. What she didn't realize was that I would go in and meet Janice Butler. We then walked a half block up the street to the movie theater, caught the latest on the big screen and returned to catch our rides home. My "devoutness" was directly tied to my hormone levels. It reminds me of the lyrics of "Walking in Memphis", a song written by Marc Cohn...

> *Now, Muriel plays piano*
> *Every Friday at the Hollywood*
> *And they brought me down to see her*
> *And they asked me if I would*
> *Do a little number*
> *And I sang with all my might*
> *She said, "Tell me are you a Christian, child?"*
> *And I said, "Ma'am, I am tonight!"*

When I ended up "going steady" with Kris Deibert, I came down with a case of "Lutheranisn". Chris Robinson was an Episcopalian and I was too. As my high school years passed, I gradually discovered there were other ways to get tight with the girls, so church lost its place in my world. But especially in my freshman year, I could bow my head with the best of them. Hallelujah!

Internally, I could never understand or accept the boogie-woogie aspect of the religious doctrine that was spooned out everywhere. When I was at my maternal grandparents' house for dinner, we bowed heads and prayed before our meals. Living on the farm in Ohio with my aunt Virginia, we went to the Methodist Church every Sunday. It was there I first had a real epiphany. I came to fully grasp and believe in the concept of consummate boredom. And the damn seats were as uncomfortable as the service was long. We prayed before every meal and thanked god for the food. I never could understand why we didn't thank my Uncle Lloyd; he was the one out on the tractor working the fields twelve hours every day. I guess that's the beauty of religion; it teaches you how to accept things that make absolutely no sense whatsoever. In fact, religion is the home of the "miracle". Checking the very definition of the word miracle pretty well sums it up: *"an event not explicable by natural or scientific laws."* In other words, a miracle is something which happens that can't happen. And I'm supposed to believe in that? Now that would be a miracle.

As My Religious Views Matured, I became increasingly comfortable in my realization that religion existed, but its supernatural content was pure fairy tale. As a result of my travels and periodic immersion into other cultures, I observed that all of them have their systems of religious belief. I have long been intrigued by the commonalities and differences between the various systems. I'm not sure if it's the chicken or it's the egg, but my lifelong interest in cultural anthropology has provided me immense pleasures of discovery that continue to this day. There have been countless books written on the subject (many of which sit on the shelves five feet to my side), but I'll try and resist the urge to delve into the subject beyond what's justified in a document of this nature. I'll just summarize my view in this way.

There are things the human mind can grasp and understand. There are other things that are far beyond the capacity of a finite human mind. It is in the realm of the incomprehensible that religion exists. One group of people, probably the majority of the human race, feels compelled to understand the incomprehensible. To this end they invent a solution. It is called God. If they don't understand why their children die from a cruel disease, they have a ready and "sensible" explanation – it was God's will. Even then they suffer. "Why would a loving God punish an innocent child?" Well, it's really quite simple. "God works in mysterious ways." Oh thanks – now it makes sense.

There are those that argue for the "god gene". They hypothesize that a belief in the supernatural has evolved right along with everything else that makes us human. View it as an evolutionary answer to the unanswerable, life's "get out of jail free" card. I wouldn't be surprised if that was the case. There is clearly survival value in getting the answers to questions. For example, I'm wondering what I'm going to have for dinner tonight. If I didn't answer that question on a fairly consistent basis, I would perish. So for some, all questions must have answers. "God!" The wildcard – when an answer doesn't exist or can't be found, play the god card and everything fits. Ah, the greatest tranquilizer history has ever known.

There are others – such as me – who don't need to have the answer to every question that can be conjured up by an uncorralled mind. Some questions simply do not have answers. I'm not going to lose any sleep over them. There are equations in mathematics that do not have solutions. As a mathematician, I'm not troubled by that reality in the least. I'm also smart enough to know I'm not going to waste a lot of my time looking for solutions to those equations.

Life is full of these imponderables. What happened "in the beginning"? In the beginning of what? What happened just before the beginning?

Who created us? To me this is a totally nonsensical question. First of all, it is generally phrased as "who" as opposed to "what" created us. The use of the word "who" in the question suggests mankind runs with unbridled arrogance and unlimited ignorance. My question is "Why did 'someone' have to create us?" If it has to be "who", then "who" created the who who created us? There clearly is no answer to this recursive question. For me, there doesn't need to be one. For a lot of evangelicals, they'd implode if they couldn't play the god card on this one.

Another one of the imponderables, but taken to a ridiculous and illogical extreme involves a "proof" that an omniscient "creator" exists. It involves a hypothetical pocket watch and the complexity of the human being. They argue that mankind is far too complex to not have a creator. They invoke a nonsensical metaphor. "What if you were walking down a beach and in the sand, you find a wristwatch?" They suggest that the watch is far too complex to have just appeared. It had to have been created by someone. Mr. Evangelical sayeth, "So it is with mankind. It couldn't have just appeared. It had to have been created by someone." I hate to break it to them, but the watch "evolved" from its creator (a horologist in Cleveland) who evolved from his ancestors both recent and distant. It doesn't mean god dropped his watch in the sand. The general explanation for the watch is patently obvious. For those with an education, the explanation for mankind is also patently obvious. We don't have the minute details for either case, but science looks for and finds the history of mankind continuously. We don't give a damn about the watch; we just buy another one. They're cheap.

For me, it is sufficient to say that today's world is related to and dependent upon the world of yesterday. I'm pretty confident that tomorrow will be impacted by today. I accept that. I don't let it keep me awake at night. I enjoy and appreciate the wonder of the world around me every day, but I don't need to invent a god to explain it. I'm in the company of some pretty good thinkers that share that belief, people like Albert Einstein, Steven Hawking, Carl Sagan, a disproportionately high percentage of scientists, countless great writers, philosophers and thinkers. The works of

Bart Ehrman are well worth reading. He began his life as a devout Christian and graduated from the Moody Bible Institute and the Princeton Theological Seminary. He is one of the most studied biblical scholars in the world. But the more he studied the Bible, the more he concluded atheism was the only rational view of reality.

For those with the god gene, I respect their need to believe. It's totally understandable to me. It's part of our heritage and our "tribe". Religious belief is interwoven throughout society. It's a reality and can't be denied, but so is a tradition of non-belief in a paternal god who needs the existence of a miracle to make sense out of things.

As a metaphor for living, religion can have great value. However, the biblical literalists – in my view – should pursue careers that are more dependent upon manual labor or repetitive actions of some kind and where cogent, prescient thought processes are not a priority.

I'll share one story on how god does indeed work in mysterious ways. Liz and I were spending a week in an extremely remote area in the southwestern part of the State of Chihuahua, Mexico. The village of Areponapuchi is extremely small and poor. There is a tiny Catholic Church in this village where essentially all the villagers are Catholic. The people are too poor and the population too sparse to justify a priest so the 500 or so square foot adobe church sits empty and open. There are no doors. The Tarahumara Indians live in the canyons below the village.

In my travels around the world, I learned to appreciate the architecture and history of the Catholic Church. Liz and I walked down the mountainside from the cabin in which we were staying and entered the church. We took in the sights and as we prepared to leave, I noted a collection basket on the altar. As I often do, I thought I'd leave a couple dollars in the basket. I had received value and pleasure in the visit and felt a quid-pro-quo need to pay my price of admission. I hoped it could be used to help the needy parishioners.

We began scaling the steep hillside that took us back to our cabin. Half way up the hill, I looked back and saw a Tarahumara woman looking older than her years with two young children in tow headed toward the church. We turned and watched. We could clearly see them inside through the doorless church. I had my camera with a 300 mm telephoto lens and used it like a telescope to look closer.

The young woman knelt and prayed. The two boys, maybe five or six years old, roamed the room until one of them saw the basket and picked it up. When he saw the money, he ran to his mother and excitedly showed her the contents. She looked at it and paused. She then looked slowly in all directions and slipped the money into her pocket.

"She's stealing the money" I said to Liz. As the woman walked briskly toward the door, it dawned on me. I had left the money with the hope that the church would help the needy. It had worked. I just didn't expect it to happen so quickly. God apparently does work in mysterious ways.

Chapter Eight – Tugboats and Lighthouses

Having lived in places where huge ocean going vessels were commonplace, we often watched as ships tried to enter areas where space was limited. The big ships aren't overly maneuverable in tight spaces. They often had to be flanked by powerful tug boats that nudged them in one direction or another to keep them from running aground. So it is with ourselves. As we traverse the oceans of life, we're often in jeopardy of getting lost or running aground. We all have people who have given us a nudge when we needed it, those who served as beacons of light as we traversed the dark nights of our lives.

I'm no exception; many people have influenced me, some more than others. Some set out to influence and guide me and worked hard to do so. Others helped guide me through challenging times and to this day, probably have no clue as to their impact on the course of my life. It goes without saying that parents and close relatives have such an impact so I'll keep those references to a minimum. Here are a few of the people that truly helped me alter course, sometimes while in dangerous waters.

Edward Mollema was a history teacher at Northville High School. I had to take his classes on world history, U.S. history and U.S. Government. The guy knew his stuff and he loved it. At the time I took his classes, I never would have dreamed that I would even remember his name beyond high school, let alone rely on his teachings nearly every day of my life. I truly don't understand why he made such a tremendous impact on me. At that time, I had no particular interest in history; it was far down on my list of priorities. When I was in the Honors College at Michigan State, I could and did waive any and all requirements for history courses. I didn't think they were important, let alone interesting.

Somehow, Mr. Mollema without knowing so planted the seed that would later in my life sprout into a tree of learning that would give me endless hours of joy. By the time I was in my thirties, I had fallen in love with history. I read voraciously. To this day, history serves the same purpose in my life that religion does in the lives of others; it gives me the "answers" as to why things happened the way they did. And by extension, it gives me insights into why they will happen in the future. I remember as if it was yesterday why the "flying buttress" was a great architectural advance in the Middle Ages. It's fresh in my mind why the Alsace-Lorraine area was so important in World War II. I could go on and on about the lessons I remember coming from Mr. Mollema. For some unknown reason, either through his teaching methods or the force of his personality or his love for history, he made a huge impact on me that would stay with me throughout my years. If he were alive today, I would give him a hug that would go down in history.

Armando Delicato was another history teacher. I only took one class from Mr. Delicato. After a hiatus in the world of news reporting, I returned to college. My first year back in school, I enrolled in some of the more basic courses to "refresh" the mind and ready myself for the academic life in a major university. Mr. Delicato taught a class on world history. Unlike the case with Mr. Mollema, I frankly don't remember a single lecture from Mr. Delicato's class. However, two factors came together simultaneously that made my experience in his class life-changing. The first was that after a few years of life in the real world, I was ready to apply myself to learning. I had an insatiable hunger. Learning had become something I wanted to do, not something I had to do.

Mr. Delicato fanned the flames of that desire to learn by encouraging me to view things differently. The text book described the situation from the perspective of the author, but I was encouraged to view them from a completely different angle. I was encouraged to research the events in an attempt to support my position. Given my previous experiences with the educational system, I had been taught I was to learn and regurgitate what I had read or been told. Those were the "correct" answers. Mr. Delicato showed me the answer is dependent upon the perspective of the viewer. If the conquest of the American West was to be described from the vantage point of a Navajo Indian, it would definitely have some different perspectives. Mr. Delicato allowed and encouraged me to "think", to look at both or all sides of an issue. He made history interesting and fun. I owe him a debt of gratitude.

Bruce Dayton was a high school classmate. Bruce was generally liked by everyone, but he wasn't at the top of the "popularity" list. Bruce was a decent athlete, but he wasn't one of the "gifted" ones. Bruce earned respectable grades, but he wasn't even close to National Honor Society quality. Bruce was just ... Bruce, a nice guy. As a freshman, Bruce went out for the football team. He made the team in large part because he had mass and could fog a mirror. Whatever was the last string, third or fourth, Bruce was on it. Every Monday through Thursday, we practiced. The first stringers scrimmaged against the fourth stringers. Four afternoons every week during the football season, we kicked the living hell out of the fourth stringers. We bloodied their noses and delighted in decorating them with bumps and bruises. Many came to the realization their futures didn't lay on the gridiron and they eschewed spending time in the hospital, so they quit. Bruce stuck it out. Friday night would roll around and we played under the lights in front of the cheering crowd. Bruce got to wear a uniform, but his greatest risk was picking up a splinter in his ass from sitting on the bench.

During the sophomore year, Bruce did it again. He was pummeled four days a week and rode the bench Friday night. He didn't quit. The first team got all the glory. The cheerleaders and "Pep Club" would make signs and tape them on the lockers of the starters. We were introduced to the crowd at pep rallies before the games. Bruce kept the bench warm on Friday nights and bled Monday through Friday.

Bruce did this in his junior year and his senior year. He never made first string. I don't think he ever got into the game until his senior year and then only when we had already demolished our opponents and the outcome was no longer in doubt. Bruce spent four years without the glory and cheers. He took his lumps. He never complained. He never gave up. He never quit. To this day, if I get the urge to turn and walk away from something because it's tough or not as rewarding as I had hoped, I remember Bruce Dayton. If you make a commitment to something, you stick it out. You suck it up and remain true to your teammates and more importantly, you remain true to yourself. This attitude has served me well over the years. I know how important it is in life because Bruce Dayton taught me. Most people have forgotten my exploits on the gridiron fifty years ago. But I remember Bruce Dayton.

Carl Cooper was a professor of Chemical Engineering at Michigan State University. He was a diminutive man perhaps five foot four or five. I doubt he weighed 130 pounds. I can assure you that if Carl was ever challenged to a fist fight, he was not the winner. He was meek and quiet. I'm certain Dr. Cooper's I.Q. was somewhere in the immeasurable clouds of Einstein. He was brilliant. I took a number of classes from Dr. Cooper and he was inspirational and effective. I remember walking down the hall of the Engineering Building at M.S.U. carrying a box of computer punch cards. I had perhaps 400 cards in my deck. They were intended to run a program that would solve some mathematical problem we had been assigned. Dr. Cooper came slowly toward me hugging the wall as he walked as if trying to be invisible. He had a stack of cards in his hand and was rhythmically slapping his thigh with them as he strolled down the hall. There were probably twenty to twenty-five cards in his deck which had been designed to solve the same problem for which I was carrying 400 cards. If I had really tried, perhaps I could have reduced my card count by twenty or so cards, but it was unfathomable to me how it could be done with the deck Dr. Cooper carried. He was a genius.

At least I'm pretty sure he was a genius. Now that I think of it, he never – not once – answered a question I asked. In every single instance over my three years at Michigan State, he responded to my question with a question of his own. His question was cryptic and merely served to get me to think about my question from a different perspective. He made me step back, simplify the challenge and rethink it. He encouraged me to think critically and analytically. To this day, I'm pretty confident Dr. Carl Cooper was brilliant, but in that he never answered a question, I guess it's possible he never knew the answers himself. Somehow I doubt that's the case. But even if it is, he still taught me how to think and you'd have to be brilliant to get me thinking clearly.

Bill Fischer is my cousin. He is the son of my mother's sister, Virginia. Bill is four years my senior and when we were boys Bill was a hero to me. He was fearless and tough. The more dangerous and adventuresome the challenge, the wider his contagious grin grew. On one occasion on the farm in Canal Winchester, he had rounded up a motorcycle. He and Stanley, a friend, were riding through a field a mile from the house. They ran it into a hollow and the bike went airborne. Stanley broke his leg. The bike landed on Bill and the brake lever on the handlebar punctured his lung. With his hand tightly held against the wound, Bill walked home to get help for Stanley. His toughness and thirst for adventure carried him throughout his career as a jet fighter pilot.

It was Bill that encouraged me to attempt difficult dives into the swimming pool or lake that ultimately earned me an athletic scholarship in college. It was Bill that dared me to push myself beyond what I perceived as my limits. It was Bill that taught me you're not defeated until you quit. There was one particular incident I vividly recall as if it happened yesterday.

It was one of the summers I lived on the farm in Ohio. Bill was taking a summer school class. The school bus dropped him off in the mid-afternoon and he'd walk the quarter mile or so up the road to the house. I would sometimes meet him at the bus stop and walk along with him. I'm guessing I was seven or eight and his was eleven or twelve. As we walked down the tree lined lane, we approached the fence that kept the animals in. Bill had his books and papers under his arm as we approached the gate. "I can jump over the gate" he said as if challenging himself. "Want to see?"

Bill broke into a run and headed full speed toward the gate. I'm guessing he jumped roughly three feet eleven and a half inches into the air. This would have been a great effort had the fence not been four feet high. Bill landed face down on the road. His books and papers scattered to the winds. Bill stood up, brushed himself off and began gathering his books and papers. He was bleeding from both arms and from his forehead. Most kids would have gone directly to the house to lick their wounds.

Once Bill had collected his belongings, he went to the corner of the gate, laid down his school materials and walked briskly back to his original starting point. He said not a word. He broke into a run and with a determination that would not be denied, he cleared the gate with room to spare. He turned to me, smiled, picked up his books and we walked on to the house. Bill had that attitude that was characterized in the old movie Blazing Saddles when someone said about Mongo, "Don't shoot him; you'll just make him mad." He made a huge impact on me that day and many of the successes I've enjoyed in my life are no doubt related to Bill and that pesky fence.

Jeff Pastorino was crazy. I don't mean like "a wild and crazy guy". I mean he was nuts. He was a schizophrenic who had been institutionalized more than once and most assuredly, he was subjected to electro-shock therapy where they cooked bits of his brain. He walked into Point Loma, California one day, sat down on a bench and stayed there for twenty years. He never asked for anything, never bothered anyone and never engaged anyone in discussion. In fact, he would always look away if anyone even came close. He sat on that bench every single day, rain or shine, for twenty years. He died on the bench.

I used to walk by the bench nearly every day for three or four years. I wondered what could possibly be going through the mind of someone like Jeff. (At the time, I didn't know his name; no one in the neighborhood did.) My curiosity got the best of me over time and I vowed I was going to find out. (Thanks to Bill's gate, I wasn't to be denied.) Over the course of many months, I gradually got Jeff to wave back to me when I waved at him early in the morning. It was an arduous process, but after a couple years, I became Jeff's best friend. We had many discussions. They were always interesting to say the least. They would frequently start off in a seemingly "normal" manner, but after two or three sentences, Jeff's schizophrenia would hijack the train and I'd never know what planet I was off to or in what giant conspiracy I was about to become entangled.

Jeff was mentally damaged. He didn't choose to be crazy. He was only playing the hand he had been dealt. He was a fundamentally good person. He meant no evil. He was simply another human being who had some challenges in life that few of us could deal with as effectively as did he.

Jeff opened my eyes to the reality that the homeless and disenfranchised members of our society are people just like we are. They may be different in many ways, but they're still human beings and deserving of the same courtesies and consideration we all hope to receive from others. After I got to know Jeff, I never again viewed the homeless and those down on their luck in the way I had in the past. Obviously, I have chosen my path in life. Others may not have the same choices. I no longer look down on them with contempt.

When Jeff died, no one knew his name. No one knew his history. Everyone seemed to have a theory, but no one knew. I felt that if I had become his only friend, I owed it to him to bring a sense of closure to his existence. Liz and I did exhaustive research and finally found Jeff's history. It turned into a huge story in San Diego, appeared "above the fold" on the front page of the San Diego Union Tribute – twice. It was featured on NPR radio and San Diego television. I wrote a book about Jeff Pastorino. "The Man on the Bench" (ISBN 978-0-9845545-0-8) is available on Amazon, Barnes and Noble and other fine booksellers. The book tells the amazing story of Jeff's path to the bench. The amazing events following his death opened the eyes of many San Diegans, but none more than mine.

Jim McCarty was one of the most amazing men I've ever known. I may be right on the fringe of violating my self-imposed rule of "no immediate family" in this discussion. Jim was my father-in-law, Liz's father. Jim was truly an enigma. He came from the humblest of backgrounds. His father was a construction worker who followed the jobs. In the Depression years, Jim was a cute, charismatic little boy who sometimes made more money with his smile selling apples on the streets than his father did working as a construction laborer. He was the third of four children and the only boy.

When Jim got out of the Navy, he married a woman who apparently looked down her nose at him because of lack of "financial status". When she left him shortly after they were married, he suffered a wound that would never completely heal. He spent the rest of his life proving to himself and to the world that he could be financially successful. He succeeded beyond even his own wildest dreams. No one would ever look down on him as being financially "unworthy" again. He became so successful that the Museum of the White Mountains has a room dedicated to Jim's contributions to the growth of the area. He lived in a world with yachts, airplanes, hotels, water companies, real estate developments, banks, restaurants and myriad other business ventures. Yet, in spite of his immense success in the business world, Jim never abandoned his humble roots. I used to only half joke about how you could take Jim and put him in a line-up with a half dozen homeless men and no one could pick him out as the multi-millionaire. He wore his boots, jeans and western shirts to the end. He drove a well-worn pickup truck all the time. When Sam Walton of WalMart fame came to Show Low to buy land from Jim, the two of them drove around in Jim's seasoned truck and hit it off famously like they'd been friends for life. I remember going into The Waterfront, a famous old bar in San Diego with Jim. One of the patrons saw Jim and thought he was down on his luck. "Hey buddy. Can I buy you a beer" said the generous customer. Not one to pass up an opportunity, Jim graciously accepted. If the guy had only known that Jim could have just as easily bought the entire bar out of pocket change, he would have been more than shocked.

After the bitter collapse of his brief first marriage, he came to Show Low to work on a construction project. There he met and married Doris Kay, Liz's mother. After I married Liz and had begun to feel comfortable with my growing friendship with Jim, I approached him.

"Jim, you've obviously had a lot of success financially. If you were to distill your success down to one bit of advice, what would it be?"

He took my question seriously – as he should have; I was serious. He thought about it for a long minute. Finally, he looked at me and said, "Think about how to make something work. Too many people think about the reasons something won't work. Successful people come up with ways to make it work."

I tried to put his advice to work in my life and judging from where I sit today, it must have served me fairly well. But over the years I knew Jim, he showed me a lot more than he ever told me. He was a master at identifying a person's greatest strengths and using them to his advantage. It was an approach that often allowed someone else to succeed to Jim's advantage. It was (usually) a win-win arrangement.

Jim had an uncanny knack for keeping business and pleasure separate. When in his mind an activity was "business", he was a cheapskate, a skin-flint of the highest order. In his business operations, he was the last to give up rotary dial phones. When fax machines were relatively new, he would send an employee over to our offices to fax when necessary rather than buy his own fax machine. He had eight-track tapes long into the digital music era. He finally gave in to the need for a copy machine, but it was a thermal copier. He "duplexed" by saving previous copies and printing on the back side of the paper. We used to joke that when vehicles were first equipped with airbags, he opted for the manual version where just before impact, you had to inflate them by blowing into the filling tube. He was strict in keeping business and pleasure separate. I recall one time where a man was willing to pay him a few hundred thousands of dollars for a piece of property, but could only meet him on a Saturday. Jim told the man, "I don't work on Saturdays" and the deal never came to pass.

When he was "off the clock" and into the world of pleasure, Jim spent money like a drunken sailor (which at times, he was). Between his Show Low house and his house in Tempe, he had well over a quarter million dollars tied up in his barbeque areas – this at a time when the average house cost less than a hundred thousand dollars. Jim loved to party. Some of us contend he only went to one party in his life. It started when he was about fifteen and he never left it. He picked up the nickname of "the Energizer Bunny" because no one could possibly keep up with him in a party atmosphere. Liz and I made a legitimate effort to do it one time in San Diego and failed dismally.

Jim set an interesting example with regard to family relations. He believed that no matter what happened, family was family. Regardless of how acrimonious the conflict or argument, Jim gave no quarter to those who would harbor a grudge toward family members. He had family members with whom he didn't have much in common and few shared viewpoints, but they were family. They were never excluded from events or consideration of any kind. When Jim died, he had left a will that split his estate between the mother of his children, his three sisters, his concubine, his three daughters and each of his six grandchildren. Unfortunately, between a collapse of the economy and an outrageously aggressive I.R.S., the concubine was the only person to truly receive anything. However, the message was clear – family came first, followed by family and then finally – family.

Chapter Nine – Siblings

For the first five years of my life, I was an only child. For most of those years, we lived with my doting grandparents so it's probably safe to say, I was spoiled rotten for five good years. In 1952, Brian Clay Jones arrived. Two years later, Jeff Francis Jones came into this world. For the rest of my life, I experienced the joys, the challenges and the tribulations of having to interact, share and get along with two brothers.

For as long as mankind has left its footprints somewhere on the planet, siblings have been the source of social adjustment, learning and growth for nearly everyone. I certainly wasn't an exception to the rule. Even though I was two months shy of my fifth birthday, I still remember the first day Brian was home from Providence Hospital in Detroit where he was born. I wanted to see this "thing" that was my brother. He was wrapped in a white blanket, an expressionless form looking eerily similar to a human being. I didn't have the first clue as to how to react or interface with a new born brother. I would have the next seven decades to figure it out. I'm still working on it.

It was perhaps ten weeks or so after Brian was at home on Moss Street when we experienced our first bit of sibling trauma. My mother had acquired a little seat designed for infants. It was canvas and was stitched onto a metal frame. A little tray sat in the front where a toy or bottle could sit. The metal frame was "C" shaped such that it acted like a spring. If the infant wanted to exercise its budding skills as a daredevil, it could use its little legs to bounce the seat. Brian wasn't real adept at bouncing himself in the chair, but would grin wildly when my mother or father lightly bounced the chair for him.

One day, my mother put the chair and Brian who was inside it onto a coffee table in the living room. She left the room, probably to round up a bottle for Brian. I tried my hand at giving him a bounce or two. He grinned. I gave him another bounce and he grinned all the wider. There's something innate where most human beings get pleasure by pleasuring others. Even at the ripe old age of five, I was pleased that I was pleasing Brian. With a little bigger bounce, his grin grew into a laugh. With a bounce that was bigger yet, I discovered the concept of the "catapult". I accidentally launched Brian into the air in an arch big enough to clear the boundaries of the table. I still remember the sound a young head makes as it bounces off a hardwood floor. Brian screamed and cried. My mother came running. After a fuss of the fourth order, everyone including Brian settled down and everything with the possible exception of my psyche returned to some semblance of order. Brian didn't seem to suffer any permanent damage, but in retrospect, I'm not certain that was the case. Brian's thought processes in the ensuing years frequently defied logic and explanation. It's not out of the question I contributed to the situation.

The Jones boys – Jeff, Howard and Brian

As the years went by, the three boys grew into their rolls as brothers. Being five years older than Brian and seven years in front of Jeff, I was the dominant brother in all accounts. There are countless books on birth order and its impact on personality development; I've read a few of them. In many respects, we fit the mold. As the oldest child, it was my job to be the trail blazer, the one who taught the parents how to be parents. Don't forget, kids don't come with instruction manuals and a lot of parenting is trial-and-error. I was the test case. As the middle child, Brian seemed to be pre-destined to try and do everything differently. As the youngest, it was incumbent on Jeff to take full advantage of having two older siblings. He was also the political swing-vote whenever there was a dispute between Brian and me. On countless occasions, Jeff would be called to settle a dispute. He carefully weighed all of the facts and evidence and invariably sided with the brother that was substantially larger and better able to kick the crap out of him if he sided with the evil middle child. I must say that I was up to the task. As the oldest of three boys raised in a family where Dad was Mr. Macho Muscle Man, it was my job to be the bully of the younger brothers, but only when necessary.

For the most part, the three of us got along. Jeff and I seemed to have a lot in common despite our seven year age difference. We both had the good fortune of being very accomplished athletes especially on the baseball field and hockey rinks. Jeff might have been as good as I was in football, but by the time he reached high school age, his priorities weren't focused on the football field. We were both pretty quick mentally with keen wits and strong deductive capabilities. With all that said, Brian wasn't. His skillsets developed in different areas. He played some baseball, but without getting close to the level of accomplishment Jeff and I attained. He didn't play football or hockey. He did wrestle in high school and did very well. The question is "Why?" Here's my theory.

Brian had an older brother that could be out-and-out mean to him. I spent a significant amount of time thumping Brian as we grew up. If we got into a feud that ultimately ended in a physical confrontation, a five year growth advantage is all but impossible to overcome without a gun and murder was frowned upon in our household. Brian always came out on the losing side of the confrontations. He dreamed of the day when he would be old enough to settle the score. This isn't simply speculation on my part. He gravitated toward the martial arts. Not only did he become a very accomplished wrestler, he ended up with Black Belts in Taikwondo, Karate and Jiu Jitsu or Judo. As he became increasingly proficient in the marshall arts, I still managed to press his hot button with some regularity. Getting him mad was sort of like trying to better a previous record.

I will never forget a particular confrontation we had after I had left home and he was a senior in high school. I was at the old house in Northville. I don't recall the specific source of the conflagration, but it must have been a good one. I got him so riled up that he was completely out of control. He was shirtless and as we stood just outside the door leading into the garage, his anger reached a crescendo never before witnessed. He was trembling. Tears rolled down his face. His fists were clenched. His face red as a beet as he said in a quivering voice saturated with rage, "So help me Howard. When I get bigger, I'm going to kick your ass."

I stared at him and saw someone who was already taller and weighed nearly as much as did I. Even though I was pretty fit myself at that point, I looked at his body as it flared out like that of a flying squirrel. His musculature should have been on the

Brian "in flight" with a kick

cover of a weightlifting magazine. He knew tricks from wrestling and his other marshall arts that he could have used to tie me in pretzel knots in an instant. I knew that if he made a move, he could have avenged every beating I'd administered over the past fifteen years in the blink of an eye. I knew I was toast, but fortunately, he didn't know it. It hadn't dawned on him that at that point, he was bigger, tougher and more dangerous that I had ever been or would ever be. I slowly back away, got in my car and drove away. Fortunately I got away before he realized the tide had turned. I never pressed his button again.

It's probably normal that the oldest child and the next oldest have conflicts as they grow up. Brian was more vulnerable in the eyes of my mother so she was more protective of him. As a result, he would get away with things for which I would be chastised. In the grade school years when my father actually ate dinner with the family most of the time, I was always held to a high standard of etiquette at the table. Heaven help the guy that didn't sit up straight and eat his dinner with some semblance of civility as defined by my father. If I happened to chew something with my mouth open, the gates of hell opened up directly in front of me. I learned that such behavior would bring negative consequences and just like Pavlov's dogs, I was a quick learner. Brian on the other hand would chew his food as if he was eating at the trough along with a 4-H Club ribbon winning pig. Nothing was said to Brian. This confused me and I would let it get to me. "Chew with your mouth closed" I would bark at Brian.

"Mind your own business" my father would say to me. Frankly, it pissed me off. If I complained about the apparent injustice, my mother told me Brian had a breathing problem that prevented him from doing so. I was the child with a touch of asthma and I had to eat like a West Point cadet. Brian showed no signs of nasal problems to me, but was allowed to snort and grunt like a farm animal. As silly as it sounds, this grew into a source of envy and friction over time. It seemed like Brian was always defended by my mother for the same transgressions against social decency that would have put me in my room for the night. But such perceived inequities tend to be remedied over time. Remember, I was five years older and five years bigger than Brian.

Looking back on it, some of the things I did to Brian were just plain mean. In the 1950's and early 60's, firecrackers were legal in Michigan. M-80s were supposedly the equivalent of about a twentieth of a stick of dynamite. They were loud and extremely dangerous. Some company came out with a fake M-80. It looked identical to the red cylinder of the actual M-80, but had no powder inside. It was outfitted with a real fuse. I remember one summer taking one of these fake M-80s, lighting the fuse and quickly grabbing Brian. I swung him around and held him face down over the fake explosive as the fuse burned down. I'm not particularly proud of that act, but it happened. I'm not sure what it proves other than young boys can be very mean and that Brian should have chewed with his mouth closed.

When Brian and Jeff got old enough to throw a ball and sometimes even catch it, I would coerce them into playing baseball every chance we'd get. Brian was the reluctant player; Jeff took to baseball like a duck to water. Even though he was two years his junior, Jeff began outplaying Brian at an early age. This resulted in another alliance of sorts where we'd best Brian on the ball field and Brian felt like the odd-man-out. Brian seemed to be somewhat of the outcast at the lake during summers as well. In large part, I suspect it was because he had a very fair complexion and was extremely prone to sunburn. Regardless of the reason, he was again on the outside looking in. Whether Brian tended to seek other pursuits because he lacked the competitiveness of Jeff and me or he lacked the competitiveness because he was prone to other pursuits is a matter of conjecture. The fact remains he was the stereotypical "middle child" and had to be "different".

One of the earliest signs of his need to go against the flow came to pass around the New Year of 1958. My father's sister, Jackie Lou and her husband had left Detroit and moved to Phoenix, Arizona. They were trying to convince my father to follow them to Phoenix. We went to Phoenix for Christmas of 1957 and to welcome in the New Year. Brian was not quite five, yet he insisted he didn't want to go with us. He ended up staying with my maternal grandparents while Jeff and I rode in the backseat across the country to look at life in Arizona. It was more time for Jeff and I to bond and for Brian to become odd-man-out.

Brian took another hit to the head when in 1958 we were riding in the backseat of my mother's "new" 1948 four-door Dodge.

We were part way up the block on Griggs Street in Detroit headed for home when Brian decided to experiment with a lever. Unfortunately, the lever he tested was the door handle. One instant, he was sitting in the seat – the next instant he was gone. He had opened the door and fallen into the street. Luckily, he bounced away from the car and didn't end up under the wheels, but unluckily, he had taken another shot to the head.

Despite the frequent trouble-making on my part, for the most part, we all got along pretty well (except when we didn't). Like all brothers, we spent a lot of time together. Jeff and I seemed to follow similar paths while Brian often headed off on a road less travelled. The older he got the more intent he seemed to be on being contrary on pretty much anything and everything he did.

In our college years, we all had the advantage of having a father who owned a successful commercial construction business. We had first crack at high paying summer jobs in the field. We were expected to work hard and we worked hard on devising schemes to hardly work. They didn't always work.

It was when we worked for our father that another aspect of Brian's contrarianism came to the fore. Frank was a member of Plum Hollow Country Club, a prestigious private club just north of Detroit. From time-to-time, I would join my father for a round of golf. He loved the notoriety of being the big shot at the club, at least in the eyes of his sons. He also loved to put on a hyper-theatrical display of how he would beat me in golf (if he did) and how he was doling out alms to the poor by bringing his underprivileged sons to the club occasionally. I made it a point to always go into the pro shop after a round of golf and buy something. It might be a golf glove, a shirt or even a new pair of golf shoes. I charged it to my father's account. I did this not so much because I needed or wanted the item I purchased; I did it for the sole purpose of giving my father the joy of putting on a hyperbolic display of outrage that night at dinner. He got to play the role of the magnanimous benefactor and supporter of the poor and he played his part well. He loved it more than you could possibly imagine.

Brian was not content working in the construction world. He wasn't content with the way our father ran the business. Brian always had "better ideas" on how things should be done. Brian came to me with his complaints about how Frank was running "his" show. I tried to tell Brian that Frank had earned the right to run the business in whatever manner he thought fit. I encouraged Brian to not only accept that, but to go the extra mile to make Frank feel that he was in fact the commander-in-chief when it came to the company – if not the family. I related the story about charging things to Frank's account at Plum Hollow and how my feigned abuse made him feel important. As had been the case in times past and would prove to be the case for the next half century, the "message" from the story flew well over Brian's head. He didn't grasp anything I was trying to tell him.

Brian was going through a particularly tumultuous time with Frank. One afternoon, the situation erupted in the office. Brian had his feelings hurt and blew up at my father. He was out of control and said anything that fell from his head as long as it was hurtful toward my father. There must have been a bus coming down the street about that time because Brian threw me under it. In an effort to hurt my father, Brian gave him his interpretation of the story I had told him about the club. Brian said I charged things at the club just to screw my father out of money and that I was callously using him for my own personal gain. It never dawned on Brian that in putting his own perverted bent on the story he was hurting both my father and me. To Brian at that moment, loyalty to family and friends was a bankrupt currency. He threw me under the bus like a gum wrapper with no thought or concern as to the consequences of his actions. Sadly, I discovered this was not to be the last time Brian tossed kin into the dumpster to serve his own needs.

My father approached me about the things Brian had said. He was clearly hurt by the words and the perception that I was shamefully using him. We had a lengthy discussion and after I explained to him everything I've written in the previous paragraphs with regard to my motives, the air cleared and our relationship was exorcised of the demons Brian had brought into it. Although, he never knew it, Brian's relationship with Frank was not unchanged. Some irreparable damage had been done. My relationship with Brian in the wake of the incident also suffered some damage. It took a while to put it behind us. It has been forgiven, but obviously, it hasn't been forgotten.

No person on the planet is more similar from a genetic standpoint than a sibling. In most cases, no people share a more common set of personality building experiences than siblings. It shouldn't come as a surprise that siblings make assumptions that they have nearly everything in common. They tend to assume they think alike, believe alike and feel alike. These assumptions can get people in trouble.

Jeff and I were very close growing up and well into our adult lives. We're close to this day. However, something happened when I was in my mid-forties. To this day, I'm not sure if it was something I said or something I did. I'm unaware of anything that would justify a reaction where one brother doesn't speak to the other for fourteen years, but that's what happened. Members of the Jones clan have been known to be stubborn and hard-headed. Apparently, Jeff felt compelled to carry on that tradition. Over the course of those fourteen years, children grew up and married, our mother died, careers were built and lives were lived. After nearly thirty years working for F.J. Jones & Company, Jeff took a new job and moved to Arizona. Liz and I had long owned a house in the same area and at around the same time chose to make Arizona our primary residence. Here we were all but neighbors and we hadn't had any meaningful contact in a decade and a half. I had long since given up on trying to make any sense out of the situation.

One day, out of the blue, I received an email from Jeff. To paraphrase the message … "This doesn't seem to make a lot of sense. Can we meet for coffee and talk about putting this behind us?"

We met at a local coffee shop. Jeff began the discussion. "This has gone on long enough. Can we maybe put this all behind us?" He seemed serious and sincere.

"Jeff, I don't have a clue as to what it is we have to put behind us" I said. It was not unlike the statement I had made the last time I spoke with him fourteen years earlier when I said, "I don't know what it is that's bothering you, but whatever it is, I think we probably should put it behind us." Jeff seemed to be a little surprised when he realized I truly didn't understand the problem or its roots, but we didn't talk about it any further. We just moved forward. We now communicate regularly. We get together for dinner and social events frequently. All seems well, but I still don't know what it is that got in the way or what it was we put behind us. I guess it was just the fact that we were Joneses.

As relations thawed with Jeff, another ice age set in with Brian. Brian had spent his life trying to be something he wasn't and doing his best to avoid being who he was. He tried to convey authority when he spoke by lowering his voice in the manner Frank would when he spoke. Brian talked at length on subjects about which he knew almost nothing. He seemed to equate word quantity with thought quality. He received a degree from Eastern Michigan University. It had something to do with education, but he elected to work for his father in the construction business. He had as much aptitude in that business as I did as a ballerina. Frank worried that Brian couldn't earn a living in another field and kept him on the payroll almost as an act of charity. Jeff did well in the business, but was frustrated by Brian's interference. Nonetheless, Brian and Jeff both worked for F.J. Jones & Company for roughly thirty years. Frank had numerous discussions with a number of people (myself included) about Brian's lack of aptitude. He was told repeatedly that he wasn't doing Brian any favors by allowing him to continue to flounder, but he always worried about the consequences of putting him on his own.

The frustrations did nothing but grow over the years. They were a significant part of the reason Jeff left the company. Frank's frustration led to ever increasing frustration on Brian's part. It was a train wreck just waiting to happen. Brian approached me seeking advice. In summary, I told him to look for something else or to buy the company so he could make the decisions. I didn't think he could begin to raise the money to buy the company let alone run it once he did, so I considered that option a non-option. Brian thought it was the best option and started pursuing the idea. The next time he brought up the subject with me, his questions revolved around how to value the company for purchase purposes. He said he thought it was worth about a million dollars. I asked him how he arrived at that number. He was dead serious when he responded, "Because the company has about a million dollars in the bank." I had known "business" wasn't Brian's long suit, but this was the first clue I had as to how completely ignorant he was in the area of business economics.

With this information in mind, picture the situation where Frank was getting up in years. The two sons in which he had the most confidence in their business savvy both lived a couple thousand miles away. Brian lived in Frank's backyard. In the last couple years before the construction firm was completely closed down, Brian had gone to college and actually received another degree – this time in nursing. He never was able to get a job in the nursing field, but he had the degree. He convinced himself that he would become Frank's care giver and his financial consultant. He also pulled the old "throw them under the bus" trick on both Jeff and me. He worked hard to convince Frank that he was the only one who truly cared about him and that he was the only one capable and qualified to help him. Frank never completely bought into Brian's façade, but ultimately appointed Brian as the "administrator" of his estate. The logic of the selection was apparent to everyone except Brian. Brian was the only one of the three boys that was in Michigan. There really was no other choice, especially when considering the estate administrator's function was to act as one of three equal partners and in the interest of all three equally.

Unfortunately, as a result of Brian's near complete lack of business knowledge, he somehow thought he was the "chosen" one rather than the one who had been stuck with the duty. When Frank died, Brian "ascended" to his throne. It resembled more of a coronation than a business activity. With cavalier disregard for the law, business practice and his other two brothers, he unilaterally decided what should be done on everything from investment decisions to disposing of assets that needed to find their way into his possession. When asked for information about the estate, information that he was obligated by law to provide, he ignored the requests with haughty arrogance. "I'm not your employee" he once said. In his defense, he was unable to produce balance sheets or other requested financial reports because he truly didn't have a clue as to what they were in the first place.

Nonetheless, his performance as the administrator of the estate further soured the relationship he had with both Jeff and me. He threw Jeff under the bus, Frank under the bus and me under the bus. I still maintain some contact, but only because Jim McCarty would get mad at me if I didn't.

Chapter Ten – Chow

What the hell does food have to do a person's history? Frankly, it says a lot. Food reflects culture and history. It reflects a family's roots. The food a person eats tells you a lot about his personality. Is the person adventurous and willing to step outside the lines? Food mirrors economic standing in the community. It may be an indicator of health. Food speaks volumes.

My childhood diet was what you would expect for someone growing up in the 1950s in a working family with roots firmly tied to the British Isles. Meat, potatoes, green beans, lots of bread and butter. With my mother on a budget, the meats didn't include Filet Mignon or New York Strips. We're talking hamburger and lots of roasts. We ate chicken, but beef was the mainstay. Thanks to pressure cookers, my mother could take tough, almost inedible cuts of beef and elevate them to chewy, barely edible delights. We occasionally had roasts where the meat was so tough and dry that I would chew a piece for five minutes before pretending to have to go to the bathroom. I would then walk through the living room and fling the masticated piece of the cow's ass behind the piano. Sadly, cooking wasn't my mother's greatest strength, but she dutifully prepared dinner every night. She would mix it up as best she could. She would serve macaroni and cheese at least once a week. Hungarian goulash was another of her favorites; it was basically beef and noodles with as much of a vegetable snuck in there as she could get away with before mass revolt. From time to time, she would throw in good old fashioned "shit on a shingle"; I'm not sure what it's called in polite society. It was white gravy with some cheap meat and peas mixed in and served over a piece of bread or toast. A couple times each month, we'd get a piece of liver, probably because it was cheap and supposedly healthy. Mashed potatoes and brown gravy accompanied nearly every meal.

I tended to be a picky eater as a kid. In part, I'm sure it was because I didn't have a lot of variety, only because I was never given a lot of variety, probably because I didn't like a lot of variety. We didn't have a lot of access to fresh vegetables so they came mostly from the can. Canned veggies can sour anyone. I tolerated canned green beans and canned peas because I had no choice. The rest of the canned stuff was way over the line in my book. My rules of thumb as a kid were:

- Green – bad. Potato – good.
- Campbell's chicken noodle soup – very good. Campbell's vegetable soup – good. Everything else – bad.
- Cereal with lots of sugar – great. Cereal with less sugar – health food.
- Broccoli, cauliflower, brussels sprouts, bell peppers, etc. – poison. Spinach – deadly poison.
- Candy – good.

Meat and potatoes - such was the diet of the Jones side of the family. Later in life after spending a month or so traveling the countryside in England, Wales and Ireland, it all began to make sense. The Jones side of the family was only a couple generations removed from Great Britain. I guess I shouldn't have been surprised to see that cooking styles and the contents of the meals were incredibly similar. With perfect hindsight, I could trace much of what I ate as a kid right to the heartlands of England and Wales. What would have been a miracle was if my family would have specialized in cooking Chinese food or Italian food. The fact of the matter was we were the people from where we came.

I mentioned beef was our primary source of meat. Actually, there was a five year period in which I had no beef in the home. No, we hadn't become vegetarians. Quite the contrary, we had meat with every meal. It was moose. My father went to northern Ontario around White River each year. For five consecutive years, he shot a moose. As it happened, one moose provided a family of five more than enough meat for an entire year. We had moose roasts, moose steaks, moose burgers, spaghetti and moose-balls and all things moose for five straight years.

My mother's side of the family was from the South. They were farmers and were frugal before the Depression. After the Depression, they redefined the word frugal. I'm certain the word "extravagant" has never been uttered in the context of my Grandmother's cooking style. When I lived with my grandparents during most summers of my youth, nearly every meal included cornbread. Now and again we'd have hush puppies which are essentially cornbread balls. Biscuits and gravy ruled the evening table and sometimes the lunch table as well. Often she would mix hamburger meat in with the gravy. Our vegetable was almost always corn or potato; sometimes we'd have potato or corn. When we had one of the more exotic dinners, chances are it was meatloaf. A simple peanut butter and jelly sandwich usually covered lunch. For breakfast, we could have anything we wanted as long as it was oatmeal or as we called it then, porridge. Canned "Pet Milk" was usually available to add a bit of luxury to the porridge. The only other staple as we grew up at the lake house with my Tennessean grandparents was the classic marshmallow. Many nights were spent in the front yard roasting them over the flames of the barbecue as we swatted mosquitoes and wound down from another rough day of play.

Surely it's obvious that by the time I stepped out on my own, my culinary horizons were not very wide. Not long before my Senior Prom in high school, I asked my parents if they'd front me the money to go to a nice restaurant. I told them that with the prom coming up, I'd be taking Barb Bogart to an upscale restaurant and that I'd be expected to exhibit a hint of class and manners. In that I'd never eaten in a fine dining establishment, I thought a dress rehearsal might be a good idea. My parents nearly laughed themselves sick at the concept. I had expected a bit more empathy from my mother. The first time she was ever taken to a high end restaurant, they put a finger bowl in front of her. She had no idea what it was and proceeded to pick it up in her hands and drink it. Despite that bit of trauma, she didn't seem to be too worried about me suffering a similar fate in front of my prom date.

By the time I was nineteen and had flown from the nest, I had never tasted lobster, mahi-mahi or Dorado. I knew there was Italian food other than canned spaghetti, but I had never tasted any. I thought a mango was a dance rather than a fruit. Iceberg was the only lettuce that existed. Onions were an exotic fruit or vegetable, but they weren't to be eaten. Mexican food involved eating a hamburger while wearing a sombrero. Chinese food was a mystery. The mere thought of eating fish raw or sushi was so abhorrent it would make me queasy just to think about. Eat a raw oyster? You've got to be joking! At that point in my life, to describe me as "worldly" when discussing food would have been a bit of a stretch.

When Lucy and I married, she was a little more adventurous that I was, but not by much. Constrained by traditional stereotypes, Lucy was the mistress of the kitchen and did her best to prepare meals. She had other strengths, so cooking was pretty much put on the back burner. She was undoubtedly hampered by my pickiness, but she was still a nice Midwestern girl from a meat and potatoes background. For the first twenty-five or so years of my life, I thought being adventuresome in the world of food meant trying a new jelly on my toast. Then I moved to San Francisco.

It began on the interview trip. The people at Chevron knew how to host a prospective job candidate. I had been selected for interviews with five separate divisions at Chevron. I was to spend a full day at each. In the evening, I was taken out by engineers that – if I was hired – would be my peers and coworkers. Their job was to show me the town. A blank check and five nights in San Francisco? If that isn't winning the lottery, what is? Each group tried to outdo the other. I had some of The City's finest dining. I still recall being taken on the first night to the Buena Vista for Irish Coffee and then on to the Marrakech for dinner. We sat on pillows on the floor and had fabulous Moroccan food. One course after another came with foods I'd never seen prepared in ways I'd never imagined. It was a show and the experience was delightful. The following evening we went to a wonderful sea food restaurant on Fisherman's Wharf. I discovered more great food I'd not dreamed existed. The top of the Hyatt Regency Hotel had breathtaking views as the entire restaurant slowly rotated above The City and San Francisco Bay. Tuxedo clad waiters catered to our every desire. On the fourth night, my hosts took me to The Shadows, a German restaurant perched high on a hill in the North Beach part of The City with the lights of Sausalito dancing on the bay waters below. Another night, I was taken to the famous Empress of China restaurant in Chinatown. In a period of one week, my food world had exploded. Forty years later, I still vividly remember many of the meals I enjoyed that week.

I took the job with Chevron Research and as luck would have it, I soon became one of those engineers who were given the blank check and instructions to take prospective job candidates into San Francisco to show them the town. It was a tough job, but someone had to do it. Over the course of the next couple years, I discovered a fabulous Greek restaurant, a world famous steak house with the best cuts of beef I've ever experienced, some awesome sea food restaurants, marvelous Japanese establishments, unparalleled Italian, super Mediterranean cuisine and I was in the heart of the land of Ghirardelli Chocolates and world class Boudin sourdough bread. I had come from a dining landscape like the back side of the moon into foodie's paradise and I enjoyed every bite of it.

I tossed my old dining habits (and cook Lucy along with them) into the trash bin of life. When I met Eleonor, my tastes took another giant step forward. She was born in Mexico and grew up eating obviously authentic and rather "blue collar" Mexican food. When we setup housekeeping together, Mexican food became my primary calorie source. I had heard of tacos and enchiladas, but soon learned the stereotypical food of Taco Bell was to Mexican food as peanut butter and jelly sandwiches are to American food. Real Mexican food doesn't end with tacos; it only begins there. I soon became somewhat of a connoisseur of Mexican cuisine. I discovered and fell in love with great mole sauces, some of the spicy peppers, buñuelos, rompope, buchis, huevos motuleños and an almost endless list of other regional foods from south of the border.

I quickly learned working class Mexicans don't waste their food like Americans. If it can be digested, chances are someone in Mexico is eating it. One of my favorite finds in the Mexican kitchen was menudo. If I would have had a bowl of this stuff put in front of me in high school, I'm certain I would have thrown up. Frankly, that probably would have made it look better. Menudo is a soup with a base of ground red chili. The principle ingredient is the lining of the stomach of a cow, i.e., tripe. It usually has onions, lime, oregano, more ground chiles and cilantro. To the uninitiated, it is not a pretty dish. Once you get past the appearance, it is delicious.

I remember going into a family run restaurant in Ensenada, Mexico where they get quite a few gringo boaters passing through the marinas en route north and south. In such places, restaurant owners try to have a few menus available in English. The problem arises when the restauranteur speaks no English. They typically get a Spanish-English dictionary and do a literal translation of their Spanish menu. Liz had one such menu and broke out in a hardy laugh. I looked at the English menu only to see they were offering "Guts Soup". If someone thought it looked bad, the description on the menu sure wouldn't help make it look any better.

In Mexico, menudo has a reputation of being a cure for a hangover. "Menudo para los crudos" goes the well-known expression. For that reason, in Mexico, California and the American Southwest, Mexican restaurants commonly serve menudo late Friday and Saturday nights and Saturday and Sunday mornings. Give it a try. It's great stuff. Just keep the lights low.

By the late seventies, my knowledge and appreciation of the world's various cuisines had come a long way from the meatloaf munching potato man from Michigan's farm country. I still had a way to go, but I was ready and willing. I remember a co-worker at Chevron asking me if I liked abalone. At first I thought he wanted to know if I like bologna. I thought it a strange question. When he realized I had never heard of abalone, he explained it was a large mollusk that lived on rocks in the ocean. He said that when they're properly prepared they are delectable treats. He said you can buy them in the grocery stores for a little in excess of seven dollars per pound. This was at a time when a good sirloin steak was selling for a buck eighty per pound. I thought to myself, "What an outrage that some glorified clam commands four times the price of a steak." Dave Mooney continued on. "We're going abalone diving this weekend near Jenner By The Sea sixty miles north of San Francisco. Would you like to come along?" He said the water was cold and a full wetsuit would be necessary.

I still had my wetsuit from my diving days in the Caribbean. I didn't have gloves or boots for the suit, but in the belief that I was somehow genetically related to Superman, I assumed I would be just fine without them. When the time came to climb into the surf, I had almost everything – including an "ab-iron" – that I needed. These critters lived on the sides of big rocks ten to twenty feet below the surface. The trick was to quickly slip the ab-iron, similar to a long chisel under the abalone and pry it off the rock. You had one and only one chance. If you didn't get in there quickly, the abalone would suck its hard shell down tightly onto the rock and you weren't going to get it off without dynamite. Because of the endangered status of abalone, State law prevented the use of scuba gear. You had to free dive. There was a minimum size and a limit on the number of abalone you could take. Spotters worked the cliffs above ready to arrest and fine violators. In I went.

I quickly learned I hadn't anticipated a couple of things. First of all, the water was cold. Yea, yea … I know, Dave told me it was cold, but didn't tell me it was really, really cold. Without boots and gloves, I risked hypothermia and couldn't take it. Within five minutes I had to get out of the water. I was trembling and my teeth were chattering. There was another big surprise. I was accustomed to diving in the Caribbean where the waters were generally not only warm, but generally fairly calm. On the coast of northern California, the surf is huge. Big waves buffet the rocky shores. Giant rocks are all over the ocean floor just off the shore. As the big waves crashed overhead, the areas between the submerged rocks became torrents and divers are thrown about like cherry pits in a kitchen blender. If you found an abalone ten feet below the surface and prepared to pop him off the rock, you might find yourself missing him by five feet as your body is tossed hither and fro. It was everything I could do to keep from breaking my own bones as I repeatedly bashed into the rock surfaces all around. If abalone could laugh, I'm sure it found the scene hilarious.

After climbing out of the ocean, I got in the car and drove to the nearest dive shop and purchased gloves and boots. At least I'd be ready for the next day's dive. The following day, I was better prepared for the cold, but still spent more time bouncing off of rocks than capturing abalone. It was a brutal pursuit. We finally caught our limits and left for home. All I could do was lick my wounds and wonder how the hell the grocery store prices of abalone could possibly be so cheap. As far as I was concerned, abalone should have carried a price tag of about a hundred dollars per pound. Only then would I ever be remotely interested in diving for them again.

Little did I know, the work wasn't even close to done. That night, we met for our abalone feast. It was there I learned that to properly prepare abalone, it had to be carefully sliced and the little "steaks" had to have the hell beat out of them with a wooden mallet. Before we were done, my arms were worn out from swinging a hammer. When you order abalone in a restaurant today, the prices are still high, but the technique of "farming" them has come a long way. I can assure you that back in the "old days", their prices couldn't be set high enough to justify all the work that went into putting them on the table.

In 1979, I left California for Arizona and unbeknownst to me, my food world was about to broaden far beyond its already expansive borders. My experiences on the Navajo Indian reservation served to open many new culinary doors. The life of a traditional Navajo revolves around sheep. One of the most common meals is mutton stew. I took a liking to it. I don't know if it was by taste or by necessity. "Fry Bread" is everywhere. It's easy to make and delicious. They also have their version of unleavened bread which I'll try to spell phonetically – nunnescaada. It's sort of like a thick flour tortilla. When the Navajo food world gets interesting is back in the hills where the natives waste no part of the sheep. Occasionally, a meal includes something that raises the eyebrows, even on someone as adventuresome as me. I remember eating a particular blood sausage type of thing that really took some courage. For the life of me, I can't remember the Navajo name for it, but don't worry, you'll never find it in a restaurant anyway.

One food story from the land of the Diné (Navajo word for "Navajo" or simply, "the people") is exceptionally noteworthy. Thanksgiving was approaching. Billie Owens and his wife were very traditional Navajos who lived well off the beaten path. They invited us to their home for the holiday. I probably should have been leery of the invite. Remember that after the first Thanksgiving, things didn't go all that well for the Indians. Surely, Billie Owens wasn't trying to win the rematch. Nonetheless, we promised we'd be there. I wondered what I would find at a Navajo Thanksgiving day feast.

It was a cold fall day with temperatures hovering near freezing as we approached the traditional hogan. We walked through a dusting of snow and entered through the east facing door of the log and mud structure. Blue smoke from the fire drifted upward through the smoke hole in the center of the hogan's roof. We were greeted warmly and encouraged to sit down at the folding card table that had been set for the dinner. I took my seat and slowly glanced around the hogan. There by my chair on the dirt floor staring up at me was the head of a sheep who had been kind enough to donate the rest of his body for the meal we were about to eat. As I looked at the table, I noticed that everyone's place had been neatly set with plates and silverware. I say "plates" and I guess that may be semantically correct. Mine was a white, slightly worn Frisbee. It definitely added a touch of charm to the meal.

So what did we have for a Thanksgiving dinner on the far reaches of the Navajo reservation? Turkey, stuffing, mashed potatoes, sweet potatoes, cranberry sauce, corn and some lamb. We pretty much had everything you'd expect in a traditional Anglo home in the middle of Michigan. There was no electricity so there was no football to watch after dinner and no TV upon which to watch it. Our hosts were magnificent, gracious and welcoming. It had to be similar to the first Thanksgiving in Plymouth Colony four hundred years before except I'll bet the Pilgrims watched football after dinner.

In 1984 with my marriage into the McCarty family, I reached foodie heaven. Liz was already a talented and experienced cook when we met, but was bound to get better and better with age. Her father loved to cook and was a master himself,

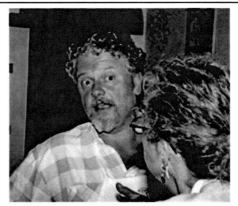

Liz with her private chef in Italy

especially when it was done outside in or near the barbeque. Her grandmother was a pie maker of some renown, Liz had good teachers. She learned to improvise. She creates masterpieces out of leftovers. The secret ingredient in all of Liz's work is her love for cooking. There's absolutely nothing to dispute; I hit the jackpot with Liz's cooking. The kicker is that at her skill level when we met, she was a master. But she was just beginning.

Over course of the next thirty years, Liz attended cooking schools in many parts of the world. She went to a cooking school in San Francisco with James Beard Award Winning chef Mary

Risley. She has worked the kitchen with Eddie Matney, one of Arizona's best known chefs. She worked the kitchen with the famed Alice Waters at her Chez Penisse restaurant in Berkley, California. She has attended cooking schools in Arizona, Italy, Mexico, New Orleans and San Juan, Puerto Rico. She was hosted on a tour of the restaurant with one of the world's most famous French chefs, Michel Roux. Liz has become what I consider an absolute master.

Liz has had three custom kitchens built for her. The one in San Diego cost more than a quarter million dollars and would be the envy of most restaurants. It was nothing short of spectacular. It wasn't built for show (although it looked like a showpiece kitchen); it was built for function and Liz used every bit of it for that.

Why am I telling you so much about Liz and her cooking in a memoir that's supposedly mine? The answer is simple. I have had to eat all this delightful food. I can't imagine anyone getting a more consistently stellar sequence of dining delights than I have for the past thirty years. Oh, the sacrifices I've had to make – poor, poor me.

Chef Liz working with the famed Chef Eddie Matney

But wait! It gets better. Ten or fifteen years ago, we met a woman at a party on the beach in San Diego. She struck up a conversation and we seemed to hit it off quite well together. In a relatively short time period, she grew into a dear friend and to this day, she's like family to both of us. We spend a lot of time with her and have traveled to lands far and wide with her. Her name is Marcie Rothman. It turns out she is a well-known California food critic and author and a magician in the kitchen. After she and Liz became close friends, they spent countless hours creating and inventing gourmet dishes together either in Liz's kitchen or Marcie's kitchen. When Marcie would review a

Liz and her great friend, food writer Marcie Rothman while traveling in Puerto Rico

fine restaurant, she would often ask us to join her so we could share the tastings and discuss the restaurant prior to her review. When Marcie was asked to review all the recipes in a book written by famed New York Chef Danny Meyer before publication, she and Liz would get together once a week to prepare each of the meals and critique it. And poor old me - I had to be there to test and taste the food. I was always generous with my time and gave them as much of it as they needed. I was the taster, the "eater" of all these spectacular foods. Wasn't that big of me? (Pun intended.) I truly can't imagine someone luckier in the "food department" than I have been.

Before I close the refrigerator door on the subject of food in my life, I want to mention one last thing – my dislikes. If you would have asked me to make a list of the foods I didn't like when I was in grade school, I'd still be writing. Chances are if it was green, it was on the list. If it wasn't well cooked or had fat or was mushy or bitter or ugly, it was on the list. Even some fruits made the list. But if you look beyond my move to San Francisco, it appears as if I had an epiphany and fell in love with any and all foods on the planet. Truth is a couple remained on the list for a lengthy period after my awakening.

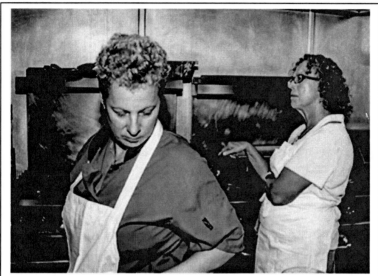

Liz working with internationally renowned Spanish Chef Maria Blanca in her kitchen at Restaurante Airenumo

Olives were probably at the top of my "do not eat" list. It had nothing to do with their appearance. There was just something about the taste that I rejected at a very core level of my being. I just couldn't bring myself to enjoy the taste of an olive, especially the green ones. I found it interesting that Liz was the same way and reacted in an identical manner to their taste. Olive lovers used to delight when they attended dinners with us where olives were plentiful; they knew they'd be getting double helpings.

Liz and I talked about how crazy it seemed that we had such broad tastes and open minds but didn't like a basic and ubiquitous food that was at the heart of some ethnic cuisines. We vowed to do everything we could to "re-program" our bodies to accept olives. When we'd go to some place that served appetizer plates of olives, we'd order them. We ate the olives and for the longest time we continued to despise them. You're never defeated until you surrender so we kept on. Then one day in 2006, we were having a glass of wine at "3rd Corner" in Ocean Beach, California. We ordered the olive appetizer plate. It came with a collection of many different kinds of olives. We started with the black ones. To my surprise, they tasted good. Liz had the same experience. We worked our way into the green ones. We liked them. We finished the bowl and enjoyed every one of them. It was as if we had exorcised the olive demon from our lives. It happened on the same day for both of us. I truly have no explanation for the phenomena. It's as if our bodies had some natural defense against something and we trained them to accept it. The fact that it literally happened on the same day after years of effort defies explanation, but it did. We have enjoyed olives ever since.

Sushi was another mountain to climb. My mother had always shuttered at the thought of eating fish that wasn't cooked thoroughly. She said it had worms. With that introduction to fish, it should be no surprise that the prospect of paying good money to eat raw fish wasn't high on my list. Liz wasn't a big sushi eater because Show Low, Arizona had no such thing. One day in the early 1990s, we were on a business trip to Salinas, California. Liz and Tempest found a nice little sidewalk café around lunch time and grabbed a seat on the patio. It turned out to be a sushi restaurant. They ordered – it was good. That was pretty much the end of the story. I tried it and loved it. Since that time, we both fell in love with sushi. Nothing beats sake sashimi (sushi grade salmon). To this day, we eat sushi an average of at least once per week.

Not all things that come from the sea were welcomed as readily as sushi. Liz has loved oysters since before I met her. However, I wouldn't consider getting my mouth close to anything that looked like a raw oyster, especially on the first date. In my mind, they were about the grossest looking things I'd ever seen. Why ingest something that truly looked like medical waste? For many years, my software business took me to New Orleans two or three times each year. Frequently, Liz's sister would join us; she was the software company's business manager. On Bourbon Street about a block off of Canal, Felix's Oyster House caters to locals and tourists alike with a host of oyster shuckers serving them on the half shell as fast as anyone can eat them. We never went to New Orleans when one of the first and one of the last stops wasn't Felix's. The staff saw Liz and Victoria so often, they recognized them the instant they walked in the door. "Assume the position" one would always say as we entered. They knew two women were about to consume a lot of raw oysters and one man would be standing there watching with contempt and disgust.

I was encouraged time and again to try one, but I had the strength of character to make a face and refrain. Finally, they wore me down. They decorated the slimy looking critter with Worcestershire sauce, horseradish, lemon juice and some of Felix's special hot sauce and passed it over. I wasn't too thrilled with the texture, but the taste was honestly pretty good. I tried another. Not bad. Then another and another. I too fell in love with them. It's been more than twenty years and Liz and I still order oysters on the half-shell as a delightful appetizer when a restaurant has them available.

So what's on my "do not eat" list now? Nothing. I'm not going to tell you there isn't a food I won't eat, but if there is, I have yet to find it. And I've looked pretty hard (especially after the oysters).

We fell in love with huitlacoche when we were in Chihuahua, Mexico. It is the black fungus that grows on corn when still encased in its husk. It makes a great soup, crepe or an omelet.

Escamole was a big surprise. We were in Mexico City and I asked the host in a fine hotel restaurant if they served anything unusual for breakfast that we couldn't get at home. "Have you ever had escamole?" he asked.

"What is it?"

"I'll tell you after you've had your breakfast" he said. An escamole omelet was ordered. When it arrived, it was a work of art. Inside the omelet was a white, cheese like substance. Liz and I shared bite after bite and tried to guess the type of cheese. It was delicious. When the meal was over, the host approached our table and asked if we enjoyed it. We assured him it was a delight.

"I'm pleased you liked it" he said. "Sometimes it is called Mexican Caviar. It comes into season for only about two weeks out of the year. You have just had omelets made from the eggs of a particular kind of ant that lives around Mexico City." Sometimes, a willingness to try new things pays handsome dividends.

During my mountain climbing years, I tried and generally enjoyed many native foods in Argentina, Chile, Peru, Mexico, Central America, Europe, Hawaii, Russia, Africa and Japan. To this day, I don't remember the names of most of them. There were a few I never knew what they were in the first place. I look back on my cloistered years of Midwestern cooking and imagine how much pleasure and joy I would have missed in my life had I not opened my mind, my heart and my mouth to so many new and exotic foods. When it comes to the world of food, no one on the planet has been luckier than have I.

Chapter Eleven – Hobbies and Idle Pursuits

Life is just one long series of hobbies interrupted by brief periods of work. A few of us have been incredibly lucky; even our periods of work were dominated by our hobbies. In the twenty-five years I ran the software company, I viewed life as one never ending computer game. How much better can it get?

As a kid, my hobbies undoubtedly fell into the realm of "normal". I'd play a game of Monopoly with friends or family. "Clue" was popular – Miss Scarlet with the lead pipe in the library. My Grandma Jones lived to gamble. Life was a game of pinochle and church attendance meant going to play bingo. I spent more than a little time playing such games with her. But all of these things were "activities" rather than "hobbies".

My first real hobby was probably bomb making. Maybe that's a tad of a stretch, but it's not untrue. I took an interest in chemistry when I was about ten years old. I had received a chemistry set from Santa Claus and learned that by mixing a couple of things together, you could make ink and other marginally useless concoctions. Bobby Ross lived up the street a few houses and he too had a chemistry set. He had actually setup a little laboratory in his basement. We worked together in a world of discovery. Imagine our surprise when we learned that by putting together saltpeter, sulfur

At age 11, Howard was in the yard with Mark LaFond mixing the chemicals

and ground coal, we could make gunpowder. We also learned how to make charming smoke bombs. Let your imagination be your guide as to what we did with our discoveries. I'll just say not everyone was as pleased with our ingenuity and products as were we. Our chemistry hobby underwent a government shutdown when Mrs. Ross evicted us from the lab after we caught the house on fire. I don't see why it was such a big deal. We got it out before it spread to the upper floors. By necessity, I put my chemistry hobby on hold until I graduated from Michigan State University with a degree in chemical engineering. Ironically, I ultimately ended up working for an explosives company making bombs.

I had a few other hobbies as a kid, but only because someone gifted me the components and I was obligated to pursue the hobby until I got sick of it, usually a few days later. Stamp collecting, coin collecting and the like are on that list. After all, who doesn't need a corkboard with a bunch of dead butterflies pinned to it? However, I can't in good conscience include such pursuits as legitimate hobbies.

I don't include baseball as a hobby either. It was more of an all-consuming way of life. It became as fundamental to me as eating. Eating didn't become a hobby to me until I met Liz.

76 Trombones -My first real hobby was probably my music. As a young boy, I don't want to say I was forced; let's just say I was encouraged without options to study piano. My mother had come from a very musical family and by damn, I was going to choose to be a musician too whether I wanted to be one or not. For two years, I went to see Mrs. Wazername every week to take my lesson. The frumpy old woman probably knew her stuff, but she damn sure didn't know that little boys have other things to do than pound out "Prelude in C" on the eighty-eights. What was worse yet is that my mother expected me to practice at least thirty minutes every day. I admire her optimism. I'd bitch and moan the entire time. I actually remember her coming into the living room one time and putting a piece of adhesive tape over my mouth. Nice try, but that didn't work either. After two years,

I won the war. I'd been force-fed a couple years' worth of musical knowledge and could make some marginally tolerable noise on the keyboard. However, I had developed a burning hatred for the mere concept of playing a musical instrument of any kind.

Fast forward a few years. I was living in the dormitory as a college freshmen in Kalamazoo, Michigan. The Beatles had just taken the country by storm. The Stones rocked. Making music was cool and I was at an age when being cool was important. Another freshman who lived down the hall from me had a guitar and could play it pretty well. He played the music of the popular groups of the day and was great when playing the folk music that was sweeping the nation. "Can you teach me to play that thing?" I asked him one day. He was more than pleased. I bought a guitar and he spent a few minutes with me three or four days every week. He gave me some things to work on and I spent a minimum of two hours each day practicing, sometimes more. The alternative was study for classes, but I had my priorities in order. My piano training came in handy during the learning process. There was one huge difference between the piano and the guitar. I didn't want to learn the piano. I did want to learn the guitar. It's amazing what a difference that can make.

After about a year of hard work, I actually became reasonably proficient as a guitarist and I had no intention of stopping there. In my sophomore year, I played with a bluegrass group that included some very accomplished musicians. One had been the banjo player for a well-known folk group called "The New Christy Minstrels". Another earned a living picking a guitar for the Gibson Guitar Company. With time, I got better and better.

That was fifty years ago. I still play my Martin D-18 or Martin D-35 every day of my life. One of them sits in a stand about four feet from my desk always within reach. Even when I was working twelve to sixteen hours a day writing computer software, my instruments were always within arm's reach for stress relief and to clear a muddied mind. My music has become inseparable from my being. It has brought me joy and relaxation for more than a half century.

Note that I said, "My instruments were always within arm's reach …" As time went on, I found that once you learn to speak in the language of music, you're not restricted to just the guitar or whatever else you learned. After a couple years on the guitar, I tried my hand at the banjo. Maybe I didn't work hard enough, but it never felt good to me. I threw in the towel on the five-string. I finally put aside my love hate relationship with Mrs. Wazername and began playing the piano again. I found that I never really got very good at it, but I was good enough to bring some pleasure into my own little world. The instruments that have been sitting within arm's reach for many years are the guitar, a beautiful Weber "Big Horn" mandolin and a beautiful, soulful violin. Not long ago, I added a piano to the mix.

Even today, Howard is always flanked by his violin, guitar and mandolin. The piano is on the other side of his desk

It's probably not fair to talk about how I "learned" to play the violin. The truth is I backed into playing it. I was always in love with violin and fiddle (same tool, different spirit). For years after listening to someone play the violin, I would remark to Liz, "I wonder if I could play one of those?" I guess I didn't realize how many times I'd pondered that question aloud. Liz did.

On one birthday about fifteen years ago, Liz presented me with a violin. She smiled and said, "You've always wondered if you could play one. Let's find out." She had poured the whopping sum of a hundred dollars into this collector's piece.

However, much to her surprise and more to my own surprise, I picked it up and played what could loosely be construed as music. I'm not going to tell you I was ready for first chair at the symphony, but I could play the damn thing better than I thought. Although I could read music in a pinch, I felt best when I was playing music by ear. With the piano, I had eighty-eight keys to worry about, with the guitar six or maybe twelve, with the mandolin eight strings called for my attention. But with the violin, I had to deal with four strings and then only one at a time. I found it a kick and rewarding to play it. My playing improved rapidly.

The problem was that with only a hundred or so dollars invested in the instrument, it sounded much like a cat with its tail caught in the garbage disposal – even when it was properly tuned and played well. Perlman couldn't make that cat purr. My mother had come for a visit and I was playing the violin in my office. She thought the technique was fine, but the screeching cat had to die. She went out and bought a violin that set her back a little more than a thousand dollars. When it arrived, my skill level skyrocketed, even with no improvement in my skill level. When I realized how the instrument quality had such a dramatic impact on the quality of the sound, I waited about a year and bought myself another one. This time more than three thousand dollars brought me together with my new best friend. It has been by my side ever since. We share music every day.

Sixty plus years ago, I learned to hate music thanks to a stodgy old piano teacher and a mother who insisted I practice. It's funny that from that hateful experience, I actually came to love music especially when it comes spontaneously from my heart as I hold one of my dear friends, my guitar, my mandolin or my violin. Thanks Mom.

I Shutter to Think – Just before our trip to Arizona in 1956, my mother purchased an Argus C-4 camera. She took it on the trip and fired at will. Unfortunately, she never hit him. Admittedly, she was a novice and had no training in photography, but if there is such a thing as "natural ability", hers was clearly elsewhere. She took roll after roll of disastrous pictures. Most of them were taken from the car as we sped down Route 66. She got some interesting shots of scenery with telephone poles centered in the blurred image. Other pictures captured the snow blanketed mountains blurred in the distance and mostly obscured by the blizzard conditions directly in front of us. She captured the essence of driving cross country by shooting bug splatter on the windshield when she was actually trying to photograph the landscape that was blurred in the background. That was my first exposure to "advanced photography". Thanks to that one trip, I honestly learned a lot about what not to do with a camera.

Some years later when I entered the world of broadcast news, I worked with news photographers as we covered everything from political speeches to mass murders. Max Gutierrez was the Bureau Chief for the Portland office of the Associated Press. He encouraged me to get a camera and take it with me when I was covering news stories. He said he'd pay me twenty-five dollars for each shot that actually ran in the local newspaper, more for those that went national. He even offered to give me some lessons on taking good photos. I purchased a Nikon FTn camera. It was a high quality and extremely rugged camera and was used by the vast majority of the professional news photographers at the time.

I worked hard to learn how to use the camera and to become as good as I could be in identifying and shooting quality news photographs. I became a professional news photographer on the day I sold my first picture to Associated Press. It was of a fire fighter crawling through some brush with a raging forest fire in the background. It was on the front page of the Portland Oregonian. I realized I could have a lot of fun with the camera and make money at the same time. I never had and never will look to photography as a principal source of income. However, my photography hobby has paid me well over the years, particularly if you don't take the cost of my equipment into account. If you do that, I'd be surprised if I've broken even. That's why I classify it as a hobby.

In the early years, I took college classes in photography. I had my own darkroom, bought my film in bulk and loaded my own rolls and did all my own processing. I delighted in learning the artistic side of photography. In the days of film photography, every shot cost money. There was a premium on getting it right the first time. There was only so much that could be done in the darkroom. Those of us that learned in the "old school" probably have an advantage over those photographers that have never held a roll of film, but only if we made it a point to never stop learning. Fortunately, I made that commitment.

It didn't come easy. I purchased a series of small, digital cameras when they first came on the market. I found the quality of the images was very much inferior to those made from film. There was little or no flexibility and artistic control. Admittedly, "film" for them was cheap, but the images produced were usually worth less. I stuck with my good old Nikon FTn for twenty-five years.

When Nikon and Canon were first coming out with digital single lens reflex cameras, my interest was aroused. At first glance, they offered more flexibility and quality. They had interchangeable lenses and some control over aperture, shutter speed and "film speed". I purchased an early release of the Canon Rebel EOS. It was definitely a step up from the previous digitals I'd played with, but it still didn't make my nightlight flicker. I hung on to the old Nikon, but I kept a closer eye on the developing digital camera field.

By late 2002, I felt it was time to make the plunge. I spent a lot of time talking with Zach Reynolds, the Photography Editor of Climbing Magazine. Canon had just released its first full-frame digital SLR camera, the Ds-1. Zach had one and insisted it was the only way to go. He said it produced professional quality images and was rugged enough to withstand the environs in which I did much of my photography. At nearly ten thousand dollars for just the camera body, I thought I'd better be pretty certain before I jumped into it. Zach didn't let me down. I bought the camera and a couple of versatile lenses and went wild into the world of photography. Over the course of the next few years, I augmented my collection of lenses and upgraded my cameras to Canon's latest and greatest. The digital cameras produced today offer awesome power and flexibility. I've been able to enlarge some of my works to four by five feet and still have good quality prints.

With digital, the darkroom is no longer necessary. There's no film to process. However, with computer software, images can be processed as if you're in the darkroom. Programs such as LightRoom and Photoshop give photographers powers never imagined in the "old days". Sometimes, I feel as if I'm cheating, but somehow, when I see the end results, I can live with myself just fine.

My photography has been purchased by governments, collectors and newspapers. It hangs on the walls of individuals and businesses. It has been auctioned at charity events. I was unanimously voted into the Point Loma Artists Association for my work. As you can tell, I'm pretty proud of some of it. But it's still just a hobby. If someone asks me if I'm a professional photographer, I have to answer "Yes" to be honest, but only because I have received money for my work. The truth is ... I do it because I love to do it. That makes it a hobby.

I find it both interesting and humorous that for years, Liz and I had been engaged in a cordial dispute over photography. I have long insisted the art can be "learned". Liz has argued that you have to be born with "the eye" of an artist. I think it's safe to say I have finally won the argument. Here's how.

I had the good fortune to go with one of the world's great photographers on a photo-shoot in Cuba in the winter of 2011. There were eight professional photographers that went along with official permission from the U.S. State Department. I was able to list Liz as my photographic "assistant" and she too got clearance to enter Cuba before travel restrictions had been lifted.

Liz ended up sitting as an observer through some of the instructional seminars and training sessions. The group rented a bus and drove from Havana on the northwest side of the island to Trinidad on the southern coast. The six hours of travel was not to be wasted. Loren Resnick, one of the world's most accomplished photographers, took the rear seat on the bus and basically setup shop. He was going to meet with each of the other professionals and critique their work one-on-one. He covered techniques, artistic issues and anything relevant to professionals wanting to take their work to the highest level. Liz and I sat in the adjacent seat. This meant Liz got to observe the one-on-one instruction of eight professionals as they were taught by one of the masters. She took it all in like a sponge.

That night, Liz said "I think I could do this."

As luck would have it, on the last day of the visit, we were back in Havana and had a big photo shoot scheduled. I ended up with a little "health issue" and didn't feel like I could go along. I handed my gear to Liz and asked her to go in my place. When she returned, I reviewed the images and discovered she had taken some outstanding shots. She seemed to be enthusiastic. From Cuba, we went on to the Dominican Republic and then Puerto Rico. Without her knowledge, I got on the internet and placed an order. When we returned to Arizona, she had her new camera gear awaiting her. She's become an outstanding photographer in her own right and gets better with every attempt. I guess it can be learned. Or maybe she was born with "the eye" and just didn't know it. The argument continues.

Because It's There – I've told the story about how I experienced an irresistible urge to climb to the top of a small mountain in Arizona when I was ten years old. It turned out that wasn't the last time I experienced that urge. In fact, I experienced it pretty much every time I saw a big mountain since that time.

I did a training seminar for my software company at the lodge on Mount Hood in Oregon. A friend of mine, Bob Quackenbush, had a heart attack a year before when he was forty-eight years old. One morning, I stood outside the lodge and looked toward the summit of Hood. Although only 11,250 feet high, Hood is a majestically beautiful mountain. As I stared and wondered what it would be like on the summit, it dawned on me that it might be a good goal for Bob. It would give him a focal point for his physical rehab from the quadruple heart bypass surgery he had undergone. I pulled my cell phone from my pocket and called Bob back in Arizona. "Would you like to climb Mt. Hood?" I blurted.

"Sure. Why not?" he responded. Bob was always willing to give something a try, but I was surprised he made such a snap decision. Regardless, we had agreed and would begin training to get to the summit in a few months.

I had never been one to undertake something without going all in. So it would be with alpine mountaineering. I began an intense training regimen. I studied climbing. I practiced techniques with ice axes, belaying, arresting falls, crevasse rescue and any and everything necessary to safely climb a mountain. I lived within a thirty minute drive of Mt. Baldy, an 11,421 foot mountain on the White Mountain Apache Reservation. It was a nice hike, but involved no "technical" mountain climbing skills. It became a frequent weekend destination simply for physical conditioning. We did practice climbs of the highest mountain in Arizona in the middle of winter (Mt. Humphries – 12,635 feet) and the highest in New Mexico (Mt. Wheeler – 13,167 feet). Every conditioning climb involved carrying a pack with eighty to one hundred pounds.

As my skill set and conditioning improved, my enthusiasm increased. Even before the scheduled climb of Mt. Hood, I set my sights on higher peaks. I travelled to southern Mexico to climb the third highest peak in North America. Pico de Orizaba touches the sky 18,491 feet high in Veracruz, Mexico. My ascent began with one of our guides arriving with a frozen body of a climber on his horse as the 17,802 foot volcano Popocatépetl nearby began a violent eruption blackening the sky with ash. It was an exciting time and only served to further fuel my passion for the peaks.

Finally, the time came for our climb of Mt. Hood. Shortly after beginning the climb, the clouds came in and held Hood tightly in their grasp. Light snow soon became a violent blizzard. We had heard of "white out" conditions where the snow was so dense you couldn't see anything but white; now we were experiencing them. It was difficult to tell where the ground ended and where the sky began. It turned into a harrowing climb. I had to get back to the lodge to dump my gear and turn around and climb back up the mountain to rescue Bob.

By the time I got Bob back to the lodge, he was close to exhaustion and slumped to the floor. He leaned against the wall and closed his eyes trying to recover. It took him a while, but he finally recovered and went to his room to rest. The following evening, our group had dinner together in the restaurant in the lodge. One of the

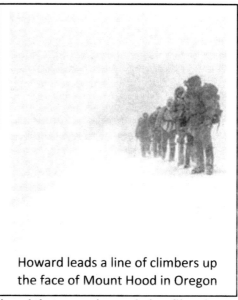

Howard leads a line of climbers up the face of Mount Hood in Oregon

people in our party mentioned that a movie was being filmed on the mountain and that Tommy Lee Jones was its star. Bob's eyes widened and then he smiled. He said that while he was lying in a semi-conscious state the night before, he thought he had been hallucinating. Apparently, Tommy Lee Jones had walked up to Bob, bent over and shook him gently. When Bob struggled to open his eyes, Jones said "Don't worry. You'll be alright buddy." Bob was now laughing with the realization that he hadn't been hallucinating and that Tommy Lee Jones had actually been trying to rattle him alive.

It turned out to be a little more difficult than Bob had imagined, but he vowed to return to get to the summit. In the meantime, I continued my training regimen and set out to climb more big mountains. A winter ascent of Mt. Whitney in California (the highest peak in the forty-eight contiguous States, 14,505 feet) was a good challenge. Mt. Rainier was a super training climb. It was covered with crevasses and offered some great training areas for rope work. Back home, Humphries, Baldy and others continued to present some good physical training grounds.

Finally, I was off to tackle my first of the world's "Seven Summits", Cerro de Aconcagua. At just shy of 23,000 feet, it is the highest mountain in the world outside the Himalayas. We took a tougher route than most climbers and it took us nearly a month to get to the top. Some of the members of our team were hit hard with altitude sickness and had to be rushed down the mountain to save their lives. There was a great feeling of accomplishment to stand on the top of the Americas.

By now, it was time to get back to Mt. Hood so Bob could claim his prize. The first day at the lodge, we climbed a few hundred feet up the mountain to practice self-arrest techniques. In the unlikely event someone did fall, we thought it would be important they knew how to stop before they got to Portland seventy miles away. Bob's wife, Janet, was there. She and Liz were also going for the prize. Janet mentioned there was a helicopter hovering up near the summit. I looked up there and concluded some climber must be in trouble and the helicopter had to be there for a rescue. I mentioned to Janet that we'd probably see it on the local news that night. She didn't believe me, but I had been a reporter and newscaster in Portland and knew what made the evening news.

As Liz came close, Janet mentioned to her that the helicopter had been hovering there for a long time. Liz turned, looked and turned back toward Janet and said, "What helicopter?"

"The one right there." Janet turned and pointed. The helicopter was gone. I knew that section of the mountain and knew there was no place for the chopper to land. It had to have crashed.

"Now you're going to see it on the national news" I said to Janet. "No way" she responded.

We finished and headed back to the lodge. As we approached the Timberline Lodge, we were the first people off the mountain since the mishap. We were mobbed by reporters. News teams had set up their broadcast trailers and were hungry for the story. We were their first pigeons. We did on-camera interviews with CBS, NBC, ABC, CNN and others. When we finished one interview, we were dragged over to the next network's set to do it again. And we hadn't even been close to the accident. They just wanted someone that looked like a mountain climber.

When we walked into the lounge, all televisions were reporting the story. Someone had fallen and was unable to arrest the fall (the skill we had just been practicing) and dragged his entire team of nine climbers into the little crevasse up close to the summit. The rescue helicopter had indeed crashed near the crevasse. Three climbers were dead; others were hospitalized.

We sat with a cold beer watching the networks' reporters interview mountain climbers – us! Janet, the woman who didn't believe me when I told her it would be a national story, was quoted on the front page of the New York Times the following morning.

In the aftermath of the disaster on Mount Hood, Howard and Liz were on all the national network news programs

Unfortunately, because a military helicopter was lying on its side on the climbing route and bodies were wedged in the crevasse, the government closed the mountain. Bob's quest for the summit of Mt. Hood was again foiled. Bob and Janet flew back to Arizona. Liz and I headed north to Seattle to climb Mt. Rainier again. Bob vowed to stand on the summit of Mt. Hood.

While Bob waited for his next chance, I continued going after the Seven Summits. I traveled to Russia to climb Mt. Elbrus (18,510 feet) and after stopping at Mont Blanc in Switzerland, traveled on to Africa. I met Liz and we climbed Mt. Kilimanjaro (19,341 feet) together. I now had three of the Seven Summits in the bag, but Bob still stalked Mt. Hood.

In May of 2003, I stood with Liz and Bob and Janet Quackenbush looking out the window at the summit from the Timberline Lodge. We were to leave the lodge at 2:30 a.m. to begin Bob's third attempt. I had climbed the back side of Hood the previous day and knew that conditions looked good high on the mountain. They say the third time is a charm. In this case, they were right. A half hour from the summit, snow and cold forced Janet to go down the mountain. An old climbing friend of mine had joined us and he graciously agreed to take her down. He seemed to be as excited about Bob's chances as the rest of us. As the sun broke the horizon, we stood on the summit of Mt. Hood. You couldn't have removed the smile from Bob's face with a scalpel. He was the poster boy for a "Never Quit" promo. It seems a little odd to think that with three of the world's Seven Summits behind me and a fourth just around the corner, that one of the highlights of my climbing days was when Bob Quackenbush stood atop an 11,250 foot peak, but it was.

I continued climbing after that with additional climbs of Mt. Rainier, Mt. Whitney and a few others. But my most brutal climb involved the fourth of the Seven Summits. The highest mountain in North America is Mount McKinley or as the natives and climbers refer to it, Denali. At 20,237 feet, it wouldn't be the highest peak I'd ever climbed, but it would be the toughest. When scaling a mountain, there's much more to the challenge than simply the elevation. When the mountain is accepting visitors, you may get lucky. But when she's in a bad mood, no one is welcome.

We had decided we would take a tougher route up the mountain. Most attempts are along the "West Buttress". We were taking the "West Rib" route. It involved a lot more technical climbing including a lengthy stretch on a near vertical wall of ice. I had to spend a few days in Ouray, Colorado just practicing climbing vertical ice walls before leaving for Alaska.

It took us a couple days before our plane could punch a hole in the clouds and land at base camp at around 7,000 feet. Landing a plane on skis with snow whirling in all directions is an experience I'll never forget. For the next three to four weeks, it would be one tough day after another. At about 17,000 feet, we found a ledge about ten feet wide just below the cornice that hung over the bergshrund. For those not fluent in the language of the mountain, the bergshrund is a giant crevasse at the top of a glacier where it is pulling away from the mountain. On Denali, such crevasses can be thousands of feet deep. If one of us fell in without a rope, there would be no rescue attempt. Ten feet away from that welcoming crack in the world was the edge of our little ledge. If you accidentally stepped over it, you might be found. Unfortunately, it would be as a crumpled heap of flesh after you landed a couple thousand feet below. I guess it was possible you'd fall into one of the thousands of crevasses below and spare your climbing partners the discomfort of having to pack your remains out. Nonetheless, we had just enough room to pitch our three two-man tents on the ledge.

As we sought some much needed rest, the weather began to turn. A storm was arriving and it was going to be a humdinger. It began snowing heavily and took no pause for seventy-two hours. It wasn't long before we heard the rumble. We knew what it was and hunkered down waiting for the worst. Seconds later, it came – a massive avalanche from above. But because of the cornice of snow that protected our ledge, the overwhelming mass of the avalanche flew right over our heads and continued on down the mountain. There was enough sluff that fell downward to completely bury all three tents. When all was calm, we dug our ways out of the now crushed tents. After nearly ninety minutes of shoveling, we had been able to repair our tents well enough to climb back in for that rest we'd been longing for. After about five minutes, there was the rumble and then the roar. Then the silence. In anticipation of the getting hit hard, I quickly rolled over and got on my hands and knees. I used my body to try and keep the tent from totally collapsing as it was again completely buried in snow. This process went on every ninety minutes like clockwork for three days. You're probably not surprised to learn we were getting rather tired of it well before the end of the first day. In that location alone, we experienced dozens of avalanches and survived to talk about it.

Howard nearing base camp after scaling Denali

At the end of the third day, the weather cleared. We surveyed the damage. With some repairs, the tents would be usable, but they'd never stand straight again. We searched for the gear we had stored outside. After some digging we found some of it. Some was gone either into the crevasse or far down the mountain. At least we were able to move on and continue our climb toward the summit.

Some things changed for me in those three days. The weather and the operator's end of a snow shovel had given me plenty of time to think things through. Here I was a happily married man. I would spend a lot of time and money to put myself in harm's way. I would be away from home for weeks at a time. I presumed Liz was wondering if I would come back alive; many climbers didn't. And all of this was done for selfish reasons.

Sure, I got to see places in the world that few people ever did and that were indescribably beautiful. I got to enjoy all of the personal "benefits" of climbing all over the world, but it seemed I was asking Liz to pay a price that was far too high. At 17,000 feet on one of the world's Seven Summits, I vowed my next climb would begin and end where the sand would be below my bare feet, where the breeze was refreshingly warm, where it was comfortable and where Liz could and would be there with me. Hell, in baseball, going four for seven was a great day. My quest for the Big Seven would end at four.

Anchors Away – To live up to my vow on Denali, Liz and I looked for, found and purchased a sailing yacht. Sailing Vessel Tempest was a forty-seven foot "blue water" ship with nearly every creature comfort imaginable. The ocean blue replaced climbing as our "hobby". For the next few years, we enjoyed much of our time sailing in Mexico or off the coast of California through the Channel Islands. It was a great life. It brought us countless hours of pleasure and relaxation. What I haven't mentioned is the suffering and trauma that went into getting enough expertise and confidence to survive our own follies.

When we purchased the Tempest, our knowledge of sailing was somewhat limited. We knew it involved water and a boat. We strongly suspected that wind came into play at some point. Beyond that, our sailing experience would have fit on the head of a pin. But ever the optimists and with confidence dripping from our pores, we knew we could learn and learn quickly. We believed a short and steep learning curve would be much better than sinking a quarter million dollar vessel especially if we were on it.

The boat was designed to handle the roughest of seas and the longest sails imaginable. We were outfitted such that we could stay out to sea for months on end without ever getting close to shore. We had the capability of making our own fresh water from salt water. We had two different systems to generate all the electricity we would need – a diesel generator and an extensive solar generation system. We had a waste management system.

We had a stove, oven, refrigerator, freezer, even a wine cabinet. We had radar, short wave radio and a satellite communication system that gave us telephone and high speed internet service from anywhere in the world. An onboard sound system was as good as found in most homes. We had television and DVD systems. A diesel engine (the iron sail) carried us forward when there was no wind and more than a thousand square feet of sails jetted us through the water when we had wind.

The only problem was that on the day we took delivery of the yacht, we didn't know how to operate any of these systems. Because the ship had a transom entry (rear), we had to back it into any slip in which we would stay. We took a one hour lesson from a licensed captain on how to back up without losing control. Everything else we would learn by reading about it or through trial and error. We bought a copy of "Sailing for Dummies", but only because no one had yet published "Sailing for Blithering Idiots".

We read incessantly. We studied the rules of the road, the laws of sailing on the open ocean, setting sails, navigation, emergency preparedness and what to do with a man overboard. We read about dealing with storms, reefing sails, weather forecasting and anything else we could find that would help us survive our pending adventures. However, there is absolutely no substitute for direct experience. We dove into the task and started racking up the experiences. We had to. Because of the California tax laws, we had only thirty days to get the yacht out of the country and into Mexico to save $25,000 in taxes. We had four weeks to build our skill level high enough to survive a lengthy sail into a foreign country. That's a pretty good incentive. On day one, we could back our boat up, but we didn't know how to go forward. We had some work to do.

We decided we would take it one system at a time. We took day trips at first. We learned how to raise and lower the sails, how to set them for maximum efficiency, how to avoid getting into "the irons" and how to get out of them when we failed to avoid them. We studied and learned how to use the electrical systems, generate our own power. Managing the waste system was non-trivial. Every trip became an adventure.

On one particular venture, the study subject was to be "anchoring". As a kid on the lake, anchoring was simple. You picked up the anchor and threw it over the side of the boat. When dealing with ocean going yachts, it's not nearly that simple. In our case, we had two anchors. One weighed fifty pounds. The other weighed forty pounds. Unlike the anchor on my childhood rowboat that might land in twenty-five feet of water, our main anchor had two hundred fifty feet of anchor line. The chain portion alone was far too heavy for a normal human being to handle. Properly "setting" an anchor took knowledge and skill and we were determined to learn how to do it and do it right.

We set sail out of the San Diego Bay to Mission Bay a few miles to the north. We would hone our anchoring skills in Mariner's Cove, spend the night with another couple who would sail with us and return the following day. We arrived at our destination and circled looking for a good spot to anchor for the night. We hooked up the "windlass control", the device that allowed us to raise and lower the anchor. We found our spot and hit the button. Nothing! I fiddled with the connection to no avail. We retrieved a spare control unit and the unit remained unresponsive. I even disassembled the electrical unit to check for the proper connections. Everything appeared to be connected correctly. No matter what we tried, we couldn't get the anchor to budge and the wind was picking up. We didn't want to run aground without even deploying the anchor. We decided to try and drop it manually. I loosened the anchor brake with a wrench while my friend held the chain in preparation to drop the anchor by hand.

We quickly verified one of the fundamental laws of physics – the one about gravity. The instant the brake released, the fifty pound anchor fell with great force and speed. My friend narrowly missed having his fingers dragged through the pulley system. He would surely have lost some of them.

We let out enough anchor line, reset the brake and successfully set the anchor. Despite our less than routine arrival, we enjoyed a fun day and night in Mission Bay. The following day, the electronics were still not functioning and we had to manually break the anchor free from the bottom and get it back into its home onboard. It was tedious, but we finally succeeded.

When I was securely back in port in San Diego, we celebrated our weekend and retired for the evening. The following morning, I called the Jeanneau dealer from whom we purchased the boat. I explained the problem and asked him about getting the system repaired. "Did you turn it on?" he asked. "For hell's sake," I jumped, "I'm an engineer and computer guy. That's the first thing I'd check." What kind of sap did he think I was?

I softened my tone and said, "So, how do you turn it on?"

"There's a switch below the bottom step on the gangway. It should be clearly labeled." I searched the area he suggested and assured him that although I'd found three switches, none of them were for the anchor. "What do they say?" he asked. I read the labels to him. The third one simply said "guindeau".

"Where was your boat made?" he said with a hint of sarcasm. "France" I replied.

"You wouldn't happen to have a French dictionary there would you?"

"Actually, I do." I grabbed my translator. The French word "guindeau" means "windlass" in English. Why didn't they say that in "Sailing for Dummies"? Some lessons were easier than others.

We had another hard earned epiphany on our first northbound sailing excursion. When exiting the San Diego Bay, boats are headed south. Many of the northbound boats continue in a southerly direction for about five miles before heading west and then ultimately north. I was a math wizard in school and you can't be a math wizard without having a solid foundation in geometry. One of the most fundamental proofs in geometry is that "the shortest distance between two points is a straight line."

I watched as all the boats put an extra ten or so miles onto their path for no apparent reason. I could only assume they had not taken or – if they had taken it – had failed geometry.

As I exited San Diego Bay bound for Catalina Island a twelve hour sail north, I steered clear of the shoreline, but made an immediate turn to the northwest. Our dear friends, the Quackenbushes, were onboard for our first trip to Avalon. I could see the surface of the sea was interrupted by patches of sea weed or kelp. In fact, navigational charts for the area showed it as hosting one of the largest kelp beds on the west coast, but my boat was the "big boy on the block" and surely wouldn't be hampered by pissy little kelp patches. If necessary, I'd just pour a little more throttle into the mix and let my prop do the rest of the work. We wouldn't miss a beat.

There had been many times in my life when I have seen the power of nature first hand and stood back in awe at its magnificence. I'd been in hurricanes, tornadoes, earthquakes, avalanches and devastating forest fires. But I couldn't bring myself to respect, let alone fear a few pieces of kelp. I'm here to tell you I was wrong, very, very wrong. The kelp grabbed my prop and propeller shaft and rendered the boat an aquaplegic. We were stuck. The Quackenbushes, especially Janet, were already apprehensive about sailing into the open ocean so I tried to maintain the utmost calm demeanor while I evaluated our predicament. I reversed the engines in the hope of reversing our course. That only served to wrap us up in more kelp. The more I did, the worse our situation became. We were dead in the water.

I considered diving into the water with a big knife and trying to cut us free by hand, but I feared that if the kelp bed had crippled a fifty foot yacht, I would have no chance of survival if it got pissed off at me. I could always call Vessel Assist, the yachter's answer to road service, but that would have been so embarrassing, I would have rather been eaten by a shark. I elected to remain at the controls and slowly go to full throttle in one direction and then full throttle in the reverse direction. It might take me a few months, but I would ultimately grind up all of the kelp west of San Diego. The questions would be "Would I be able to maintain my smile and relaxed expression for the Quackenbushes that long?" and "Would the boat's engine survive the physical abuse I was administering?"

After about a half hour of the insanity, the Quackenbushes still had no clue as to our survival concerns. "How about another beer Bob? It's such a nice evening." I asked Liz to take the controls and to continue the engine reversal game while I went below to make sure everything was alright with the engine and the other systems. I said we had decided to take on one system at a time on the climb of our learning curve, but now we had to take on another one. The instrument panel showed me our engine was performing well, but there was another indicator I'd never really noticed before. There was a big, flashing red light. Fortunately, it was labeled in English – "Bilge Pumps". Holy crap! What was going on?

I lifted one floor panel after another until I found the "bilge" closest to the point where the propeller shaft passed into the engine compartment. The little bilge pump was working away trying to empty the bilge. Shit!!! We were taking on water. The constant reversal of the propeller had begun to wear the bearing or somehow had opened up a gap in the seal that now allowed sea water to flow into the boat. We might be sinking!

"How's your beer holding out, Bob? Would you like another one?" I said with my best imitation of a relaxed smile. I calmly asked Liz to join me below for a minute, ostensibly to get another beer for Bob. I quickly explained the situation and we agreed to alternate trips below to check out the situation without arousing the suspicions of the Quacks.

The bilge pumps handled their tasks admirably and after a couple hours of fighting the attack of the giant kelp bed, we finally broke free and sailed into the normal shipping channel. We pointed the bow south and sailed about five miles before turning west and ultimately to the north. Once the propeller shaft was allowed to rest, the leaks seemed to heal themselves. We sailed all night and arrived in Avalon Harbor the following morning.

To this day, the Quackenbushes have no idea that their lives were in jeopardy and that we were preparing for "Plan B" which included inflating our dingy for a life-saving escape at sea.

We enjoyed many exciting and interesting sailing and learning experiences over the ensuing couple of years. But with time and practice we actually attained a fairly high level of competence on the high seas. Even then, nature had a way of feeding me a periodic dose of humility. On one occasion, we had been out to sea during a minor storm. With more than light winds, we approached the rocky entry to Ensenada Harbor in Mexico. Under calm conditions, an inexperienced sailor would drop sail and crank up the diesel before trying to pass through the rocky entrance. By now, I had become a reasonably accomplished pilot. Never one to be burdened by humility or fear, I elected to enter the harbor under full sail. As I executed the maneuver to perfection, I noticed the Carnival Cruise ship was at its dock. Many of the passengers were on the rail of the eleventh deck watching the beautiful sailing vessel enter the harbor. That wasn't good enough for me. As I approached the cruise ship, I pulled my violin from its case and stood astern playing the violin as the winds rattled the rigging on the boat and I sailed past the cruise ship. I humbly envied the passengers because they not only got to see a great demonstration of my incomparable sailing skills, they also got to hear the enchanting sounds of my violin. I tried to look humble, but failed dismally.

As I reached the bow of the massive passenger liner, it was time to lower the sails and prepare to enter our marina. With a couple hundred spectators, we prepared to come-about. We had to turn directly into the wind to drop the sails. It was a bonus show for the Carnival crowd, but I'm afraid we didn't follow the script. We made a hundred eighty degree turn into the wind and began lowering the sails. As I continued on my counter-clockwise turn, I heard a noise and realized we had put out some fishing lines while out to sea. I had completely forgotten and was now wrapping the boat, the shaft and the propeller in fishing lines. I quickly went into the "oh shit" mode and tried to unwrap the boat in full view of the previously adoring crowd. I turned a work of sailing art into a Three Stooges movie as the boat careened in this direction and that in front of an amused crowd of onlookers. It was a masterpiece.

On another evening, my plan to showcase my skills was transformed into a comedy worthy of the ages. Liz had been undergoing treatment for breast cancer and was unable to safely help manage the boat. Her sister, Victoria, was onboard and was ready and willing to help demolish the boat, the dock or the entire port of San Diego if asked. By this time, I had become a master at bringing the Tempest into her slip even in the most difficult of times. This night was to be the performance for the ages. I would perform the entire operation without anyone's help. Even though the last light of day was barely a memory on the horizon and the westerly winds were approaching ten knots, I had laid out a plan to bring the boat into the slip with such aplomb that TV news crews would swarm me for interviews.

With the precision of a surgeon, I eased the boat into the slip gently backing past the dock on one side and another yacht on the other – never touching either one. It was going flawlessly. With about twenty feet to go, I reversed the engine with such skill that it was immediately obvious I had absolutely nailed the landing. I could see I had reduced speed so flawlessly that the boat would stop with the stern a hair's width from the dock. I could have placed an egg between the transom and the dock and kept it from falling into the water and yet not broken it. I casually left the controls and stepped toward the dock where I would lightly step ashore and tie of the boat with not so much as a subtle bump. The crowd in my mind went wild.

The one thing that I didn't anticipate was that boaters help other boaters. Another resident of our dock had seen us coming in and assumed that given the windy conditions we would need some help. Unbeknownst to me, Victoria assumed she'd be helping if she tossed a dock line to our neighbor standing on the port side. The neighbor grabbed the dock line. She wrapped it around a cleat. As the boat approached a point about a foot or so from the dock, I realized I had accomplished my task with heavenly perfection. It was then my marina neighbor cinched down the dock line. I had one foot in the air when the boat came to an abrupt halt. I went flying off the transom onto the dock picking up splinters as I landed. "I saw you coming in and thought I'd help" she said. It was to be the pinnacle of my yachting career. I ended up picking bloody splinters out of my hands and arms in the marina bar after trying to recover my dignity. Oh, my! It would have been so, so good.

There are countless stories about our adventures on the high seas, but one event had the greatest impact on the life of a young girl. I offered one of my employees at the software company a chance to bring his family for a three day trip on the Tempest. He was excited about the prospect. So was his wife and two out of his three children. His twelve year old daughter, the middle child, didn't seem to share the enthusiasm. She said she didn't want to go. As departure day crept closer, she became more resolute in opposition to the trip. Her father counseled with her and she finally admitted she had seen the movie "Jaws" and had developed a dreaded fear of being eaten by a giant shark. Now that the source of her reluctance was out in the open, her family members could deal with it. They educated her on sailing, sharks and the realities of the ocean world. Just before departure, her fears had been sufficiently reduced that she went along. The first couple days of the trip went off without a hitch.

On the final day, we were headed north toward San Diego. The youngest child, Sam, thought it would be fun to fish. We rigged the pole and set a line. We thought the odds of getting a hook-up were pretty low, but Sam was satisfied just with the prospect. About five miles out, the pole lurched violently and the high pitched sound of fishing line being ripped off the reel could be heard by everyone on board. We had something and it was not small. We quickly outfitted my employee, Gary, with a heavy leather fighting belt and he began to work the fish. Whatever it was, it put up a good fight. I tried to keep an eye on the surface of the ocean in the hope that the fish would break the water so I could identify it. I could sometimes see the water churn a hundred or so yards behind the boat, but I couldn't get a good enough look at the beast to see if it was marlin or tuna or whatever. Gary kept up the fight and gradually brought the fish in closer to the boat. His wife and three children anxiously watched.

When Gary had worked the fish to about fifty feet from the boat, it finally broke the surface. It rocketed out of the sea with its massive head coming directly toward us. Its mouth was wide open exposing what at first glance appeared to be a million large razor sharp teeth. We had a good sized Mako Shark on the line. Shelby, the young girl who had been traumatized by the Jaws movie, nearly fainted. Her face went white and she headed below deck to await her imminent doom.

The battle with the shark went on much longer than we anticipated. We didn't want to bring it into the boat for fear the ensuing slaughter would further traumatize the girl. I hated to cut the line; the lure was worth forty dollars. After another half hour, the shark finally broke free. We recovered the lure and found the shark had actually bitten a big chunk of the wood out of it. The lure now sits in a glass case in Gary's home. Shelby did not pursue a career in fishing.

Fore! – There's one more "hobby" I'll mention here just so I won't be accused of omitting something I've done for pleasure for sixty years. When I was eight or nine years old, my father took me to the driving range. He bought a large bucket of golf balls for himself and a small one for me. He handed a golf club to me and told me roughly what to do with it. I did my best to murder these little white balls. I'm still doing it.

I've had periods in my life when I played seven days per week. You don't suppose that's part of the reason Lucy and I went our separate ways? I've also had periods when I didn't play at all. I had begun to take the game far too seriously. My golf handicap was in the low single-digits and I began worrying about not staying on top of my game if I missed a day of practice. If I wasn't playing for money, it wasn't as much fun. One day, it hit me that I'd lost the vision of why you "play" a "game". It had stopped being fun so I put the clubs up and didn't touch them for five years.

I took it up again when I moved to the White Mountains. After getting paired with Liz in my first tournament after returning to the game, I won a wife. It seemed like a fun game again. I joined a nice country club and played regularly. But soon the handicap started dropping and the game started to take on the feel of a job. I sold the membership and put the clubs away again, this time for twenty years.

Around 2009, a good friend of mine invited us to his wedding. It was to include a two day golf outing. I figured that for him, I'd dust off the clubs and play again. However, I made a solemn commitment to myself that I would never again take the game so seriously that it would cease to be pleasurable. I would accept higher scores and I would smell the flowers. I wouldn't practice as much, but I'd smile more. I would derive pleasure from the good shots and laugh at the bad ones. I would rejoice in the beauty of nature that came with playing the game of golf. I've now been golfing three or so days per week for the past six years and I'm having nothing but fun with it. I'll never be the golfer I was and that is good.

Chapter Twelve – Who's Your Daddy? (Parenting)

When I was a kid, I watched my parents and made mental notes on how I would do things differently when I became a parent. When that day finally arrived, I had misplaced my mental notes. Like other parents from generations long past, I discovered that when you become one, no one gives you a manual. There's no autopilot. You're flying blind and doing things by instinct or trial-and-error. It's not always fun and it's damn sure not easy.

Most of what I thought I knew about being a parent was learned as a child from my parents. There's an a priori assumption there that my parents knew what they were doing. It wasn't until later on in life that it dawned on me they hadn't been issued an instruction manual either. They were flying by the seats of their pants or in some cases, the seat of my pants. Nonetheless, that's how it's been done for generations.

My parents were raised in families where corporal punishment wasn't the grave offense it is today. I was never abused, but definitely had a spanking on more than one occasion. It wasn't a common occurrence; if it had been, its purpose would have been defeated. It was supposed to be "something special", a consequence for "special behavior".

Looking back on it, I do believe corporal punishment as meted out by my mother's side of the family came from a different place than that administered by my father's family. The Radcliffes seemed to view a spanking in a more biblical sense. It was administered as a form of "justice" or "atonement" and was intended to instill the child with a fear that all sins would be dealt with in a manner prescribed by God who was in this case decorated as the parent. A Radcliffe spanking would more than likely involve a belt or paddle and would supposedly carry an appropriate number of lashes to suit the crime. On the other hand, a Jones spanking seemed to be more of a "don't cross that line" message. It was more of a didactic tool, more Pavlovian. It didn't take long to learn that certain signals existed as the eruption approached. In this way, I learned to approach, but not get too close to the boiling point. Such events were quite rare, but memorable. For that reason, a Jones spanking seemed much more logical to me. After all, how many times do you have to pull a cat's tail to learn not to do that? I guess I can't speak for you, but I can assure you that after the first time an angry cat fileted my hand, I learned not to do that.

My father was a Second Lieutenant in the Army and pretty much expected his boys to act like new recruits. When he issued orders or we otherwise rolled into the quasi-military model, all answers were to be "Yes Sir" or "No Sir". I don't remember even having the third option of "Sir, I don't understand the question, sir" that I had during my brief exposure to Army life. I guess he expected us to always understand the question.

My mother was far more gullible than my father and it was much easier to pull the wool over her eyes. I'm not sure how I pulled it off, but I somehow convinced her I was always perfectly honest and truthful. The guise probably worked well because I was (almost) always up front and truthful. The trick was to hide the "almost" qualifier. One of my most artful escapes from the gallows took place when I was twelve years old and lived in Detroit. I had become interested in a most intriguing animal called "girls". Pat Keeler was one such animal and we got along quite well. One afternoon after school, I decided it would be nice to walk to Pat's house and spin a bottle or two. My next door neighbor, Jimmy Foley, was a year younger and about seven years dumber. He wasn't allowed to leave the block without permission and he was anxious to walk along with me. There was some question as to whether or not either one of us could get permission to hoof it a mile and a half. I assured Jimmy I could get permission even if he couldn't. I went into my house and told my mother I was going up to Mumford High School to play baseball. It was three blocks distant. This is something I did regularly; my mother had no reason to question it. I took my baseball glove and headed out the door. I clued Jimmy in on my ruse and he decided if it worked for me, it would work for him.

Out he came with his baseball glove in hand. We headed off in the direction of Mumford, but once out of sight, we turned and headed toward Pat Keeler's house.

Just before we got to Pat's house, Jimmy's mother drove up in a rage. She hadn't trusted Jimmy's story (he didn't normally play baseball) and had followed us. She confronted Jimmy and she tossed him into the car. Jimmy sang like a prisoner on death row. He told her we were going to a girl's house and that I had set the whole thing up including the fake baseball story. Mrs. Foley was one pissed off mama. In the meantime, I marched on my merry way to Pat Keeler's house. No one was home – ah the best laid plans of mice and men. I had some time to kill and a baseball glove in hand. What the hell; I'll go play some baseball at Mumford High.

Meanwhile, Mrs. Foley took her captive home and gave him an extended piece of her mind about the evils of running around with the hooligan next door, i.e., me. Once she completed her lengthy lecture and locked her prisoner in solitary confinement, she headed next door. She and my mother were not the best of friends. Mrs. Foley lit into my mother. She let her know what a diabolical and deceitful son she was raising and her little purebred retard wouldn't be allowed to play with me anymore (again). Mrs. Foley's unrefined diplomacy pissed off my mother. My mother assured her that I had said I was going to play baseball and that unlike her shit-headed little bone-brained son, I would never lie to my mother. They parted as they usually did with venom spittle clouding the air. The story that I was actually visiting a girl seemed far-fetched to my mother, but in the unlikely event that there was substance to the Foley charges, my mother grabbed her keys, went out and cranked up the old blue Dodge. She drove directly to the ball field at Mumford. As she pulled up by the fence, I was just rounding first base after lining a solid single to centerfield. She went home comforted with the proof that I would never mislead her. That damn Foley boy was a creep. It was hard for me to play baseball with that halo always floating above my head.

Another parenting lesson I received from my father was that no one should ever, under any circumstances, show disrespect to his mother. If I was to misbehave or exhibit disrespectful conduct in my mother's presence, I was well advised to do so when my father wasn't present. I'm not certain, but I strongly suspect my father was given that lesson by his father who no doubt got it from his father. Whatever the root, it was well planted and heaven help he who didn't heed the warnings. Even thirty years after his bitter and acrimonious divorce from my mother, it would anger him if he heard any one of his sons say something that could even be remotely construed as disrespectful to her.

There you have it. That's what I had to work with when on August 18, 1967, Amy Kristin Jones arrived. Here I was, not yet grown up myself and I (along with her mother) was in charge of a critter that couldn't take care of herself without our help. If there was a panic button, we should have hit it. We were in for some serious learning experiences.

I'm confident that neither Lucy nor I were nominated for any parenting awards. We just tried to figure it all out. If Amy cried, we fed her or changed her diaper. If she laughed, we did whatever we were doing again. I suspect most parents can figure that part out. It doesn't really start getting complicated until the child stops being an automaton and starts developing into a prescient human being. That's when the game of life truly begins.

Amy was a pretty sharp kid and for the most part was easy to raise. We read to her often. We exposed her to music. We played games with her. As an only child, she tended to be involved in adult environments. She could pass a joint with the best of them, but she couldn't indulge. What do you think we were – liberal parents?

Our biggest challenge with Amy involved asthma. She had a serious case of it. When we lived in a small apartment at Michigan State University, as soon as she went to sleep in the room adjacent to ours, she began the wheezing and rattling associated with severe asthma. It sounded like she was suffering terribly and it often kept us awake at night. After countless doctor's visits, allergy testing, medications and anything we could think of to help, the condition improved somewhat, but still weighed heavily upon us. There is an inexplicable suffering in a parent's heart when a child suffers. It frustrated us that we couldn't seem to tame the monster. From that standpoint, parenthood can be hell. It got better over the years, but never totally went away. I suspect it still haunts her.

I was only the parent for the first ten years of Amy's life. She was ten when Lucy and I split the sheets. The year we separated, we spent a month or so in Peru. We stayed at the home of a good friend from Michigan State, Rosa. Rosa's daughter, Samantha, was Amy's best friend. We enrolled Amy in school in Lima. Every day Amy and Samantha went to school

Lucy and Amy in 1977

together. On the first day of class, Amy spoke no Spanish. A month later, she was a chatty ten year old and the chat language was Spanish. Looking back, it was probably one of the best things we did for Amy. It gave her a jump start on a second language and opened up her world to different cultures and viewpoints.

Sadly, Amy would never live in a two-parent home again. Lucy and I had irreconcilable differences and went our separate ways. To hear Amy tell it, from that point forward, she had to raise herself. Lucy apparently had an agenda that didn't include parenting high on the priority list. I was no longer allowed to be the parent and Lucy elected not to be. Amy was the victim. The situation caused some long term problems and I regret to say Amy and I haven't had contact in a many years.

Nataanii (Chief) Jones – With my marriage to Roberta, I was instant parent to three children, Kevin, Karen and Kenny and the official Head of a Native American Household. Kevin and Karen were eleven and ten years old. Kenny was about five. Kevin and Karen were both well mannered, fun loving kids. They were a delight to be around. Kenny was a little different. He wasn't born with Kevin's mental horsepower and lacked Karen's innocent charm. Realizing I could have been a better parent to Amy, I made it a priority to be a more dedicated and helpful parent to my new brood. With the two oldest ones, it was an easy job. They were receptive and seemed to love the attention they were getting. They hadn't had a father in the home since they were old enough to walk.

I spent a lot of time with Kevin and Karen. I took my baseball background to the field as a Little League coach. Kevin became one of my star players and we won the championship. We spent a lot of time camping and even more time in Ganado on the reservation. To tell the truth, that was pretty close to more camping,

Step-Daughter Karen Tso Age 11

but it was great family time. Kevin had an aptitude for math and I spent time coming up with math challenges that he seemed to enjoy and that helped him get ahead of his classmates in school. Kevin was nicknamed "Otter" and was always quick with a smile or a laugh.

Karen was as sweet as a young girl could be. She was shy, warm hearted and a delight to be around. When she asked for help with her homework, we sat down and went over it until she felt comfortable with it. For one school project, we spent a week building a Navajo hogan, sheep corral, sweat-lodge and she ended up with an "A" in the class. Forty years later, she still has fond memories of those days (and the hogan).

I was confronted with a new parenting challenge I would have never dreamed I would have to face. One day Karen came home from school with tears running down her face. When I asked her what had happened, she told me a group of the kids had ganged up on her and taunted her about being an Indian. I recalled how young kids could be ruthlessly cruel and insensitive. I had been so myself as a young kid. I am ashamed of it to this day, but I knew it could happen. Karen and I had a long talk on the subject of discrimination, cruel and immature boys and about how she should be proud of who and what she was. I shared her pain and frustration. In the end, the best medicine turned out to be a big hug. Maybe I was finally learning how to be a parent.

As Roberta's health declined, everyone's life was turned upside down. She would spend her dying days on the reservation in Northeastern Arizona and the kids would go with her. When she died, Kevin and Karen were whisked away to a Mormon home in Provo, Utah. I wasn't told where and lost contact with her. For twenty-five years, I made attempts to find her, but was unsuccessful. Finally, I vowed to drive to the old homeland and not give up until she was found. With my old friend, Bob Quackenbush, I drove to Ganado. I found old hogans in which I had stayed abandoned. One had been burned. Family members I had known were dead and buried. I finally found someone that knew Karen was living in St. George, Utah. I scheduled a trip to St. George. We had our long awaited reunion. We hugged just like we did when she came home from school with tears in her eyes. We remain close to this day. She has returned to the reservation and leads the life of a traditional Navajo near Ganado. She is always happy to see us and insists I'm the only "real Dad" she's ever had. Maybe I had finally become a parent after all.

The Storm Approaches - When I moved to the White Mountains and fell in love with the spunky Irish girl named Liz, she had a four year old daughter she had adopted just before her first marriage had broken apart. Tempest had fiery red hair and a personality to match both hair and name. She was a kick to be around. She was fun loving and showed not a hint of shyness. At the time, I didn't imagine I would ultimately marry Liz and adopt Tempest. But as fate revealed itself, I became a parent for the third time.

One might think that with enough practice, I'd be an expert in the art of raising a daughter. Oh how I wish this was true, but unfortunately, every song comes with different music. Tempest was a wonderful kid, but she was far from perfect. Looking back, she was a pretty normal kid. She wasn't an outstanding student, but when considering her rootstock, she probably performed at close to her full potential in school.

Many years ago, there was a television comedy called "Kids say the Darndest Things". Tempest had a few that I'm sure would have qualified. Liz and I both believe that communication skills are critical to success in life. We tried to work with Tempest in every way possible to help her develop those skills. I remember one day talking with Tempest when she was about seven. She wanted to tell me about someone who couldn't hear. "She's death" Tempest said. I understood what she was trying to say and spoke up to gently correct her.

"You mean she's 'deaf'", I calmly told her. "'Death' is when someone dies. 'Deaf' is the word that means someone can't hear."

"Well someone can't hear when she's dead" she said. Point, set, match to Tempest.

Our greatest regret as parents was that we chose to raise Tempest in Show Low. The dominant social group in the schools corresponded with the dominant religious group in town – the Mormons. If your child was a member of this cliquish and cultish demographic, you were welcomed and included in all the activities. Many of the teachers were Mormon and beyond a shadow of a doubt favored the Mormon kids over the non-

Mormons. The end result was Tempest was forced to be in the outcast group of non-Mormons. Her friends tended to be those who were viewed as nonconformists, hence they tended to become nonconformists. Even with high achievement, it wouldn't be viewed as being as good as a Mormon kid's mediocre performance. On one occasion, the principal of the junior high school punished Tempest for the fact that we took her out of school to do a history tour in Boston while her classmates went bowling. Parenting in that environment definitely presented some challenges above and beyond the usual obstacles faced by parents.

Tempest with a tarantula in her hair about 1990

My brother Jeff once talked about a discussion he had with his son when Derek entered his teen years. "Son," he said, "You're about to enter a dark tunnel. I'll see you when you come out the other end in about ten years." When Tempest became a teenager, like most teenagers for countless generations, she entered that tunnel. It was a time when she discovered she knew far more than her parents. It was nice for Liz and me; it was as if we had our own animated version of Wikipedia to clarify any misconceptions we might have … and we had many. I'm sure the teen years have evolved such that the process of leaving the nest is welcomed by all parties involved. It was a period of growth for Tempest. She grew boobs and an attitude. If the truth be known, her passage into the teen era wasn't all that bad. She was still generally good natured and was usually pleasant to be around.

We were always conscious of the fact that Tempest was an "only child". She had no brothers or sisters at home who could help her learn critical social skills like sharing and conflict resolution. We did our best to overcome the problem by hosting a "best friend" on many of our frequent trips around the country. It seemed like a great idea at the time, but would ultimately prove to be the single worst parenting decision we'd ever made. For a couple of years, Kortney Eisenhour was Tempest's best friend. She was with us on a number of trips. One to San Francisco and Lake Tahoe was very memorable and delightful. Everyone had a wonderful time and the strategy seemed to be working. They acted like sisters and the socialization challenge seemed to be on track. Courtney was from a Mormon family and ultimately, she and Tempest drifted into different social and philosophical worlds.

Shelley Scott was the beginning of the end of Tempest's future. They were classmates throughout high school and for years, they studied ballet together. Shelley was an energetic and pleasant girl. She was good natured and had a quick wit. Unfortunately, Shelley was raised by a single mother that was less than an ideal role model. Jill was a welfare queen. She lived in a dirty, run-down trailer in an area we used to call the "Cedar Triangle", an area inhabited by nutcases from the fringes of society. She could drink her weight in cheap beer and had some major challenges with determining right from wrong. Her code of ethics was non-existent. Her moral compass had a bent needle and had never been magnetized. In a nutshell, she was a lazy liability to society and she was as dumb as an ox. Shelley didn't stand a ghost's chance in hell of crawling out of the moral abyss in which she was raised.

When Shelley and Tempest first became friends, her outgoing and friendly demeanor masked the devil within. Shelley spent countless hours at our house. She traveled with us all over the country. The girls became inseparable friends. Sadly, an unfortunate combination of two realities altered the course of Tempest's life and not for the better.

Shelley was a bit of a plotter. Like any and all responsible parents, we had our rules. Just little things like … no wild parties at the house if we weren't there. Actually, we weren't too keen on having wild parties at the house even if we were there, but for the most part, life in the Jones household was fairly open and reasonably permissive. That wasn't good enough for Shelley. She thought she should be able to do whatever she wanted to do whenever she wanted to do it. She could and would manipulate Tempest to lie, cheat and steal. Naturally, that didn't go over very well with us. The girls were never pleased when they were caught building a house of deception. Shelley worked Tempest without end. She tried to convince Tempest we were overbearing parents and that life would be better for her if she moved out.

Shelley's mother was too dumb to know which direction was up, but it didn't matter because she was usually too drunk to stand up anyway. She jumped right in the middle of the turmoil and when Tempest turned eighteen, Jill tried to convince Tempest to move in with them. Coincidentally, Tempest had always been a frugal kid and had a bank account of a couple thousand dollars which she was saving for college. After convincing Tempest to move out, they next convinced her she needed to buy furniture for the trailer so everyone had a nice place to sleep. There went Tempest's entire bankroll. The Scotts had now doubled their net worth.

Liz was devastated and felt much betrayed. I also felt betrayed, but seemed to be better equipped to deal with the situation. That's not to say I liked it, but I had long ago learned not to fret over things where you had little or no control. As you can imagine, Tempest's new found "lifestyle" wasn't one to elicit pride. She was now running with a crowd that looked up to the Scott household as middle America, something to aspire to. There was liquor and there were drugs. It wasn't pretty.

In the course of raising Tempest, we had never tried to deceive her about the fact that she had been adopted. We had always promised her that when she came of legal age and if she wanted to find her birth parents, we would do whatever possible to help her in that quest. When she turned eighteen, but before she moved out, she said she wanted to find them. We hired an investigator to help us with the search. It was interesting to discover that both Shelley and her mother constantly played the adoption card with Tempest telling her, "You don't have to do anything they say. They're not even your real parents."

Nonetheless, we remained true to our word and continued to pay the investigator to seek answers. A few months after Tempest left home, we found the birth-mother. She lived ninety miles to the west in Payson, Arizona. We contacted Tempest and gave her the news. A date and time was set to drive to Payson and meet the birth mother and three of her four other children. Tempest would finally have a genetic heritage, a physical link to her past, to her ancestors.

Every adoptee has dreams of their personal story. Maybe Tempest was the daughter of a movie star who had to give her up to avoid a career destroying scandal. Perhaps she was the daughter of a high ranking politician or a famous sports star. The reality rarely turns out to be so glamorous. It certainly didn't turn out to be a glorious history for Tempest. The hunt for the mother had taken a long time because she refused to return any phone calls for fear they were from bill collectors. We learned she had a total of five children by (she thinks) five different fathers. She wasn't exactly a member of society's highest echelon. Tempest was the middle child and the only one that was given away. One was in jail. Another was "mentally handicapped". The family clearly took more from society than it contributed.

Regardless of the less than dazzling discoveries surrounding the makeup of her immediate family, Tempest would at least come away with knowledge of her ancestry ... or so we thought. We were all stunned when we learned that the birth mother, Daphne, was herself adopted and had absolutely no clue as to the identities of her own birth parents. Tempest came away unfulfilled. She replaced her ancestral dead-end with another dead-end.

As a footnote to the story, we continued our search for the birth father. It took us about ten years, but we finally found him. Liz and I arranged a meeting with the man. I had never been in a maximum security prison before; it was a most interesting visit. Michael Connelly was a guest of the State of Arizona and would be for another thirty-five years if he maintained good behavior and was paroled when he finally became eligible. It seems his felonies involved use of a deadly weapon while raping people. And he seemed like such a nice guy when we met him. The prison warden assured us he had some major mental problems and our discussion with him did nothing to dispel that allegation. We met his brother about a year later. Jim Stidd said the umbilical cord had been wrapped around Michael's neck at birth. He called him a "blue baby" who suffered some oxygen deprivation. He speculated that Michael had some brain damage as a result.

When all was said and done, we did our best to live up to our commitments as parents. When we look at Tempest today, we sometimes feel like we could have done better in our roles as parents. But all things considered, we feel like we did a pretty good job. I've gained a deeper understanding that we all have to deal with the forces of nature and of nurture. Both are powerful and irresistible.

As I reminisce on my years as a parent, I realize how it is the epitome of the education process. What I didn't realize on the front end was that it isn't just the child that is the beneficiary. The parent learns patience, understanding, caring and love. Parenting is like flying a kite; you can't let it get too high and you can't let it get too close to the ground. Sometimes you've got to take fast action to avoid trouble. You let it work with the wind and when things go well and it flies high in the sun laden sky, it becomes a thing of beauty and a source of joy.

Chapter Thirteen – Vice, Evil and Avarice

I saved this chapter as the last to write. I've been afraid that I might have to tell some sordid stories about things this angelic gentleman could never have done. I hate to tarnish my halo. However, if the truth be known, I wasn't really a perfect kid. I didn't grow up to become the perfect adult. George Bernard Shaw once said, "Morals are a luxury of the rich." Any student of history quickly figures that one out. In fact the cynics in the crowd carry the belief that even amongst the rich, impeccable morals are in very limited quantity.

Sticky Fingers - When I was seven or so, I developed a mild case of the sticky fingers. My mother took me to Hudson's Department Store. It was the Macy's of Detroit and carried everything under the sun. As she shopped for clothing, I wandered nearby fighting the boredom of a seven year old trapped in the dress racks of women's fashions. I drifted into the nearby men's area where leather goods were on display. I slowly looked at the offerings and came upon a rich looking, beautifully tooled leather wallet. It had a ten dollar price tag in 1954; it wasn't a cheap one. I wanted that wallet in the worst way (pun intended), but knew my mother wouldn't spring for it. I certainly didn't have that kind of money; my weekly allowance was one thin dime. Security cameras had yet to be invented. No one was watching. I slipped the wallet into the position for which it was intended. I put it in my pocket. Soon we were on our way home.

The following day, I was in my room admiring this thing of beauty. My mother walked in. "Where did you get that wallet?" she stammered.

"I found it," I said. I wasn't lying. As the interrogation intensified, it became increasingly apparent to my inquisitor that I had walked with the wallet without waiting to pay the tab. She was angry and frustrated. Remember, parenting comes without the instruction manual. After some deliberation, she dragged my ass back to Hudson's. She stood in the background as I presented my explanation, apology and the wallet back to the sale's clerk. She knew that would forever expunge the klepto-urge from her otherwise morally pure son. It didn't work.

A couple years later, I had developed a passion for chemistry. I never dreamed I'd ultimately become a chemical engineer and work making bombs and dynamite, but the allure of making black powder and smoke bombs was too much to resist as a nine year old in Detroit. After receiving a "chemistry set" from Santa Claus, I set up my lab and went to work. It didn't take long before I was running out of ingredients for my diabolical pursuits. There was a hobby store a few blocks from the house. It offered small bottles of chemicals. I couldn't afford to buy all the chemicals I wanted. I went to the hobby store and stood in front of the shelves full of little bottles. For twenty minutes I stared at the chemicals. I pulled a bottle off the rack and carefully read the label. I put it back and grabbed another and slowly read the label. Frankly, there wasn't much to read, but there was plenty to think about – like how to slip it into my pocket without getting caught. Looking back on it, my actions were so obvious, I might as well have had a sign on my back that said "shoplifter in training".

When I thought the coast was clear, one bottle ended up in my pocket rather than back on the shelf. I walked home triumphant and undetected. Who says crime doesn't pay. I was back the next day. If I wasn't obvious the previous day, I had to stick out like a hooker at a tent revival. I had read enough labels to have memorized the store's entire inventory. Yet another bottle magically found its way into my pocket.

The store owner came over and stood next to me. "Are you looking for something in particular?" he asked.

"No, I'm just looking." I suspect my nerves betrayed me. Suddenly, he reached over and tapped my coat pocket. He reached in and removed the little bottle of Sulphur. He held it up and with an executioner's expression, confronted me.

"Were you planning on paying for this?" He knew the answer, but I wasn't going to throw it the towel. It was then I discovered my undeveloped talent for extemporaneous speaking.

"I already paid for this," I exclaimed. "I bought it yesterday when I was in the store." What balderdash! What balls! Surely he would remember I didn't buy anything the day before, but I rambled on. "You can call my mother and ask her."

I had visions of a striped suit, a ball-and-chain and a future of breaking rocks with a sledge hammer in the hot sun. I knew I was busted, but I persisted. Somehow, I won the battle. After a two minute – seemed like a lifetime – presentation of a fabrication, I was free. I can't believe I convinced him, but I must have put enough doubt in his mind that he let me go. I walked out the door with great haste. I had a bottle of Sulphur in my pocket; I had purchased it yesterday at a store in my mind.

The whole experience unnerved me. I truly thought I was going to jail. It seemed to have the effect that my mother had tried to instill a couple years earlier. I never helped myself to someone else's merchandise again. It did not, however, mark the end of my life on the darker side.

Sticky Fingers, Part II – Sex in the Sixties – Like all adolescents, I entered those years when I transitioned from boyhood to manhood. Nature had written the script for those times and like everyone that preceded me and everyone that would follow, I was going to read my lines with enthusiasm.

When I first moved to Northville and was preparing to enter my freshman year of high school, I met Sandy Parmenter. We hit it off well together and I developed a little crush on her. At fourteen, I had developed a healthy interest in girls, but I hadn't quite put all the pieces together just yet. When Sandy invited me to visit her at her summer house on a lake about fifteen miles distant, I thought it would be fun, especially in view of the fact that she'd be in her bathing suit. Despite that observation, it wasn't about sex; it was social interaction. The trip turned sexual right after I left the house.

I walked the length of a football field to Eight Mile Road and stuck out my thumb. It was my first attempt at hitchhiking and it wasn't long before a car stopped. I jumped in the front seat and thanked the man for the ride. As we drove off, the man struck up a conversation. He asked me my name and I told him. He engaged in what I perceived as idle chat. Finally after driving a couple miles, he turned to me and asked, "So Howard, tell me. Are you gay?"

I had never heard the term used for any other purpose than to reference a state of being happy. I had no clue it carried "other" connotations. It struck me as a rather odd question. I concluded he was leading into some joke or riddle of some kind, maybe some version of a "knock-knock" joke. Still it seemed silly. I could answer the question either way. I thought "Hell, I'll play the game."

"Yea, sure," I responded. I waited for the punchline.

"Do you want to go over to my house for the afternoon?" he asked. I must have appeared totally confused by his question.

"Howard, do you know what 'gay' means?"

"Happy?" I answered.

He seemed surprised by my answer and tried to educate me. "No, it's when two people get together and have fun sexually."

I was stunned. It still didn't begin to dawn on me what he was trying to say. With a skull thicker than Lake Ontario ice in February, I jumped to what proved to be an erroneous conclusion.

"Oh no!" I said. "My dad would kill me if I ever got a girl pregnant." I was aghast.

With a bit of a chuckle he said, "No. It's not like that. It's when two men get together and have fun sexually." You could have hit me with a brick and I wouldn't have been any more stunned. As the reality quickly settled in, I promptly told the guy that my girlfriend lived on the lake just over the hill from where we presently were.

"This is where I get out," I claimed with my eyes wide open. He stopped the car. I got out and walked the two miles back to my house. I didn't make it to Sandy's lake house that day, but I did get an education. That was the day I learned that "happy" and "gay" were not always synonyms. Oh my!

By the time I was sixteen, all body parts (with the possible exception of the brain) were fully functional. I had graduated from National Geographic to Playboy magazine. I had learned a lot about that fundamental instinct upon which all human life was dependent. I had experimented with my girlfriend in the back seat of our 62 Ford Fairlane, but the lesson hadn't arrived at the "final exam" yet. I was determined to cross that one last line that separated me from adulthood.

Kent Kipfer was a good friend of mine. As soon as I turned sixteen, the two of us jumped in his 55 Ford and headed off to the west coast of Michigan. We camped for a week on the beach and did our best to meet the girls and fulfill our destinies. Although we had a great time, we fell short of our goals.

After our return to Northville, we devised a plan to drive down to John R and Brush Streets in the heart of Detroit. It was the area the ladies of the night plied their trade. When Saturday night rolled around, Kent picked me up and we pointed the car in the direction of downtown Detroit. It was well past dark-thirty as we cruised Brush Street. The buildings were well worn as were many of the ladies who approached our car whenever we stopped at an intersection. "Fi-dolla" seemed to be the going rate. Kent and I kept shopping, giggling as we evaluated our options. Finally we parked the car. We got out and walked toward a dark and weather worn brick building. Some girls were waving us over and we walked in that direction.

I'm sure most people remember their "first time". I certainly do. I suspect most people have memories of a romantic scene with a sequence of events that led to a rapturous arrival at the pinnacle of life's grandest summit. Over the ensuing years, our memories probably work behind the scenes to decorate that magic time with fineness and fluff that includes everything but the music. My memory has to work harder to dress up that night. When the door was closed, she applied a washrag and a bar of soap to make sure I was genitally spiffy. She asked if I brought a raincoat. She put it on me. And a young, nervous kid of sixteen galloped into the night with fear and trepidation, so much fear and trepidation that I still hadn't finished the final question on the exam that would have allowed me to graduate into manhood. After about five minutes, I was out the door. She bid me farewell by asking me, "Hey, you got a dollar fo da room?"

How About a Beer – No journey into the world of vice and decadence would be complete without a bottle of hooch. My Grandfather Jones drank a lot. He got pretty feisty when he did. In his later years, I'd stop by his place and take him over to the neighborhood beer garden for a cold one. My mother's mother, my Grandmother Radcliffe, never drank. She did, however, take medicine when she was ill. The potion usually had a wine label or was poured from a bottle labeled "brandy", but it was strictly medicinal. The devil made you drink liquor, but the lord gave you medicine for healing. My grandmother seemed to be a sickly woman quite often. With my family history, it should come as no surprise that I have no problem partaking. I wouldn't want to let my ancestors down and turn into one of those insufferable teetotalers.

When I was in high school, a number of my classmates were already experimenting with alcohol by the time they were freshman. With each passing year, a few more fell by the wayside. By the time I was a senior, I still hadn't had a beer with or without the boys. I told you I was an angel. My record of abstinence was blown into the winds of history when I was invited to join the other seniors on the football team to celebrate our successful season the night following our final game in November of 1964. The team's seniors were going to pitch a couple of big tents out in the woods somewhere and spend the night drinking and reveling until they could no more. Cars would be parked nearby, but keys would be hidden. No one would drive until the following day.

The beer was Carling Black Label and Pabst Blue Ribbon and there was lots of each. More than fifty years later, I still remember much of that night. There was a lot of horseplay and a lot of laughter. Bob Tuck, a two hundred forty pound offensive tackle stands out in my memory. After copious quantities of brew had been consumed, Bob climbed about twenty feet up in a tree. He took a beer and a box of matches with him. He then spent the next thirty minutes striking matches, carefully bringing them around to his back side and lighting farts. It was our own version of the Fourth of July as every minute or so, we saw a flash of light as Bob produced what seemed like a never ending supply of flammable gas. Yes, we were a sophisticated bunch. And some people wonder why football players have a less than Phi Beta Kappa image. I can't begin to imagine.

The following day, some of us had our first experience with another of life's inglorious conditions. I experienced my first hangover. It wasn't a pleasant experience, but it wasn't so unpleasant as to cause me to give up drinking for good. By the following weekend, I was ready for "Round Two".

Like a lot of people at that age, I had yet to learn how to drink responsibly. I'm not sure how other people do it, but my approach was pretty much trial-and-error. It generally involved drinking irresponsibly and then saying, "Nope, that wasn't the smartest thing to do." After hearing the accounts of others over the years, it seems I followed the most common approach. Sadly for some, that approach led to their untimely ends.

To suggest that I became a teetotaler would be like saying Mickey Rooney was a star basketball player. Neither ever happened. However, with age I learned to drink responsibly and I usually did so. There were times where I may have crossed the line. One time while in Lima, Peru I went to a party where I had so many pisco sours that I actually got on the dance floor for a fast dance. When you realize how much I despise dancing, you know I had to have overindulged that evening. One time after our team clinched at least a top three finish in the Western Regionals of the National Fastpitch Softball Tournament, I overindulged along with the rest of my teammates. I'm sure there were other instances, but the chapter on vice is already too long. My trick has been don't drive in such situations and don't get caught when you do.

Just Say Yes to Drugs – I wasn't aware of my first encounter with illicit drugs. I was a naïve college freshman who had just wasted my first semester in college partying and having a good time. When it came time for final exams, I felt like I wasn't prepared. If the truth be known, I wasn't as prepared as I thought. Nonetheless, I joined many of the other under-prepared students in my dorm in a big room to "cram". Cramming amounted to reading the books that should have been read weeks before. For many of the students, it was study until they dropped or fell asleep.

Imagine my intrigue when a friend told me about a "study pill". According to Kent, if you took one of these pills, you could easily stay awake all night, study and remember everything you read. This sounded like just what the doctor ordered for me. I couldn't take the pill fast enough.

I later learned I had ingested amphetamine or "speed". I did indeed stay up all night studying. In fact, I stayed up all night the next night too. By the third night, I still felt awake, but my body was starting to wear down. I hadn't eaten much and without sleep for three days and my tank was definitely running on empty. A little after midnight, my friend suggested we go to an all-night restaurant near the campus, I thought it was a good idea. We sat at a table and ordered breakfast. Before the meal was served, I began to feel extremely dizzy. For some reason, I felt compelled to get out of the restaurant. I stood up and staggered toward the entry. It was freezing cold outside. I stumbled across the icy sidewalk. I took another step or two into Michigan Avenue, Kalamazoo's main thoroughfare and I lost consciousness. I have no recollection of anything after that until the following morning when I woke up in my dorm.

How did the "study pill" work? Obviously, it was very effective in keeping me awake. However, the claim that you would remember everything you read is questionable at best. I damn near flunked out of college that semester. I must have forgotten something.

When I started college, I really hadn't heard of marijuana. I was too busy self-schooling on the merits of slow gin, beer and Southern Comfort to recognize the arrival of the children of the sixties. Early in my sophomore year at Western Michigan, I declared myself wise beyond my years, dropped out of college and married Lucy Byard. After a series of stabs at establishing a "career", I was hired as a newscaster and reporter. I also ended up hosting a popular jazz show in Ann Arbor, a progressive university town in Michigan. The door to the age of "flower power" opened wide.

As the host of a jazz show, much of my new found celebrity was in my own mind, but not all of it. It wasn't long before I became a fairly well known "personality" in Ann Arbor. I became a fixture at The Golden Falcon, a popular jazz club downtown. I was introduced to a broad variety of Ann Arbor's more "colorful" figures. I moved effortlessly between the university crowd and the black jazz community. Vietnam provided impetus to the counter culture; protests and riots filled the streets. It was my job to get into the middle of it all ... and I did.

It was through friends at The Golden Falcon that I was introduced to pot. I tried it and found it to be a seemingly harmless ticket to an "A" ride of euphoria. I introduced it to Lucy and she too found it to be a pleasant source of smiles and giggles. At about the same time, we discovered many of our old friends from high school and college alike had been swept up in the rush to "heightened relaxation". Like so many young people of that era, marijuana smoking became an integral part of our social scene. From late 1967 through 1975, most days were capped off with some of nature's most ubiquitous herb.

There were those who argued that marijuana was a "gateway" drug and that it led to other more dangerous drugs. In a back-door sort of way, it was true. In that society had criminalized this relatively harmless substance, its users (which amounted to a majority of college age Americans) were forced to deal with those who worked on the other side of the legal line in order to acquire their stashes. What was even more dangerous was the fact that most pot smokers discovered they had been lied to by the "establishment". It wasn't the debilitating, mind destroying drug it was made out to be in the likes of the famous film "Reefer Madness". Hence, millions of "inquiring minds" asked the logical question, "If they're lying to us about marijuana, are they lying to us about all these other naughty substances?"

There was only one easy way to find out – give them a try.

The evidence against heroin seemed to be pretty overwhelming, but without firsthand experience, I couldn't really pass judgment. I was introduced to a pretty hardcore addict through a friend at The Golden Falcon. One night, I gave it a try. With my long standing affliction with trypanophobia, you can be sure the experiment didn't include injection. It did, however, involve ingestion. The white powder was sucked up through a rolled up dollar bill into the nose. Even though this occurred nearly fifty years ago, I can still remember much of that evening. I recall feeling absolutely stupefied in a most pleasant sort of way. I was conscious, but completely without motivation. I was anesthetized to the point where I probably could have performed open heart surgery on myself and smiled throughout the process. I remember thinking that I was in a state of such complete euphoria that little or nothing mattered. But I also remember thinking that the only purpose I served on the planet at that time was as a paperweight and I wasn't real certain of that.

When the sun rose the following morning, I was glad I had undergone the experience, but I knew that I would never do it again. It was pleasant, incredibly pleasant. But life isn't meant to be that pleasant.

As The Beatles sang "Lucy in the Sky with Diamonds", we rode along with them. It was the time of Timothy Leary – "Turn On, Tune In, Drop Out". Bob Dylan was singing "The Times They are a Changing." Society was in a state of upheaval. Woodstock drew more than 200,000 members of the counter-culture and they all got along. Friends introduced us to psycho-active drugs like mescaline, magic mushrooms (psilocybin) and LSD. I had heard stories about the mind-awakening qualities of such things and felt like only through firsthand experience could I reach a valid conclusion. In 1971, I had returned to college. Mind altering substances would become a part of my advanced education.

Over the course of the next four or so years, I probably went on visits to the other side of the mind a couple dozen times. Did it alter my level of "consciousness"? Unquestionably yes. Did it alter my philosophical viewpoints on life? Beyond a shadow of a doubt. Without belaboring the matter, it opened some doors inside my mind and showed me that the mind is an incredibly powerful thing. I experienced many things that were clearly not "real", but I saw how the mind can build alternative realities that appear every bit as real as the reality in which most of our time is spent. (There are erudite scholars that suggest "normal" reality isn't.) The experiences opened my mind to possibilities that I had never dreamed. They permitted me to see my place in the universe in a very different manner. It is not coincidence that these experiences corresponded with my renewed focus on knowledge and learning. I graduated from Michigan State University with extremely high grades. The focus and insights gained during the forays into chemically induced alternative realities were to a large extent the most significant factors leading to my high academic performance. This brings into question the matter of whether or not the use of these drugs was a "vice", but they were illegal, so "vice" they are.

Shortly after I graduated from college, I was sitting at home one evening after enjoying a "doobie". I recall enjoying a feeling of being completely relaxed, but something wasn't right. The sense of pleasure was fine, but I wasn't "doing" anything constructive.

Yet the life's clock kept on ticking. I felt like my time on earth was limited and that at that moment, I was being complete unproductive. I decided I had things in my life that needed to be done and they weren't going to be done while I sat around like a happy vegetable. At that moment, I stopped smoking pot. It wasn't a statement about being better. It wasn't an attempt to elevate me from the depths of happiness and contentment. It was simply a matter of having other things to do. To this day, I don't fear marijuana. I don't begrudge anyone else for smoking it. I just have other things to do. Maybe someday, I won't.

Chapter Fourteen - The Sporting Life

The story of my life wouldn't be complete without a glimpse into the world of sports. From my early childhood on, sports have been an integral part of my daily existence. My father was a respectable athlete. He played football in high school and while at Pasadena City College in the 1940's. He used to delight in telling people he was one of a very few athletes who played in the Rose Bowl four times. After his victims raised their eyebrows in stunned amazement, he would then confess it was because the Rose Bowl stadium was the home field for his school. Both of my grandfathers were accomplished baseball players. And my maternal grandmother could throw a rolling pin with deadly accuracy.

My earliest recollection of the sporting world came four months prior to my fifth birthday. My father gave me a Remington Model 6 .22 caliber rifle, the same one he had been given a week before his fifth birthday. All the men on my father's side of the family were hunters and fishermen. It was just assumed I would follow in their footsteps. The Jones boys fed themselves with rod and rifle before migrating to Michigan from the Georgian Bay area of Canada in the mid-nineteenth century. They maintained the tradition in Michigan for as long as they lived.

My father began taking me out on weekends to teach me how to handle a gun. We would spend hours out in the woods learning how to shoot – breathing, trigger pressure, adjusting the sight, shooting at moving targets and above all else – gun safety. To this day I treat all guns as if they're loaded even if I know they're not. I never, never point a gun at someone unless I plan to shoot. Those lessons were so strongly inculcated in my early years, I'm seriously bothered if I see a child point what I know to be a toy gun at anyone, especially me.

I actually became quite proficient by the time I was seven or so. My father encouraged me to shoot a couple of his bigger guns. I still remember getting knocked backwards the first time I pulled the trigger on his sixteen gauge shotgun. I began to realize my destiny did not include following in the family's footsteps when my father first took me deer hunting. I wasn't all that enthused to begin with, but what little enthusiasm I might have had quickly disappeared when my father rolled me out of bed at three in the morning on a cold and miserable night. We had to be at our chosen spot before the first light of dawn. Out we went. I was told it was going to be fun. I don't think my father intended on lying to me; he was just wrong.

We traipsed through heavy brush, thorns, stickers, swamp, more thorns, more swamp and more stickers. It was pitch dark and I walked into overhanging tree limbs. It was freezing and I broke through a layer of ice and fell into shallow swamp water every minute or so. There was a light snow falling. My feet were now wet. And all of this was just so I could murder some cute, little, furry animal who had done nothing to me. This was supposed to be "fun"? The family tradition was in serious jeopardy at this point.

Over the course of the next twenty-five years, I did a little hunting, but frankly, it was more out of a sense of obligation and social pressure than it was for enjoyment. When I did hunt, I went after the most difficult game to bag. My rationale was that if I significantly lowered the odds of finding my prey, I wouldn't have to worry about killing it. That worked pretty well.

Liz put the exclamation mark on my resignation from the world of the great bwanas. A short time after we were married, her father and some friends were going quail hunting. He asked me to go along. I dutifully obliged. Early on in the day, we got into a small covey of quail and I took one down. I put it in my bag and continued on in search of the rest of dinner. We never saw another bird. There's something in my nature that tells me it is immoral to kill for sport. I believe it is acceptable to kill only for defense or sustenance. Clearly, the bird did not threaten me so by definition, he was in the bag for consumption. The only problem was that one quail isn't enough to feed one person. When I got home, I told Liz about the day and put the solitary quail in the freezer. I assumed another day would bring some more quail, enough for a full meal.

The following weekend, I was sitting in my office writing. Liz was preparing a meal for the three of us. I heard the call – "Howard, dinner's ready." I rounded the corner and found that she had not only cooked the solitary quail, she had served it on a huge silver platter adorned with a carving knife and fork big enough to handle a side of beef. There sat mashed potatoes, dressing, beans … the makings of a full Thanksgiving Day meal with a tiny, lone quail lost in the immensity of a grand silver platter. Liz looked at me with her big baby blue eyes and with a perfectly straight face said, "It's time to carve the bird." She then doubled over in uncontrollable laughter. To this day, she laughs uncontrollably when this story is told. I never hunted again.

My life as a fisherman followed a similar path to my life as a hunter. My paternal grandfather lived to fish. I spent countless hours with him on the lake or the river bank with rod and reel in hand. Sure, we ate the fish we caught and lots of them, but it just never felt like a sport to me. I did a lot of fishing on Green Lake as a child. When you're a boy living on a lake, it's tough to not do some fishing. But somehow, it always struck me that sitting in a boat with the sun beating down upon me while I tried to think like a bass didn't put me at the pinnacle of intellectual achievement. It gave me an acute sense of failure when the bass outwitted me and I came home empty handed. Again, my fishing experiences were more out of sense of social obligation than desire. If I really wanted fish for dinner, I'd be more inclined to grab a fishing pole, don a pair of waders and try my luck in the sea food section of the local grocery store. It would just strike me as far more efficient than sitting in a boat for hours.

My ambivalence for fishing was always shared by Liz. When our boating lives took us out to sea later in life, the crew loved to fish. The captain would ask if he should set some lines for marlin or tuna; he pretended he was doing it for us. We knew better, the crew members were the ones who loved to hook-up with the big ones. We'd tell them to go ahead and set the lines.

Liz and I would be sitting and reading or working on the computer or just taking in the view when we'd hear and feel the captain cut the engines and begin to circle. We knew we had a hook-up. We also knew the crew would feel compelled to find us and "let" us land the fish. We didn't want to so we always launched into a bit of a game running all over the boat trying to hide from the crew. They would soon give up trying to find us and one of them would reel in the catch. We'd show up on the rear deck about the time they were ready to land the fish. It was quite a show. One of them would work the line while another would artfully begin fileting the fish before it was ever completely on the deck. They had fun and we avoided the work. We were all happy, especially when we'd have the freshest sushi grade tuna right from the sea without having to work up a sweat to get it.

Batter Up – It wasn't my idea; it was my dad's. I was six or seven years old and my father concluded it was time I became a baseball player. He bought a ball and a glove and launched his campaign to have me become the next Babe Ruth. I still remember the glove; it was a "Willie 'Puddin-Head' Jones" model. He could have started me out with a rubber ball or a tennis ball, but no. If I was to become a baseball star I had to be weaned on a major league hardball. Nearly every evening, he took me out in front of the house to play catch. For the first three or four weeks, the session ended the same way. I misjudged a toss and instead of catching the ball with the pocket of my glove, I tried to snag it with a spot somewhere in the middle of my forehead. I ended up running into the house crying probably more out of frustration and embarrassment than pain. We were both beginning to wonder if the lump on my forehead was to become a permanent ornament, but with time, I started getting the hang of it. It wasn't all that long before I started to get pretty good at it – at least for a kid that hadn't yet learned how to write in cursive.

By the time I was eight or nine, the majority of my waking moments from spring through fall – when not in school – were dedicated to playing baseball. If I wasn't playing street ball with the kids in the neighborhood, I was playing catch with myself by bouncing a ball off the steps or a wall somewhere. Even at school, baseball took up a lot of time. We played baseball during recess. We played a lot in gym class. If I arrived at school early, I went to a place on the side where I had used chalk to mark off a rectangle the size of the strike-zone. I would then throw a ball up against the wall practicing my pitching control and my fielding on the rebound. On a typical school day, I might throw a couple hundred pitches before the first bell of the day rang.

Even during my summers with my cousins at Green Lake, baseball occupied a lot of my time. We used my grandfather's mower to cut a baseball diamond out of the field behind the house and we played for hours on end. When I wasn't playing with others, I went to the lake's edge with an old broken bat with its handle taped. Then one after another after another, I threw rocks into the air and hit them into the lake to practice my swing and improve my hand-eye coordination. I would do this until I literally wore the wood off the bat. I got another old broken bat and started again.

At least one of the two weekend days found me and my father on the baseball field at Mumford High School. He had purchased a dozen brand new hardballs. He would put me in the batter's box and retreat to the pitching mound with all the balls. He pitched and pitched until I'd hit all of the balls into the field. He then jogged around the field to retrieve the balls. He returned to the pitcher's mound and the ritual began again. He did this for hours on end. He worked with me on my fielding techniques. I had to stand with my back to the backstop while he hit ground ball after ground ball to me. By now I had moved on from my Puddin-Head glove to an Al Kaline model, one of the better mitts available at the time. I was getting better and better.

I played Little League ball and was the star of my team. It was the same in the Billy Rogel league, then Babe Ruth and high school ball. I played varsity baseball as a freshman. By the time I was a junior I was getting the attention of some major league scouts. Lou D'Nunnzio of the Detroit Tiger organization first approached my coach. Then he came to me and we talked about my future prospects. He said if I stayed on track, it would be reasonable to expect a minor league contract offer from the Tigers. I pretty well put an end to that when I tried to play my junior year with a broken wrist and a hard head. Who knows where I would have ended up were it not for that one fateful decision? It clearly changed the locus of my future.

Little League at age 12

By the time I was fifteen, I had developed an impressive skill set on the baseball field. I had good running speed, hit with power and had one of the strongest throwing arms ever seen in my hometown. With ninety plus mile per hour throwing speed, I had finished third in the State of Michigan Junior Olympics as a fourteen year old. It seemed the only baseball skill I hadn't yet developed was that of humility. But hey! Frank Lloyd Wright said it best when he stated, "Honest arrogance is better than false humility."

Despite my excessive pride on the ball field, I still chuckle to think that I still hold my high school record for the longest single in the history of the school stadium. The stadium opened for play in 1962 and is still in use fifty-three years later. I know I still hold the record; here's why. It was a chilly day for a ball game. Spring time in Michigan isn't all about flowers. It can get pretty cold. On such days, hitting the ball can make your hands sting painfully. I don't remember who we were playing, but I do remember the wind was blowing in from left center field. I was at bat in the middle innings and the pitcher threw me a watermelon (a euphemism for a straight pitch right in your power zone that you see so well, it looks like a watermelon). I timed my swing to perfection, made a good turn on the ball and got my legs into it well. When a batter really crushes one, he knows it before it leaves the barrel of the bat. I hit it so well, I instantly knew it was not only out of the park, it could be out of the city, maybe even the county. I worried about low flying aircraft. Being a somewhat "confident" player, I didn't want to deprive the crowd of its chance to see me strut down the base path. I cavalierly flipped the bat to the side and slowly began my victory lap around the bases. I wondered if the ball would ever be found and if it was, would it be usable or flat on one side.

The fence in left-center field was the deepest part of the ball park. To hit it out of the park at that point took a prodigious blast. No problem; this was one for the record book. The wind was blowing a little harder now, but I had nothing to worry about. I smiled at the girls in the stands as I continued toward first base. Then I heard it – a distant clinking sound. I glanced toward left-center. The strong winds had apparently caused the ball to fly much higher than I expected and much to my chagrin, much shorter. It had landed on the top of the fence at the very point of the deepest part of the ball park. It apparently bounced nearly straight up into the air and came down just inside the park. It wasn't a homerun after all. It was in play.

My first reaction was one of "Oh shit! I'm in big trouble now. The coach is going to have my head." The first base coach was yelling at me to run. The ball was far enough away that I could at least salvage a double on the hit. I threw it into overdrive and rounded first base like I'd been shot out of a canon. I looked toward second base. All would have turned out alright if I hadn't caught a spike in the ground and fallen face down midway between first and second base. When I regained my feet, I saw the throw coming into second base. I turned and scrambled back to first base diving head first just in time to beat the relay from the second baseman. I remember hearing a guy call out from the stands, "Hey coach. You want some mustard to put on that hotdog on first base?"

After throwing away my pro contract due to the broken wrist, I still could play at a fairly high level. When I returned to Michigan from Oregon, word got around that a good third baseman was back in town. Don Thompson, a multi-millionaire with more money than sense wanted to operate a championship team. He went out and built a magnificent softball stadium and used it as a recruiting tool to pull together the most talented team possible. When I got the knock on the door and the offer, I couldn't turn it down. Nearly every player on the team had played either profession baseball or professional football. It was a team with awesome talent and it went on to win the state championship that year. Although I played the first half of the season, I had to settle for the trophies and a full length cast on my leg. It was while playing on that team that my right knee was catastrophically demolished. Surgery ended that glorious season.

After playing recreational ball a few years and having a lot of fun doing it, I once again got the call. I was recruited to play on a semi-professional team out of Arizona. I still remember taking my position at third base and feeling an exhilaration looking around the field and realizing I was once again playing ball at a high level with some highly skilled – albeit no longer playing in the big leagues – players. The first time we finished infield practice, we left the field with a feeling of confidence knowing we were going places that year. And we did, we ended up going to Nationals and finishing third.

Incidentally, many people have heard the term "semi-pro" and wonder if that's similar to saying someone is semi-tall or even semi-pregnant. If you're wondering what semi-pro ball really is, let me explain. It's when you are playing at a very high level as an amateur, but that you are being paid just enough to cover your necessary "expenses". These might include things like equipment, food, lodging, travel, car payments, entertainment, dancing girls, massages, drinks and other essential items for playing baseball. If the truth be known, I wasn't being paid for all these things. I was simply getting paid anywhere from fifty to a hundred dollars per game and maybe a rare perk or two. We actually had a couple of our players that we had flown in for the big games, one from Los Angeles and another from Texas. Sometimes amateur ball gets to be pretty serious.

My last flash of glory on the baseball diamond came and went quickly. I lived in San Diego and walked a few miles every morning with Liz. On one memorable morning, we walked past a ball field. I wandered over to the field and watched as players from the San Diego Senior League played a competitive game on the diamond. I had barely thrown a ball in nearly twenty-five years, but it looked like these guys were having fun. One of the ringleaders approached me and struck up a conversation. One thing led to another. He asked if I had ever played baseball. Never having shied away from the braggadocio on the subject of baseball, I told him a little bit about my background. He asked me if I'd be interested in playing ball. What an intriguing idea!

"I'm undoubtedly not a good as I used to be, but I'm probably still close to great," I thought to myself. It seems an old ballplayer's ego lives on long past his arm and legs. I agreed to play for one of the Senior League teams. The following Saturday morning, I was there glove in hand and ready to play. I was sixty-four years old. I loosened up and the old throwing arm still seemed to function with maybe a little degradation in velocity. When the game started, I was positioned at my old home – third base. I found that I could still field my position like a vacuum cleaner sucking up crisp ground balls like a real ball player. Unfortunately, my lateral range wasn't nearly what it used to be. As long as the ball was hit within one step left or right of where I stood, it was mine. The first hint of a problem came when I first cut one loose to first base. The old gun that used to throw a ball so hard it literally rose in route to first base hadn't been fired in a while. The ball was thrown on a perfect line, but I watched with a grin as it bounced not once, but twice on its way. I had to put extra postage on it to get it to its destination.

After a couple of swings, my batting skills were obviously still pretty good. I went five for five that day, but the towering blasts that used to sail over the outfield walls didn't seem to go nearly as far as I recalled. Maybe the air in San Diego is heavier. With five hits, I spent a lot of time running the bases that morning. My activity at third base called for the use of a few muscles that had been in dry dock for a quarter century. Despite the challenges, I played well and had a great time. I was warmly received by my teammates and I looked forward to our next game.

I got in my car and drove home. It was a little over two miles and took no more than five minutes. I pulled into the driveway, turned off the engine, opened the door and started to get out. I couldn't move my legs. The abuse I administered to myself had caused my muscles to go on strike. The five minutes allowed them to tighten up so that I truly couldn't lift my legs out of the car. I laughed as a grabbed my cell phone. I called Liz. "I need for you to come and help me," I said. She assumed my car had broken down somewhere.

"Where are you?" she asked.

"I'm in the driveway." She looked out the window and hustled down the stairs. Her eyes were wide, her laugh verged on raucous. She helped lift one leg out of the car. I turned and she helped with the other one. I barely made it up the stairs and spent the better part of the week hobbled by my love affair with my youth. Talk about unrequited love!

For the next two Saturdays, I played with the team and did very well. In the fourth week of my delusional return to my younger years, I had hit a solid single and was standing on first base as a teammate stepped into the batter's box. He swung at the first pitch and hit a shot over the head of the shortstop. I bolted for second base. I heard and felt an audible pop from my lower leg. I immediately went to the ground. I had ruptured my Achilles tendon. One step south of first base on a ball field in San Diego, my illustrious baseball life came to an abrupt and painful end. Oh, but the glory over the years had been an aphrodisiac. The memories still wash over my heart almost every day of my life. Much of the satisfaction of simply doing something well gave meaning to my life that was indescribably delicious.

Many years ago after a ball game in Milwaukee in which I had played particularly well, I left the stadium. The crowd had pretty much disappeared, but when I walked through the gate toward the parking lot, I was approached by a middle aged man and a young boy. He came up to me and said he had waited with his grandson to thank me for playing such a great game. "We really enjoyed watching you play." It was moments like that that made every lump on the forehead, every bruise and cut, every embarrassment and even the ruined knee and painful Achilles heel and each and every one of the thousands of hours of practice and competition worthwhile. Baseball has indeed been very, very good to me.

Get the puck out of here – In the winter months in Michigan there is not a lot of baseball played. Ice hockey is king. In the land of Gordie Howe and Red Wings, it should come as no surprise that hockey was my winter game. I was five when my father got me my first pair of ice skates. He took me to Palmer Park where there was a frozen pond. He strapped on the skates and turned me loose. I joke with people that I became a good swimmer because that took place in July, but it didn't. It was right after Christmas. My father had played hockey as a kid and by god, so was his kid going to be a hockey player (when he wasn't playing baseball).

In those years, money was tight and skates were expensive. Parents knew that kids had an annoying habit of growing, especially if you feed them. Some parents bought skates a couple sizes too big so the kids could "grow into them". They could get a couple seasons out of them that way. They could fill up the void space by wearing four pairs of socks. Unfortunately, that approach doesn't work very well. Just like a hat five sizes too big doesn't ride well on your head, skates don't give much support to your ankles when your feet don't get close to the walls of the boot. My first couple years of skating found me doing everything I could to keep my ankles straight rather than having them collapse on the ice. After a couple years, it became apparent I was going to play hockey at a little higher level than average. I started getting skates that fit properly. It was amazing how my skills improved when I could spend my ice time actually using the blades to skate.

For young boys in Detroit, most hockey was "street hockey". When the streets were snow packed, we piled snow to mark the edge of the goal and had rousing games of hockey that went on for hours in the middle of the street. If a car came down the street, the game was briefly suspended – our version of the commercial timeout. After it passed, we'd rebuild the net markers if necessary and keep on playing.

Most years, I built an ice rink in the back yard. The snow was compacted with our feet. I piled up snow for the rink boundaries. I flooded the entire thing and let Mother Nature do her thing. If I was lucky, the rink would be playable from early December through early March. It was always sad when the ice started to turn to a honeycomb in the early spring. Then we knew we only had another day or two to skate.

By the time I was twelve, I was playing organized hockey in a sanctioned "bantam" league. We played on commercial rinks then although most were still outdoor. But we had real boards for boundaries and real hockey nets for goals. I was becoming a respectable player, but didn't have the standing I did in the world of baseball. Regardless, I loved the game.

When my family moved from Detroit into the Northville countryside, I continued to play a lot of hockey in the winter months. However, there was no high school hockey team and hockey leagues were not as common as they were in HockeyTown. Most of my playing time was spent on frozen ponds and lakes. They were everywhere. A good friend of mine, Gordy Hammond, had a good sized pond by his house and cold winter days started just after sunrise with a good game of hockey on the pond. We all took our turns shoveling the pond to keep the surface playable. We typically played well after dark; he had spotlights on the pond. We built our own nets out of two-by-fours and chicken mesh. No hockey player that has ever played in the frozen north doesn't know the ritual you go through at the end of a long day skating in freezing temperatures. We'd all convene in Gordy's family room where we'd remove our skates and drink hot chocolate made by the gallon by Gordy's mother. Then it began. As the feet began to thaw, the toes started to hurt. It was almost a burning sensation. As they regained their feeling, there was a period of maybe five or ten minutes when the pain was substantial. It was all part of the process. We didn't have to endure it again until the following night after another twelve hours of playing hockey.

I remember one thing about skating on big frozen ponds and lakes that was almost of a spiritual nature. Unless you grew up in Canada or north of the forty-fifth parallel, you've probably never heard the eerie sound. The first time you get on the ice after it has frozen well enough to support skaters, there's an indescribable sound as the ice cracks from settlement. It's almost a musical "boinking" that goes on and on as you first traverse the frozen surface. It's a magical sound and I can still hear it in the sound chamber of my mind even though I haven't actually experienced it in fifty years.

Unlike baseball where I unhumbly and unashamedly knew I was good, I was aware that my hockey skills were maybe average at best. However, I always wondered where I would fall in the bell curve of skill if I had pursued it harder. After my hiatus from college for four or five years, I had my chance to find out. I enrolled at Oakland College in Farmington, Michigan. It had a college hockey team. I was out of shape by hockey player standards, but I figured nothing ventured, nothing gained. I went out for the team. No one was more amazed than was I when I made the cut. However, I'm pretty sure it was by the skin of my teeth. What I lacked in skill, I had to make up in aggression. That's not the way to play in my mind. It was fun, but the end of the bench – although honorable – wasn't my idea of success.

I played in a few amateur hockey leagues after leaving college, but getting up at one in the morning for a game (ice time was in short supply) got old quickly. I was twenty-eight when in a single game, our team had one guy go down with a heart attack and another get cut so badly, he damn near bled to death before they got him sewn up. After that game, I concluded discretion was indeed the better part of valor. My competitive hockey days were over.

Pigskins and Proms – When it was too cold for baseball and too warm for hockey, we had a handy little season in Michigan called the "football season". I had the good fortune of having my natural athletic abilities carry over onto the gridiron. I played as a freshman right on through my senior year. I was the team's punter and I started at defensive end. Most defensive ends are large critters. I was only 5' 8" tall and weighed 175 pounds. What I lacked in size, I made up for in aggression. I probably shouldn't be proud of this, but I suspect I still hold another high school sports record. It's a tough one to beat.

We were on the road one Friday night. It was a spirited contest. When the ball was snapped I broke for the quarterback. The offensive tackle's job was to make sure I didn't get to him. I discarded the tackle's advances by grabbing him and throwing him off to the side. This immediately got the attention of the line judge who threw his flag for my "illegal use of the hands" violation. There was nothing between me and the quarterback and I went after him with the intent of making sure he would remember my visit when he regained consciousness. As I tried to deliver the message, it seems my forearm came up under his chin in a manner that was construed as excessively aggressive. The line judge's flag was already on the ground due to my previous infraction, but the umpire's flag was handy and went flying into the air for the illegal hit. The quarterback's helmet was on the ground as I rose to my feet. When I realized I was being penalized, I thought I would share my thoughts on the matter with the referee; I was just trying to help him. His flag flew into the air and I was called for "unsportsman's like conduct". In less than fifteen seconds, I had accrued forty-five yards in penalties. On the next play, I did nothing other than listen as the coach shared his thoughts with me on the sideline. I was back in the game on the next play. I had to be; I was the punter and few teams gain a first down when they have fifty-five yards to gain to get one.

I was proud of my accomplishments on the football field (penalties not withstanding). I was a four year letterman and earned honorable mention all-league honors. Believe it or not, I was actually offered a college football scholarship. Unfortunately, that fact isn't as glorious as it might appear at first glance. As a punter, I averaged about forty yards per kick, a pretty strong number for a high school punter. Now, the rest of the story: My best friend in high school was Dave Kerr. He had extremely high grades and was a very talented and gifted athlete. He was the center on the football team and a lot of colleges were after Dave in earnest. I joined Dave on a couple of his recruiting trips. One was to Denison University in Granville, Ohio. Denison was an outstanding liberal arts institution with a great reputation. However, its allure to Dave wasn't as great as some of the other colleges such as Dartmouth that were soliciting his services. The Denison coach knew he was at a competitive disadvantage. When I arrived with Dave, the coach asked a number of pointed questions and soon realized we were best of friends and that I had been a pretty strong punter and had respectable grades in high school. He went for the best friend gambit. If he offered a scholarship to me, that might induce Dave to take the offer to play for Denison. Dave ultimately attended undergraduate and medical school at the University of Michigan and didn't even play football in college. The coach's ruse didn't work, but I can now say with a straight face and without crossing my fingers behind my back that I had a football scholarship to a fine university.

My inglorious love affairs with other sports – I mentioned there was no high school hockey when I was in Northville. That left the period between the end of football season and the beginning of the baseball season without a high school sport for me. That didn't mean I didn't give a couple of them a little spin.

In the summer before my freshman year, I played an occasional game of "horse" or "around the world" on the basketball court. My natural athletic ability resulted in me being a very good shooter of the round ball. I could jump very well; not many fourteen year olds my height could jump high enough to grab the ten foot rim. One of the guys I would play with on the court kept trying to convince me to go out for the basketball team. We were confident I'd be a starter in no time.

I went out for the team. I immediately caught the eyes of the coaching staff as I put one shot after another through the hoop from long distance. They knew from the football season that I was pretty fast on my feet and a good competitor. But then they threw a monkey wrench into the mix. They said I had to dribble the ball wherever I went. This definitely complicated the matter for me. I hadn't spent my entire life bouncing a basketball around. It wasn't my strength. Then they really soiled my chances. They threw in another variable I hadn't anticipated; they put guys that were nearly a foot taller than I was in front of me. Those complications brought my basketball career to an abrupt close. I didn't make the team.

By the time my senior year rolled around, I was looking for another possible sport to add to my list of accomplishments. I hadn't tried wrestling. Hell, I was a strong kid; I'd be a natural for wrestling. I went out for the team. I regret to inform you that I made the team. It was two weeks of complete hell.

I quickly had a pair of traumatic awakenings, both on the first day of practice. I hadn't anticipated the grim reality that more than a dozen post-pubescent men would be placed in a small room with no ventilation where they would be putting forth extreme physical efforts. This unavoidably resulted in a massive quantity of sweat which dripped and oozed everywhere. It stunk! It was like spending a couple hours every afternoon with your nose planted firmly in the under-arm of Boxcar Willie on a hot summer day. The only saving grace for spending the time in the wrestling room was that when the coach was out of the room, the guys got to take turns peeking through a pinhole in a door that led into the shower in the girls' locker room.

The real deal breaker came on day one when everyone was lined up against the wall in order of weight class. We started with the little guys and paired off. I don't remember the actual breakdowns for the little guys, but it was something like the 112 pound guy paired up with the one that weighed 118 pounds. 127 paired with the 135 pounder. I weighed 175 pounds and ended up being in the "light-heavyweight" class. You can probably already see this isn't going to have a happy ending. The only guy left for me was the "heavyweight". The problem was that meant he had to weight more than something like 195 pounds. That would have been twenty pounds heavier than me. However, no one in the room weighed 195 pounds; our heavyweight was the tackle on the football team. Jerry Burns (yes, the same Jerry Burns that farted in freshman English and dumped on me) was my practice partner and at 245 pounds was 70 pounds heavier than me. I immediately began to regret the fact that I had been brought up with an ideal that quitting wasn't an option.

For the next two weeks, I was in a gag-bag called the wrestling room and I was getting rolled, thrown, booted, beaten, tossed, folded and thumped by Mr. Burns. At times, I believe he practiced the art of origami with my body. I'm sure he made shadow puppets by holding my lifeless form in front of the light and asking others to guess what I was. When he was done with me, I was so thoroughly conquered, I was too tired to take my turn peering through the peep hole into the girl's shower.

But alas … good fortune finally smiled upon me. I broke my arm! I was to be out of action for the rest of the season. Yes, I took the coward's way out. Call me a chicken.

Water World – With a doctor prescribed (falsely in turns out) end to my baseball career, I was sportless as a freshman at Western Michigan University. Shortly after my arrival in Kalamazoo, I thought I'd take advantage of one of the perks associated with being a student. I went over the pool to have a little fun on the diving board. As you've noticed by now, I haven't lacked for confidence in my athletic pursuits. However, it never dawned on me that I might have some talent on the diving board. It was just something I did for fun. I didn't even know it was a marketable skill. Who can't jump off a diving board into a pool of water?

As it happened, the swimming coach happened to be at the pool that day and saw me throw a few dives. He thought I had a lot of rough edges; I'd never had any coaching other than a few dares over the years. Nonetheless, he apparently concluded I had enough talent to be on what at that time was one of the nation's finest swimming teams. He came up to me and struck up a conversation. When all was said and done, we shook hands. He had just awarded me an athletic scholarship. Suddenly, I was obligated to take diving a little more seriously. I never dreamed I would letter in intercollegiate athletics in swimming, but that's what ended up coming to pass.

Over the course of the next two seasons I competed around the country as the number two diver on the team. I got better and better with practice, but I never approached All-American status. Hell, I never got to the number one spot on the team. I never missed the pool on a dive; I came close. That doesn't mean I didn't try to kill myself a couple of times.

Throughout my freshman year, I was pretty much confined to the one-meter board. Halfway through the season, our coach, Ed Gabel, decided I needed to start working from the three-meter board. If I was to score higher in meets, I needed to be throwing dives from the higher board where the degree of difficulty made higher scoring dives possible. The first thing I learned about the higher board was that it may only be three-meters up, but it's about fifty-meters when looking down. The coach said, "Do a forward one-and-a-half in the pike position."

Oh sure; easy for him to say. He's standing on the ground. I was looking down into what I feared would be my sepulcher. Our future Hall-of-Fame diver, Ron Bramble could see my apprehensive expression and tried to simplify it for me. "It's easy," he said with a smile. "You just get into the pike position and fall off the board."

One of my strengths was sometimes also one of my greatest weaknesses. I had the ability to follow coaching instructions extremely well. Ron was being a little simplistic – I was taking him very literally. I stood at the end of the three-meter board and slowly went into the pike position, i.e., where you bend ninety degrees forward at the waist. I simply fell forward as instructed. I held my pike position very well. When I thought it time to come out of it, I discovered I was a bit early. I made what turned out to be an inappropriate decision. I tried to get back into the pike as fast and forcefully as possible. I hit the water squarely face down. It would have been a painful problem even if I hadn't tried to refold my body. As it happened, I added all the force I could muster onto the forces gravity had already contributed. The sound of my body hitting the water so hard caused everyone in the building to instantly stop whatever they were doing and turn to see if a plane had crashed in the pool. I was in immediate pain and did my best to keep my wits about me. I got out of the pool and stood by the edge. People resumed their activities. Within seconds, I watched as red welts began to rise horizontally

Always up for a little excitement at Formula One racing school

across my body from the waist up. They quickly grew together. It wasn't sixty seconds before my eyes had been totally enveloped in the swelling. I could see nothing and feel everything – especially a screaming pain. Someone led me into a cold shower.

On another occasion, my quest for higher points caused a problem. I learned to dive up, then down – not out. The more vertical a dive, the higher the point total. But the more vertical the dive, the closer you are to the diving board when you pass it by. I made another noise rarely heard when I was so close to the board that I actually hit it with my nose. I removed a good part of the skin on my nose, but finished the meet. I don't remember if I got a deduct for the nose, but it wouldn't seem fair to lose part of your nose and part of your points. I would think it should be one or the other.

Looking back, baseball and all of the other sports in which I participated, brought me a great deal of pleasure, a little pain, a modicum of glory and a lot of trophies (which I always gave away as soon as they were received). Beyond that, some of the greatest lessons of my lifetime came from the fields of athletic competition. To win, I had to learn it was to be a team effort. With an infinitely small bit of extra effort, an out might have been a base hit. All of the work you do before the game is what goes toward the win – what you do on the field comes only as a result of the work you did before the game.

In 1982, I played ball on a semi-pro team that was highly ranked nationally. I personally had an exceptional year. I was singled out in many tournaments for my outstanding defense and throwing ability. I earned MVP awards and was even selected for the all-region team at the western regional finals in Nevada. But here's another confession. Those trophies weren't really mine. Sure, I played well and for that I'm proud. But I had the advantage of having a first baseman named Edmundo Mesa who could catch balls that few other human beings could get close to catching. I can't begin to count the number of times when I threw a ball that would have gone as an error were it not for Mundo. He made me a star that year. He was my hero. When playing on a team, it's truly not about me; it's about "we". Baseball has been very, very good to me.

Chapter Fifteen – Life's Lessons

In the course of passing through life, everyone experiences events that serve as awakenings or epiphanies. They provide lessons that are not only memorable, but life changing. Here are of few of those stories.

The Myth of Justice - You heard it – just like I heard it, every school day for years. "I pledge allegiance to the flag … with liberty and justice for all." We said the words over and over and over. "With liberty and justice for all." Can you blame me for believing it? Isn't that what the government wants us to believe? We're bombarded with the jingoist propaganda every day of our lives.

Well stop the presses, Bubba. I've got some bad news. If justice does exist, it is rare and elusive. And the crap about "liberty and justice for all" is just that – crap! I learned my lesson in Orchard Lake, Michigan.

I had just turned twenty-one. I was driving home one afternoon on the winding lakefront road. With a thirty-five mile per hour speed limit, I wasn't about to push my luck. I kept it under the limit. I came to a stop sign and dutifully stopped. When I pulled away, a little bit of beach sand came up from my rear tires. I had barely touched the accelerator, but the sand gave way just a smidgeon. I saw a car about a quarter mile up the road coming my way and I soon discovered he saw me too. Soon he was behind me driving what appeared to be a family sedan. He reached up and placed a flashing light on his dashboard. I wondered if it was a joke, but just in case, I pulled over.

Officer Sniblefarp approached my car. He asked for driver's license and registration. In that I was certain beyond doubt that I had done nothing wrong, I asked for an explanation. He told me I was speeding. I assured him he was in error. He began writing something down. "What are you doing?" I asked.

"I'm writing you a ticket," was his cold reply. I was incensed. I knew I had nothing to worry about. Obviously, he was the one that didn't know about "liberty and justice for all." As he continued writing, my anger meter was entering the red zone. I entered into the process of educating the clearly uneducated officer. As I spoke, my tact level started approaching the low end of cordial. He made additional notes on the ticket suggesting that my conduct wasn't becoming. He handed me the ticket.

"This is bullshit," I informed him. He said I could protest the ticket with the Justice of the Peace at the city offices. I didn't need to protest it. I was completely innocent and if there was justice for all, surely I was covered under that umbrella policy. As he walked away, I wadded up the ticket and threw it at him. Yes, I was mature and brilliant all in one hot-headed package. He drove away as I had a fleeting flash of common sense. Maybe I'd better pick up the ticket and protest it at city hall.

I drove directly back around the lake to City Hall. I was speeding all the way. I charged into the building and went to the only desk that seemed to have anyone sitting at it. I threw the ticket on the desk and told the woman, "I want to protest this ticket I got from some imbecile riding around pretending to be a cop."

She looked at the ticket and dryly told me, "The 'imbecile' to whom you're referring happens to be our Chief of Police."

With a mouth full of dumb ass, I said, "I don't care who he is. I wasn't speeding and he's an imbecile." I was going to tell her the part about liberty and justice for all, but I figured she'd probably heard it before. She looked down at her calendar. "Your court date is next Monday at 2 p.m. in the judge's office."

By the time Monday rolled around, you might think any prescient human being would have started to put the pieces together. Not this future rocket scientist. I was still listening to the lyrics of the Pledge of Allegiance and had full faith that justice would prevail. I had never been in a courtroom before. As it turned out, it wasn't a courtroom; it was the office of the

Justice of the Peace. I was so confident of my innocence, I didn't even bring a checkbook or any money.

When I walked in, I was surprised there was no jury or court clerk or any of the other players I'd seen countless times on the Perry Mason Show. It was just the judge. He told me to put my hand on the Bible and swore me to tell the truth. Finally we were getting somewhere. If I had to tell the truth, so did everyone else. I was told to take a seat in front of his desk. At about that time, the Chief of Police walked in and took the other seat next to me. The judge called the proceeding to order. He looked at the Chief and asked him what happened. The Chief told the judge I was speeding and he gave me a ticket. That was it! The judge told the Chief he could leave and he did.

The judge turned to me and asked for my side of the story. "I wasn't speeding," I told him. That was my ironclad defense. "If it doesn't fit, you must acquit" hadn't been invented yet. Besides, I was innocent; there was no way I could lose. The judge tapped his gavel on the desk and said, "The defendant is guilty and will pay a fine of twenty-five dollars or spend two weeks in jail." I had an easy out. "I didn't bring any money," I told him. Surely, he now had to let me go.

The judge showed not a hint of emotion. He turned toward the table behind him and began writing. It was at this point that the light in my mind began to flicker – ever so faintly at first. "What are you doing?" I asked the judge.

"I'm filling out the paperwork committing you to the Oakland County Jail." Suddenly, the light came on brightly. I was going to be locked up with mother rapers and father stabbers. Oh did my attitude suddenly change. The judge said, "You do get one phone call."

I called my father and explained the situation. I asked him if he could come immediately and bring twenty-five dollars with him. I was livid, but more so, I was incredibly disappointed. All those people that had forced me to recite that Pledge of Allegiance had sold me a bill-of-goods. I wasn't sure about the liberty part, but I learned beyond a shadow of a doubt, there was not justice for all. I had been suckered. As I waited for my father to arrive with the money, I sat brooding in the chair. I felt like I had been robbed. If there was to be justice, I was going to have to administer it myself. When the judge left the room for a minute, I reached over, wrapped my fingers around the judge's gavel and stealthily slipped it into my pocket. Yes, I stole the damn gavel. I guess you might say I bought it for twenty-five bucks. My father arrived moments later. We paid the fine and left the building with a gavel in my pocket.

Finish the Job – Boys will be boys. I was known to get in my fair share of scraps when I was a kid. As a general rule, I didn't finish in second place. I was athletic and a strong kid. One boy on our block was a friend of mine, but that didn't mean we didn't have our disagreements. Larry Vaishvila was the stereotypical "tough guy" sort of like Butch was to the Little Rascals Gang of the 1930s. Larry was bigger than me and had a fight card with twice as many bouts as I had logged. We were probably nine years old and we got into an argument over something. One thing led to another and the next thing you know, we were trading punches. I out-maneuvered him and managed to knock him onto his back. I immediately jumped on him, sat on his chest and used my knees to pin both of his arms to the ground. He was helpless and defenseless. I could have pummeled him into oblivion, but I didn't. "Do you give up?" I said as I smugly looked down upon his chin that was begging to be punched. He didn't say anything so I badgered him again. "Give up?"

He looked up and said, "Sure. I give up. You whipped me." I got off of Larry and we both rose to our feet. I was pleased that I had so readily defeated Mr. Tuff Guy. I didn't even see it coming. He hammered me with a hard right hand, then a left and another left. A couple more solid rights and my nose was bleeding like it had been amputated. The next thing I knew, I was on my back. He didn't ask me if I was willing to give up. He just kept punching me until the option of going on had been removed from the table.

Larry taught me a valuable lesson that day. If you're going to do something, don't do it half way. If you start the job – finish it. If you don't someone else will.

Don't Spill Your Milk – It makes a mess, but if you do spill it, don't cry. I had two good teachers for this lesson. The first of my awakenings came when I had finally been brought in to work in the office for my father's company. For weeks, he had been preparing to submit a bid on a large school construction project. Because the school was being built for a public entity, the bid opening had to be public. There was a specific deadline time to submit the bid; if it was one second late, it wouldn't be considered. The bids were opened in front of a crowd of onlookers and the low bidder celebrated winning a ten million dollar job.

The process leading up to the bid deadline was intense and hectic, especially on the day of the bid submission. An employee was stationed at a pay phone near the bid location. He would take the final bid amount, fill it into a bid form and run it to the person accepting bids – sometimes only seconds before the deadline. The phones buzzed in the office with constant chatter with subcontractors trying to get them to refine their bids. Although F.J. Jones and Company was successful and on a solid financial foundation, to some general contractors, winning a bid of this magnitude could mean the difference between success and closing their doors. Before the bid deadline, engineers and architects were scrambling to double check their numbers and refine the bid as best as humanly possible. It was a frenzied atmosphere.

At five minutes to two in the afternoon, Mike Terlicki was on the phone from the bid site waiting for the final number. My father picked up the phone in his office and spoke with Mike. "Are you ready?" he asked Mike. "Nine million three hundred sixty five thousand, four hundred twenty seven dollars" said my father. Mike read it back to him as he wrote it into the bid letter. "Go!" said Dad.

I had never been in the middle of anything involving so much money. To me it seemed almost like a life-and-death situation. The lives of dozens of people rode on the strength of that number. We all waited. The anticipation was almost unbearable. Finally, after about thirty minutes, the phone rang. My father picked it up and spoke with Mike. We finished in second place two thousand dollars behind the winner. In this case, second place was the same as last place. I expected a massive show of disappointment and anger from everyone in the office, especially from my father. To this day, I vividly recollect seeing him sit at his desk with an air of complete calm. Here was a man prone to hyperbolic displays of emotion when Bobby Lane's pass to Jim Doran fell incomplete in the Lion's game, yet he sat almost content after missing out on a ten million dollar job by two one-hundredths of a percent. I remember standing there with a look of stunned amazement asking him "Aren't you upset?"

"That one's behind us," he said with a smile. It's time to move on to the next one. "There's nothing to be gained from worrying about something that's in the past." The rest of the day was strangely normal.

Many years later, Jim McCarty, Liz's father, gave me a refresher course on the same subject. We had spent the previous forty-nine hours cruising in his seventy-five foot Hatteras yacht from San Carlos, Mexico to Mazatlan, Mexico. It was close to lunch time when Captain Ramon entered El Cid Marina. Jim, Liz, Victoria and I were all in the galley having lunch as Ramon began the process of carefully backing the ship into its slip. I was standing by the table. Jim was seated with his back to the window. He took a bite of his ham sandwich. As I looked in his direction, I saw the background of other boats and the docks begin moving faster than I would normally have expected. As our speed increased, there was a frantic call from the bridge where the Captain was maneuvering the boat. "Howard!" he cried out in a panic; he normally looked to me for help because I spoke Spanish far better than he spoke English. The throttle had bound up and we were now accelerating to a very unsafe speed. In a matter of a second or two (it seemed like an eternity), the boat kept gaining speed. The dock was flying by outside the window and it was apparent to everyone we were in trouble. Suddenly, there was a deafening crash, almost like an explosion. The dock rocked and trembled. The boat abruptly stopped. Pieces of the wooden swim platform that had been on the transom could be seen flying through the air. Jim sat at the table expressionless. He casually took another bite of the ham sandwich he still held in his hand. He seemed to be enjoying it.

When I later asked Jim about his unexpected lack of reaction, he said, "At that point, there was nothing I could do. The damage had been done. There was no sense in worrying about it then. And the sandwich was good." There were a couple of great lessons and I have taken them to heart.

The Milk of Canine Kindness – Man's best friend? There are exceptions. Seems odd that one of my more memorable lessons came from a dog, but such is the case. Liz and I were in San Carlos, Mexico. We've always been early risers. One morning we went for a walk before the town had begun to come alive. There was a golf course nearby and we took in the sights and sounds of morning as we strolled along one of the fairways. As we approached the clubhouse, we saw movement in the swimming pool. Our pace quickened. As we got close enough to see into the pool, we spotted a dog. He was near exhaustion as he paddled for his life. There was no way for him to get out of the pool and it was only a matter of time before he perished.

I thought about grabbing him by the nap of his neck and pulling him out. Surely, he'd welcome someone who was saving his life. But I remembered another old lesson – an ounce of prevention is worth a pound of cure. I thought I'd still better be careful. I looked around and found a piece of wood about eight feet long and carried it to the pool's edge. I slid it gently under the dog and worked him to the edge where I used the wood as a lever to get him up out of the water. I struggled for a minute or so, but finally got his front paws onto the pavement and then wedged his body out of the pool. I saved his life.

He was too exhausted to move for about thirty seconds. He slowly got to his feet. Then he tried to attack me. Luckily, I still had the wood and used it to fend him off. Life is full of stories that convey this lesson in one way or another. No good deed goes unpunished. My favorite parable is the one about the frog and the scorpion. Regardless of your favorite, this dog really brought the message home to me.

Michael Rowed the Boat Ashore (It just wasn't his boat!) It was during my mountain climbing years. My daily training regimen was vigorous. Every day began with a brisk walk of five or so miles. We were in Las Vegas for a convention. As the night put its darkness away, Liz and I were on the street hoofing it a couple blocks from the Golden Nugget Hotel. As we reached a corner, what appeared to be a homeless man emerged from the bushes. Despite his obvious hard times, he had an irrepressible charisma. The morning brightened when he smiled and introduced himself.

"Hi. My name is Michael." His smile widened when he went on. "You wouldn't happen to have a dollar for a cup of coffee?"

I typically carried enough money on our morning walk to round up a couple of lattes for ourselves. I looked at Michael and said, "I don't have a dollar Michael. All I have is a twenty dollar bill in my pocket." Liz's eyes widened.

"I'll tell you what. I'll give you the twenty. You go up to the coffee shop and buy a cup of coffee and bring the change back to me. I'll wait right here."

Liz was now giving me the look with which I'd become so familiar over the years. A loose translation goes something like this: "Are out of your god damned mind?"

As I handed the twenty to Michael, his smile widened still further; his eyes betrayed his feeling of "Damn! Have I hit the jackpot this morning." He turned and walked away. A few seconds later, he turned, pointed across the street and said, "I'm goin right over there to the coffee shop. I'll bring your change back in a minute."

I watched as he pulled the handle of the door. It was too early. It wouldn't open for another hour. Michael cast another smile my way and pointed to another coffee shop in the next block. I watched as he crossed the street again. When he pulled on the door of the next diner, he looked my way and signaled that it too was not yet open. By now, he was far enough away, I couldn't verify that it was even a coffee source or not. For all I knew, it could have been an empty warehouse.

He pointed toward the next coffee shop, smiled and headed toward the next block. Even if he had been within hearing distance, I couldn't have heard his words. Liz was filling my ears with nuanced truisms about misguided trust in human nature and something about me being an idiot.

"Look," I said to Liz, "We don't gamble. Someone else would have thrown the twenty onto the blackjack table and wasted it in a flash. Look at this as a show ticket. The entertainment value is priceless. And I'm sure Michael will bring back the change." I was clearly lying there, but that was to become part of the show.

Meanwhile, Michael had reached the intersection two blocks south of where we awaited his return. His smile glistened in the early morning light as he gestured and pointed toward yet another coffee shop. He then rounded the corner and disappeared. Although we no longer had visual contact with Michael, I'm sure he was continuing his trek in search of a coffee shop that opened earlier than the others. Liz wasn't as sure as was I. She shared further insights she had no doubt learned about human nature in her psychology classes at A.S.U. as I waited.

"I'm sure he'll be back soon," I assured Liz, "but we really need to get going. We've got to be somewhere soon." We walked away. Poor Michael wouldn't know what to do with the nineteen dollars he assuredly would bring back to the corner of Idiot Street and Dumb Ass Avenue.

Twenty years later, Liz still reacts reflexively with "You Idiot!" whenever this story is broached. But the truth is that twenty dollar investment proved to be one of the best show tickets we've ever purchased. It continues to entertain even to this day.

I assured Liz that Michael invested that nineteen dollars (if he didn't give it to charity) and has parlayed it into millions. I'm certain he periodically cruises the streets of Las Vegas looking out the windows of his limousine in search of the man who gave him the double-sawbuck that led to his financial success.

If you're ever in Las Vegas and see a thin black man with the smile of a lighthouse looking longingly out the window of a stretch limo, ask him if his name is Michael. Tell him I said hello.

The lesson from this encounter was not unlike the story of the frog and scorpion. Someone is what he is. Only a fool would expect him to be anything else.

Chapter Sixteen – Regrets

Don't you love it when people are asked, "What would you do differently if you had it to do all over again?" and they respond, "I wouldn't change a thing"? That's the kind of answer that got Pinocchio in big trouble. They're lying through their teeth. Hell yes, I'd do some things differently.

I truly am very happy with the collection of experiences that have made me who I am today. I've had an incredibly exciting life and have no reason to complain. I'm delighted I made the choices I did, but that's not to say I couldn't have improved on a few of them. My list of regrets will be in random order and of varying levels of significance. I'm sure if I listed them all, I'd create of tome that would rival the great books of the western world in length and a 1965 phone book from Hoboken, New Jersey in significance.

I regret that I didn't become a foreign exchange student for one of my high school years. If I had known then what I know now about how an immersion into a foreign culture expands one's horizons exponentially, I would have done everything possible to have the experience. I can't begin to imagine what path my life would have followed other than to say I'm certain it would have been very unlike the one I did follow. I can't say it would have been for the better or for the worse, but it would have been drastically different.

I regret that I exhibited such a mean streak when I was a little kid. I didn't know it was mean. I treated Norman Appel, David Goodman and many others – including my brother Brian - unfairly and meanly. In retrospect, I suspect it was a natural part of growing up. I hadn't yet learned how to empathize. I hope that's not abnormal, but I wish I would have learned sooner.

I regret not making certain the car was in neutral. When I was twelve or so, my mother would give me her keys and let me go outside and start her old Dodge car. It had the manual transmission and step one was to make sure I put the car in neutral. Step two was to insert the key and start the car. I quickly learned I had been unsuccessful in step one when step two brought the car to life. I panicked as the Dodge crashed through the gate and drove itself into the backyard of the house on Griggs before I could get it turned off.

I regret not working harder. I was lucky so many things came easy to me. Sports, academics, especially math, public speaking and myriad other things were easier for me than for most. In so many areas, I could do twice as well as my peers by putting forth only half the effort. Throughout my grade school years, report cards had a grade for "effort" and another for "achievement" in each of the subjects. I was always getting "A"s for achievement; I don't remember ever getting anything above a "C" for effort. I shudder to think about how well I could have done if I had only applied myself. When I finally put forth a serious effort academically, I graduated number one out of a class of seven thousand students. What if I had applied myself like that in grade school and high school. Where might it have taken me? When I went to work at Chevron and Union Oil, I was being groomed for the highest levels of management. I chose to apply myself to other pursuits rather than my career. Where might I have ended up? I played baseball semi-professionally. What if I would have put in the extra hours of practice and worked harder? Would I have made the major leagues? What would I have done if I'd practiced my music two or three hours every day? But in my mind, I could also put forth the extra effort tomorrow after I had fun today. Where could I have gone? What could I have accomplished?

I regret not learning a foreign language at an earlier age. I studied (assuming attending the class qualifies as "studying") French, Latin and German in high school and college. Sadly, I really wasn't interested in learning the languages. French helped me a little bit when communicating with French-Canadian hockey players, but other than that, I saw no value in learning another language. When the day finally came when I actually wanted to speak another language, Spanish, I dove into learning it head-first and soon became fairly fluent. It opened doors into the hearts and minds of people all over the world. For me, it was a great awakening. There's no way I could begin to put a value on having a second or third or fourth language. I wish I would have done it sooner.

I regret taking foolish risks. Just because I got away with it doesn't mean I'm glad I did it. When I was in high school, I put myself in some pretty hazardous places by driving a car or a motorcycle like an idiot. It wasn't as if I gained something other than a little bit of time. It was just foolish. I have known others who gambled like that and didn't live to write their story.

I regret saying hurtful things. Most people have done it, but it doesn't make it right and it damn sure doesn't make it smart. Sometimes things were said in anger. Other times they were spoken in a poorly ill-conceived attempt at humor. Occasionally, there was no mean spirit, but the words accidentally brought hurt.

I regret passing cars in the right lane. I was sixteen. I had been to the basketball game in Clarenceville. Kris Deibert, my longtime girlfriend, was my date. It was a cold winter night and Kris was sitting close to me on the ride home. After all, we had to keep warm. Eight Mile Road was a two lane highway except at the intersection of Farmington Road where a second lane had been created for those wishing to turn right at the light. As I approached the intersection, someone was going to turn left and had four or five cars waiting behind him. I saw the light turn yellow for traffic on Farmington Road and knew we'd have the green light in a second or two. Always one to look for ways to improve things, I adroitly dipped into the right turn lane and with perfect timing, blew by all the waiting traffic and zipped back into the single lane heading west toward Northville. I knew my amazing skills had overwhelmed Kris who had to be nearly as impressed with me as I was with myself.

I slowed back down to the fifty miles per hour limit and slipped my arm around Kris to get warmer yet. After a minute or so, I saw a pair of headlights gaining quickly in the rearview mirror.

The car was suddenly right on my ass and the driver began flashing the lights. I could tell it wasn't a police car; I assumed it was another high schooler flexing his motor muscles. I told Kris to watch as I applied a bit of psychology to the hot-rodder. I pressed the accelerator and soon had the speedometer reading one-hundred miles per hour leaving the challenger far behind. "Now watch this," I told Kris with an air of erudition. I slowed back down to fifty miles per hour and waited. "The guy will take that as a challenge and try to outdo me. He'll get up here quickly and have an uncontrollable need to show me he can go faster. He'll pass us and we'll drive the rest of the way to the apple orchard without any other traffic." Oh damn, I was smart.

As predicted, the car's headlights reappeared in nothing flat. It pulled out to pass. "What did I tell you?" I asked Kris with a smug grin. That's where my plan starting falling apart. The other car stayed next to me and began blowing its horn. I glanced to my left and saw my father with his "prepare to meet your maker" expression on his face waiving me over to the side of the road. He had been in one of the cars that I had blown by at the light. When I hit a hundred miles per hour, he had for some inexplicable reason, become even angrier. I had to use every bit of salesmanship that I could muster to convince him to allow me to even take Kris home. I had to drive her directly to her house, drop her off and come directly home. I lost my driving privileges for a month. On the upside of the story, I gave my father a great story to tell about Dunderhead for the next forty-five years.

I regret that I don't have a relationship with my oldest daughter Amy or her children. It's unfortunate, but that is the reality. There may be some that suggest putting the past aside and moving forward with a fresh view of the horizon. As sad as it may be, the situation came to pass for reasons that left no honorable alternatives. Pieces of what could have been are gone. What can be is determined by the reality in which we live. Wishing it were different does nothing to change the facts. I regret there's no relationship, but that's what reality dictated. It would be as foolhardy to expect anything else as it would be to hope the moon's rotation suddenly stop.

I regret punching Gary Williams. We were in gym class playing volleyball. He was a less than accomplished player and wasn't overwhelmingly knowledgeable of the rules. He kept infringing upon my space and I warned him a couple of times to stop. Finally, he jumped in front of me again. I offered him some physical encouragement to not do it again. I wheeled around and punched him. As luck would have it, I suffered what is referred to as a "boxer break" of my wrist. Due to a combination of too much macho and too little smart, I refused to get the break set until after the baseball season. It cost me my chance at a pro baseball career. To this day, the wrist doesn't flex above a point directly in line with my forearm. It has been a lifelong nuisance and a pretty constant source of pain. It wasn't one of my smartest moves.

I regret not looking both ways. I believe it was Christmas of 1958 when I received my Schwinn Black Phantom bike. This was the ultimate bicycle for a kid. As soon as the snow was gone, I was out riding this behemoth past the envious stares of my friends. As spring rolled around, my mother would let me ride the bike up to the Federal's Department store about a mile west of home. Rather than ride along Six Mile Road where sidewalks had not yet been outfitted with curb cuts for bikes, I preferred to ride through the alleys behind the businesses. There were no curbs to slow down my progress. About four blocks from my destination, I began to cross Cheyenne Street. As I entered the street, I saw a hotrod turn the corner and the driver had his foot to the floor. It was too late for me to stop and too late for the hotrod to stop. That left only one sound – the sound you hear when a car strikes a boy on a bicycle. I must have briefly blacked out, but I still remember being face down on the pavement two houses down from the impact point and sliding toward my bike which was now four houses down the block. I was bloody, but no bones were broken. My bike was not so lucky. All of its bones were broken. It was pronounced dead on the scene and ended up in the scrap heap.

I regret riding the Ferris wheel. I regret passing up a chance to use the bathroom when there would be none for the next three hours. I regret passing the gas station and the sign that said "Next Services – 70 miles" when I had enough gas to drive sixty miles. I regret not listening closer to a golfing buddy that wanted me to invest in an idea he had that ultimately became "Pac Man".

Yes, I did a lot of things that could have been done better. Even so, each and every one of those experiences went into the mud from which I was molded. My life has been nothing short of spectacular and without the missteps and fumbles, I wouldn't be the person I am. I'm happy and content. So do I have regrets? Sure. But ask the question "Would I do anything different?" Probably not. Otherwise I'd be somebody else and who would be here to write this book?

Chapter Seventeen – On Death and Dying

Sooner or later, death is going to win. But so far, I'm still in the game. There have been a few instances where victory came with the narrowest of margins. At the risk of sounding contrite, a serious confrontation with impending death is a major enlightenment. I've learned a lot about myself and a lot about the human animal by staring into the eyes of the Grim Reaper. I now know that we are truly programmed to survive. Sometimes death is the easy way out, but humanity doesn't go on generation after generation by taking the easy exit. We're predestined to fight. We don't have a choice. Consider an incident that took place in "The Bermuda Triangle".

It was early in the summer of 1968. I was living in southern Florida and trying to earn money as a scuba diver. I had a reasonable amount of experience diving, but no doubt overrated my skill set a touch. If I was half as good as I thought I was, I would have been twice as good as I was. Nonetheless, I had a number of commercial dives under my belt. I went with a couple of friends for a mid-day dive off the coast of Fort Lauderdale. We had a small boat and took it about a mile and a half off shore and dropped the anchor. The three of us went over the side and headed for the ocean floor. We were in thirty-five to forty feet of water.

As soon as I got to the bottom, I began having trouble getting air. My regulator was acting up. I surfaced and assumed my dive was over. I surfaced maybe forty yards from the boat. The seas were strengthening. I was in a four to five foot chop. Rather than fight the swim back to the boat, I decided to take the easy way. I pulled the cord on my life vest and had an easy float back to the boat. Once in the boat, I disassembled my regulator and found that a small piece of rock had wedged itself against the rubber diaphragm. Once I removed it, the regulator worked fine. I had a nearly full tank of air and had to wait for my two diving companions to return. I hated to waste the opportunity, but one of the cardinal rules is never dive without a life vest and I had expended the CO^2 cartridge. It was then I made what proved to be one of the most foolish decisions I've ever made. It nearly cost me my life.

I rationalized that if I dove in and followed the anchor line straight down to the bottom and stayed right there until my air supply got low, there was no risk of anything ill coming to pass. I could just take in the sights of the reef below. I left my life vest on the boat floor and overboard I went. I headed nearly straight down. When I got to the sandy bottom, I turned around and looked for the anchor line. I didn't see it. I guessed I must have veered a little too far in one direction on my descent and I swam in the direction I guessed it to be. Fifty yards later, still no anchor line. I went the other way for a hundred yards or so. When the elusive anchor line didn't materialize, I went in another direction, then another. There was still no sign of the anchor line when my air supply ran out. I made my way to the surface.

I surveyed the seascape and spotted the boat about two hundred yards to the north. I was surprised I had veered so far from the boat. I was faced with a lengthy swim in rough seas with heavy scuba gear on my back. I might have been a little heavier, but my life vest was in the boat. The shore was visible nearly two miles to the west. The choice seemed to be simple -- swim for the boat.

I swam for roughly twenty minutes, but the boat didn't seem to be getting much closer. It didn't dawn on me that the boat was drifting with the current and wind. I later learned that when I jumped into the ocean, the anchor line had snapped. I couldn't find it because it wasn't there.

I was tiring and began to worry about getting to the boat at all. With my paltry income, it was a major decision to drop my weight belt. Those things weren't cheap, but survival started to become an issue. After another fifteen to twenty minutes, I was nearing exhaustion and finally made the choice to drop my scuba tank and regulator. That was a major cost item and was a sign of the seriousness of the situation. I was now fighting for survival.

Minutes turned into hours. Fatigue morphed into exhaustion. My body and mind were forced into a realm they'd never known before. The only thing that became clearer as time passed was that I might never again see a sunrise. The boat remained on the horizon and I was becoming convinced I was going to die that day. As hope was fading, I spotted a pleasure yacht heading south about fifty yards away. I tried to raise my arms out of the water to wave. With all the strength I could garner, I couldn't lift them above the surface. I tried to shout, but my voice was so weak as to be inaudible even at close range. The yacht continued on out of sight. That was the moment I knew I was destined to die that day.

It was then I learned something about the human spirit. I was suffering physically. I had just seen my last hope speed off over the horizon. I remember thinking I would soon lose consciousness. I remember thinking how futile and unjust it seemed to have to struggle and suffer more. Fortunately, somewhere in the human psyche, the survival instinct is programmed to take control over the mind. If I could have just turned my head into the water and drowned, I would have done so. But that instinct stepped in and said "Out of the way. I'll handle it from here." I kept swimming. I felt as if I had no hope remaining, but I couldn't quit.

Hours passed and I caught the boat. I'm sure I wasn't thinking clearly in my exhausted state, but I still remember the details about the rendezvous. The bow was pointing west toward shore still a couple miles distant. The ladder was on the opposite side. I tried to hold onto a thin metal ridge on the hull. I knew I had to get to the ladder. It would have been the ultimate irony to have put forth a supreme effort only to die after reaching my destination. It seemed like it took forever to slowly work my way around to the other side and grasp the bottom rung of the metal ladder. What remained of my muscles screamed as I tried to climb the ladder. Every ounce of strength I had was put into the effort to lift my body from the water and climb into the boat. I recall finally reaching the top and simultaneously throwing up as I fell toward the bottom of the boat. I vaguely remember hitting the bottom, but the next thing I recall was waking up to the sound of a siren. I was in an ambulance headed for a hospital.

When my diving partners surfaced, they had the presence of mind to realize the boat was adrift. They made the right choice and headed toward the shore. They hastily found another boat and headed back out to sea where they found my unconscious body in the boat.

If I had the choice, I would have died that day. But the human animal is an amazing creature. You and I have more strength and stamina than either of us can possibly imagine. You learn that only when you must and it's not necessarily going to be fun. It is, however, incredible. You have a power within and if you learn to access it, you can do some truly amazing things.

What Goes Up Must Come Down – Pico de Orizaba was my first mountain attempt over 18,000 feet. It was a character builder. I have been to the summit of a number of other mountains that were substantially higher than Orizaba, but none that presented such a unique challenge. It took about a week of climbing to reach the summit of Mexico's highest peak, but the last day was a monster. Although the climb up the Jamapa Glacier was only about a mile as the crow flies, it was many

Solid ice at 18,000 feet on Pico de Orizaba in central Mexico

miles as the climber walks. It was a shear sheet of ice at about a forty degree angle. In a typical year, about a dozen climbers die after falling while on the glacier. If you lose your traction and can't quickly arrest your fall, you're doomed to a high speed fall to the rocks thousands of feet below. The good news is your body would be so torn up during the tumble, you'd be long dead before kissing the rocks below.

Our summit day would take twenty hours for the round trip. Nourishment and above all, hydration was the key to our success. Each of the four of us would take two water bottles with a liter of water in each. That was cutting it close, but we were trying to keep weight to a minimum. About six hours into the climb the sun was just chasing the night away. We stopped briefly to rest. On a sheet of ice, resting doesn't mean sitting down; it means standing in one spot without moving. I reached for one of my water bottles. My fingers were ice cold and the bottle slipped from my hand. I looked in horror as half my water supply rocketed down the face of the glacier. I watched as it shot faster and faster until it was finally out of sight. I had fourteen hours to go and would have to do it on less than the one single liter of water I had not already drunk in my remaining bottle.

For the next seven hours we steadily progressed toward the summit. It was physically demanding, but no one complained. I finally stood on the summit 18,490 feet high with a view of the Gulf of Mexico seventy miles to the east. We spent perhaps ten minutes on the summit before beginning the most dangerous part of the journey, the down-climb on a sheet of ice while we were extremely fatigued.

After another six hours, we finally reached the base of the glacier and could finally sit down or lay down and rest. We hadn't slept in twenty-four hours. We were all exhausted. I was suffering from serious dehydration. I had little solace in the knowledge that my climbing partner, a dentist from Illinois, was in worse shape than I was despite having had twice as much water during the climb. We had another hour or two to get back to camp. With the weather quickly worsening and temperatures falling, it's unlikely we could have survived the night where we were without shelter. We agreed we'd take fifteen minutes to rest our weary bodies. Anymore would have put us in greater jeopardy of failure.

After fifteen years, I can still vividly remember what a wonderful sense of euphoria I experienced by simply laying my exhausted body down. I had heard the stories about climbers such as Scott Fischer and Rob Hall who died on Mount Everest. Their exhaustion had been so extreme that both laid down and almost willingly died. We all agreed that eyes should remain in the open position. When I laid down, the physical relief was so great, I instantly closed my eyes. I recall thinking about how easy it would be just to go to sleep and not wake up. The next thing I knew, someone was shaking me. "Wake up! We've got to get going before the blizzard hits. Despite the delightful prospect of simply staying where I lay, I got up and began the last leg of the climb to camp.

A couple hours later, I was at high camp in a raging snow storm. I had made it. My climbing partner didn't arrive for nearly another hour. We were worried and were starting to think about climbing back up to find him. It turned out, those who stayed in camp had been held hostage by the storm for the entire time we were gone. They assumed we were experiencing the same weather high on the mountain and feared we had died. In fact, we had clear skies above. But we could see everything below around 16,000 feet in the grips of the storm.

I can't say with certainty if I would have died or not that night on the mountain. The will to live filled my sails and took me back to camp so here I sit. I do believe that if I had persisted in my desire to rest where I laid down, that would have become my final resting place.

Guns and Knives – One of the best bits of advice I ever received from my father was "If you don't want to be compromised, don't put yourself into compromising positions." I took that advice to heart, but not without a few flaws in judgment. For example, when I was in grad school at the University of Arizona, I would want to get away from it all from time-to-time. By that, I mean away from the world of academia, away from professors, away from my fellow grad students and away from the campus. I discovered a bar on Tucson's south side named the Monte Carlo. To say it was a bit rough would be a great understatement. It was not uncommon to find a knife fight or shooting outside the bar on Saturday nights. It was a blue collar, Mexican hangout with a couple of pool tables and a "colorful" atmosphere. It was close to the Arizona School for the Deaf and Blind. I met a couple of old fellows that were deaf and became good friends with them. I would sit over a beer and "chat" with John and Ernie. I say chat, but actually it was in the Monte Carlo I learned American Sign Language. To make it even more interesting, I learned to sign in Spanish the dominant language in the Monte Carlo.

I visited the Monte Carlo a couple times each week. I shot a few games of pool with the hustlers and met quite a large number of the patrons over time. I was a curiosity to many of them. Why would a lily white doctoral student spend his spare time in a rough neighborhood shooting pool with the local Mexican community and have discussions with deaf people? Not everyone reached the same conclusion. Saul and Ramón decided I would be there for only one reason – I had to be an undercover narcotics officer, a narc. On one rowdy Friday afternoon, Saul and Ramón escorted me into a dark corner of the bar. Saul produced a knife and put it up to my neck and held it there while Ramón "encouraged" me to confess. In that I wasn't involved with any conspiracy to root out drug dealers, I assumed they were joking. With increased blade pressure on my neck, I realized humor wasn't the motive. I assured them of my innocence. Either because of my skills of persuasion or because the boys didn't feel it appropriate to kill someone in the bar, they let me go. Like the rocket scientist I was studying to become, I did a brilliant thing. I went back to chatting with the deaf boys and shooting pool.

A Most Compromising Situation – As I've mentioned throughout this book, my younger years were not always the most placid of times. In my wilder twenties, life was indeed an adventure. A romantic tryst was not unheard of, but one of them came close to spelling the end. How could I have known she was married at the time? Well, actually I could have asked. Actually, I did ask … and she told me. She said her husband was in a band and never got home before two-thirty in the morning. Apparently it had been a slow night at the club in which he normally played.

The band elected not to play the last set. It had been a fast night for my show and I elected to play one more set.

Fortunately, I heard the key in the door. It didn't take the mind of a rocket scientist to quickly devise an exit strategy. It involved a side door and a sprint. I moved so fast that my shadow was three steps behind me. As I reached the side door, I could hear voices. "No. No one's here" she said. I heard footsteps coming my way as I fumbled with the door lock. As I finally bolted through the door, I heard the sound of the hammer cocking on the pistol he always carried. I didn't pause to say hello. I had parked a half block up the street and I made a beeline for my car. I would have run ever faster, but I was wearing his robe. I drove off wearing his nice fluffy white robe. Oh, impetuous youth. That's sort of a Shakespearian term meaning "stupid". But at least I survived.

Motorcycles were not always my friend. In the summer between my freshman and sophomore years of college, I was enjoying a ride on my Honda motorcycle. I had just completed my first year as an intercollegiate diver on the swimming team. It probably saved my life. I was riding from Toledo, Ohio back to the Detroit area when the rear tire on the bike exploded. I was driving nearly seventy miles per hour when the bike suddenly became unmanageable. The rear wheel swayed wildly from side to side. I maintained control for a second or two, enough time to allow the bike to slow down to maybe sixty or so. But then I lost it. The bike tumbled and I went flying through the air like an unguided missile. When I first hit the ground, I tucked, rolled and bounced. My body traveled nearly a hundred feet from the point of first impact, but I employed diving techniques to tuck, roll and twist before finally coming to rest. When I finally came to a stop, I stood up. With the exception of a few little cuts and scrapes, I was uninjured and unfazed. I'm not sure how the judges would have rated my performance, but I remember it as being one of my better dives. The fact that I'm alive today serves as my proof. I don't think very many people would smile and walk away from a tumble at sixty plus miles per hour.

Fast forward more than a decade and I was again in college and the owner of a motorcycle. This time I was working on my doctorate at the University of Arizona and riding home on my new motorcycle. When the light turned green, the panel truck in front of me pulled off. I followed at a safe distance or so I thought. We reached the forty mile per hour speed limit. I glanced to my right and spotted a hyper-fancy Harley-Davidson painted yellow driving by. I looked at it longer than I should. As luck would have it, at the instant I looked right, a car pulled out of a driveway in front of the van in front of me. When I looked back, it was very apparent there was no way to avoid impact. I suspect I had one second at the most to consider the alternatives. I hit the van squarely in the back. I remember flying directly over the handle bars and placing my head squarely centered into the back of the van. I still recall the pieces of what had been the van's custom wood bumper flying in the air after it shattered. I got up off the pavement and surveyed the situation. The driver of the van was far closer to panic than was I. I stood the bike up and looked it over. The front wheel was crushed. The frame was bent, but I wasn't. Once again, I walked away nearly unscathed. My only visible injuries didn't appear until the following day when I woke up to find two perfectly etched bruises, one on each shoulder, the precise size and shape of the rearview mirrors that had been mounted on the motorcycle before my flying body removed them at the time of impact.

In the years since these incidents, I have considered getting another motorcycle. I've even walked into a Harley-Davidson dealership and fondled the Sportster model. But every time the urge struck me, the survival instinct kicked in and I walked away alive. Maybe I'm not completely without common sense after all.

Adrenaline isn't always our friend. In 1969 I was a news reporter in Denver, Colorado. I'd be lying if I said it wasn't an interesting and exciting life. I covered major news events. I got to meet sports stars. I knew the governor, senators and congressmen. I got to see the glamourous parts of life and I got to see the seediest parts of life.

A couple of neighbors had developed an acrimonious relationship over a lengthy time period. The Hatfields and McCoys had nothing on these people. They weren't sophisticated people and their problem solving skills were quite limited. I don't recall specifically what triggered it, but one of the neighbors reached the breaking point. As one man sat rocking in his chair on the front porch, the other couple walked up on his porch. The visiting neighbor held a handgun, raised it up and put six rounds into the chest of his neighbor. The guy was dead when he hit the floor, but one of the things about this story that made it all the more memorable was that as the shooter fled the scene, his wife remained on the porch beating the dead man's body with her broom.

Meanwhile, the killer ran next door, grabbed a rifle and fled on foot. He ran a couple of blocks and entered a vacant house that was surrounded by open fields. The police surrounded the house and prepared for the impending firefight. The police arrived at about the same time as the star reporter, a.k.a., me. I had my tape recorder and camera in hand and scrambled to get into position to get the absolute best sound bites and photos possible. Adrenaline fueled my tank and dulled my mind as I crawled into what I thought was a great position. I hunkered down in a little ditch about forty feet from the porch of the house. As my brain began to kick in again, I realized I had managed to position myself directly between the killer and the police line. When the firing began, I stood a good chance of getting shot from both sides. It was rather tense for about twenty minutes, but the murderer finally surrendered to the police without any shots being fired. Once again, I had cheated the Grim Reaper. Notice I didn't say I outsmarted him.

In the shadow of death even when I was six – As a first grader, I would often accompany my mother on little shopping junkets. In 1953 she didn't have a car. Everything was done on foot or on the bus. I had no experience crossing the "big street". My mother knew that and would always dutifully hold my hand when crossing one. But now I was six. I was in first grade. I was almost an adult and on my own. We walked a block and a half toward Six Mile Road, one of Detroit's main cross streets. In addition to the two lanes of parked cars, one on each side of the street, Six Mile has four additional lanes of traffic. When the eastbound lanes had cleared we slowly walked toward the center of the street. My mother paused and waited for the westbound lanes to clear. My mother was holding her newborn son, Brian and wasn't holding my hand; why would she? I was a grown up.

I was overwhelmed by the sights and sounds. It seems odd to assume that my survival instinct almost got me killed, but I'm convinced that's what happened. As confusion enveloped my mind, I was overwhelmed by an urge to get to safety as quickly as possible. How do you do something quickly? You run. I bolted into the westbound lane headed for the other side of the road. I still recall freezing in my tracks when I saw the car bearing down on me. My mother screamed my name so loudly she could easily be heard over the sound of the screeching tires that filled the air with smoke. A car came to an abrupt halt just a couple of feet from my body. My mother took my hand.

I'm sure there have been other instances where I came precariously close to my untimely end, but I obviously experienced a fair amount of good fortune. I wish I could say that all of my friends shared the same good luck, but sadly many of them are gone. I hope the good luck keeps on coming. I don't plan on spending nearly as much time tempting fate. Live and let live seems like a nice way to go.

Chapter Eighteen – Obituary

Howard Alton Jones passed away on [fill-in-the-blank]. He died of unnatural causes. He lived his life unnaturally; why should his passing be any different? He never lived up to his potential, but that was far more than adequate. He is survived by his dear wife, Liz, (hopefully), lots of friends and even more enemies. He has a genetic daughter, a step-daughter and an adopted daughter. Each falls into one of the two aforementioned categories. He may also have one or more children of which he was unaware.

There will be no service, no funeral, no burial; there may be a party. He's dead. He no longer cares. The party's over, not just beginning. He has not gone to be with his heavenly father. He's dead. In lieu of flowers, you can send contributions to Liz; she can always use extra money.

He was a provocateur, a rebel, an iconoclast and creative thinker. His best performances came when the challenges were the greatest. He eschewed the status quo, avoided "normal" at all costs and often played both the role of the irresistible force and the immovable object. He never suffered bullies well. He championed the underdogs of the world.

He embraced the philosophy that in the end, you regret most the things you didn't do rather than the ones you did. He never feared failure; he knew without failures, there could be no successes. He preferred rough seas to calm waters, thunder and lightning to blue skies. He would rather walk into the wind than retreat to the safe haven. Lightening exhilarated him. The thunder gave him energy.

For him, life was theater. It was mystery. It was hidden treasures. It was music and song. The only dance he knew was the dance of life. He danced it with all his heart, but now the band has put its music away and gone home. The next dance is yours. Dance in joy.

About the Author

You're kidding right? Only a Dunderhead would put an "About the Author" page in an autobiography. Did you know that the word "gullible" isn't actually in the dictionary? Look it up.

CPSIA information can be obtained at www.ICGtesting.com
Printed in the USA
LVOW11s1122140316

479071LV00001B/106/P

9 780984 554539